Judicial Protection
of Human Rights

Judicial Protection of Human Rights

Myth or Reality?

EDITED BY
Mark Gibney and
Stanislaw Frankowski

Westport, Connecticut
London

Library of Congress Cataloging-in-Publication Data

Judicial protection of human rights : myth or reality? / edited by
   Mark Gibney and Stanislaw Frankowski.
      p.   cm.
   Includes bibliographical references and index.
   ISBN 0–275–96011–0 (alk. paper)
     1. Human rights. 2. Courts. 3. Justice, Administration of.
   I. Gibney, Mark. II. Frankowski, Stanislaw.
   K3240.4j83   1999
   341.4'81—dc21   98–23567

British Library Cataloguing in Publication Data is available.

Library of Congress Catalog Card Number: 98–23567
ISBN: 0–275–96011–0

First published in 1999

Praeger Publishers, 88 Post Road West, Westport, CT 06881
An imprint of Greenwood Publishing Group, Inc.

Printed in the United States of America

The paper used in this book complies with the
Permanent Paper Standard issued by the National
Information Standards Organization (Z39.48–1984).

10 9 8 7 6 5 4 3 2 1

Contents

Introduction

The central question taken up by the chapters in this book is the degree to which judges have (or have not) served as protectors of human rights. Much has changed since World War II. Before that time there was very little, if any, particular focus on what we now know as human rights. Since then, however, there has been a veritable explosion of international instruments, regional bodies and domestic laws that are intended to protect individuals from pernicious governmental practices. Despite these vast legal changes, it is also commonly conceded that gross levels of human rights abuses continue to afflict a substantial part—perhaps the vast majority—of the people of the world.

Why focus on the judiciary? We are of the view that courts play a unique role in nearly every society. Although the judiciary is nominally a part of the governing structure, it is also nearly always the case that the judiciary stands apart from those entities that make and carry out policy. Thus, it is safe to say that it has not been judges who have designed or carried out the myriad of human rights violations that are so common. However, the question we ask is the extent to which courts have merely abided such practices or perhaps have even provided legitimation to repressive regimes—or, on the other hand, the degree to which courts have purposely interceded to attempt to bring about some change in stemming abusive governmental practices.

Obviously, the task could be an overwhelming one. There are, quite literally, hundreds of judicial systems in the world, in addition to a growing number of regional bodies. No book could even begin to capture this tremendous diversity. What we have provided here instead is a cross section of judicial systems throughout the world, but with a focus on those systems where the judiciary has become involved in questions concerning human rights.

EUROPE

We begin with the transformation of two judicial regimes in Eastern Europe. In Chapter 1, "Protection of Human Rights by the Judiciary in Romania," Monica Macovei documents the attempt to create an independent judiciary against a background of the rapidly changing political, social and economic forces in Romania. In Macovei's view, although important steps have been taken to strengthen the judiciary vis-à-vis the other branches of government, these efforts have fallen far short. As a result, the political branches (the executive in particular) continue to assert themselves in questions that are of a judicial nature. Macovei suggests that absent far-ranging structural changes, the judiciary's role in offering protection against human rights abuses will be challenged constantly.

In Chapter 2, "The Judicial Protection of the Constitutional Rights and Freedoms in Russia: Myths and Reality," Igor Petrukhin provides an in-depth examination of the multitude of changes in the law and the judicial system in Russia. Petrukhin not only documents this ongoing transformation, but he offers insightful commentary on Russia's attempt to (re)create a legal system that is not premised on communist values.

ISRAEL AND THE OCCUPIED TERRITORIES

Stephen Goldstein and John Quigley offer two completely differing views of the Israeli judiciary—but these views are not necessarily mutually inconsistent. In Chapter 3, "The Protection of Human Rights by Judges: The Israeli Experience," Goldstein focuses on the judiciary's role in the internal affairs of Israel, and what he finds is a Supreme Court that, in his words, has "shaped, developed and enforced the protection of human rights. The importance of the fact that in Israel legal actions challenging governmental policy are brought originally in the Supreme Court cannot be overemphasized." Goldstein concludes his chapter by suggesting that where the Israeli Supreme Court has been far less likely to act has been with regard to events in the Occupied Territories, and this is the starting point for Chapter 4, John Quigley's "Judicial Protection in Israeli-Occupied Territories." In Quigley's view, the judges of the Supreme Court of Israel share the political values of the Israeli military, not the values of the Palestinian population. Because of this, Quigley argues, the Court has been extraordinarily hesitant to offer any resistance to many of the military initiatives that have been undertaken. The ultimate end of all this, however, is a Palestinian population that has effectively been under Israeli control, militarily and politically, but with few, if any, avenues of redress.

LATIN AMERICA

Part III consists of Chapter 5, Brian Turner's "Judicial Protection of Human Rights in Latin America: Heroism and Pragmatism." Turner's focus is the

Southern Cone—Argentina, Brazil, Chile, Paraguay and Uruguay—and his time frame is from 1964 (with the military coup in Brazil) to the present. Tying his analysis to Robert Cover's study of antebellum judges in the United States, Turner finds that there were several kinds of responses to military rule, although even for the judicial "hero" the line between pragmatism and capitulation has been a rather thin one.

Turner's analysis looks at two periods of time. The first is during military rule, and what he finds is that there was some variability of judicial response—from attempts to offer some human rights protection to outright submission—although Turner raises the question whether acts of judicial heroism might actually do more harm than good by unintentionally providing legitimacy to repressive regimes. The second point in time is the period during democratization, and Turner's focus is on the various attempts to reform the judiciary. In some countries, such as Uruguay, the courts have begun to adopt a more active use of judicial review. In contrast, judicial independence has been much slower in Chile and virtually non-existent in Paraguay.

Turner concludes from his study that judicial defense of human rights depends upon two key factors. The first is that the judiciary itself needs to develop traditions that value political liberty more than formalism, which will then provide creative and strong-willed judges the necessary support for protecting human rights. The second key is the ability of the judiciary to recognize the strong need that the military has for some type of legitimacy, which should in turn allow the courts some "leverage" to prevent some of the worst abuses of military rule.

INDIA, THE PHILIPPINES AND CHINA

In Chapter 6, "Freedom from Torture and Cruel, Inhuman or Degrading Treatment or Punishment: The Role of the Supreme Court of India," Vijayashri Sripati provides both a historical account and a legal analysis of the Supreme Court's changing role in the protection of human rights. Following independence in 1947, the Court was at first hesitant to give an expansive reading to the scope of "fundamental rights." However, beginning in the 1970s, the Court has handed down a number of opinions, many of them involving the mistreatment of prisoners, that have served to promote the protection of human rights. As Sripati notes, although national constitutions will often appear to guarantee human rights, judicial reasoning can either negate those rights or uphold them instead. Sripati's analysis also shows the manner in which domestic law can be greatly informed by the rules of customary international law.

In Chapter 7, "Judicial Defense of Human Rights during the Marcos Dictatorship in the Philippines: The Careers of Claudio Teehankee and Cecelia Muñoz Palma," C. Neal Tate offers a unique insight into the lives of two Supreme Court justices who served under Ferdinand Marcos's rule but who also played a historic role in the transformation to democracy in that country. Still, Tate argues that there are important differences in how these two justices operated, and he presents an analysis of their voting records in support of this position.

The final contribution in this section is Chapter 8, "Legal Culture, Legal Professionals and the Future of Human Rights in China," by Albert Melone and Xiaolin Wang. Although the Chinese judiciary is presently dominated by Communist Party functionaries, and the rule of law subservient to political considerations, the authors suggest that enormous levels of change might very well occur in the near future. Most notably, in the past few years there has been a surge in the numbers attending law school as well as those who have opened up private law practices. The reason for this is the desperate need for professionally trained lawyers to assist China's passage into the world's financial and economic marketplace. However, the unintended consequence of this might well be a judiciary that no longer accedes to the dictates of Party ideology and that might well serve as an important protector of human rights.

THE PROTECTION OF INDIGENOUS RIGHTS: THE AUSTRALIAN EXAMPLE

In Chapter 9, " 'Retreat from Injustice': The High Court of Australia and Native Title," Garth Nettheim examines the belated recognition of Aboriginal land rights in Australia in the case of *Mabo v. Queensland* (1992). Relying on selected excerpts from the writing of eminent jurists such as Vattel and Blackstone, for two centuries Australian law relied on the legal fiction that the land rights of Aboriginal people had been extinguished when the British acquired sovereignty over the Australian colonies. Displaying a much different, and modern, conception of international law, *Mabo* overturned this principle and thereby set in motion the country's political machinery, culminating in the passage of the Native Title Bill.

THE UNITED STATES

By now, much is known about human rights litigation in U.S. courts under the jurisdiction of the Alien Tort Statute (ATS) following the Second Circuit's landmark decision in *Filartiga v. Peña-Irala* (1980). Relying on the *Filartiga* precedent, a substantial number of foreign plaintiffs have successfully sued foreign defendants in U.S. courts for the commission of human rights violations occurring in the home country. However, there is another stream of human rights litigation in U.S. courts—suits alleging human rights abuses by the U.S. government—that have met a chilly reception, and this case law is the focus in Chapter 10, "U.S. Courts and the Selective Protection of Human Rights," by Mark Gibney.

In Gibney's view, as commendable and noteworthy as the ATS litigation has been, courts in this country should have an even stronger incentive to ensure that a coordinate branch of government is not responsible for the commission of human rights abuses. The chapter also suggests that the dividing line between our transgressions (which U.S. courts will not litigate) and those committed by others (which generally will be) is not always a clear one.

For example, it is not unknown for foreign officials to be on the Central Intelligence Agency (CIA) payroll (in a country like Guatemala this seemed to occur almost as a matter of course). When these same officials commit human rights abuses in the form of torture, disappearances, summary executions and so forth, are these violations attributable to this other country? or to the United States? or perhaps to governmental policy in both countries? The larger question that is raised by all of this is how the American judiciary can be so vigilant with respect to one class of human rights abuses but then so completely deferential to the political branches of government in this country when there are allegations of human rights violations by the United States.

ACKNOWLEDGMENT

We would like to thank Mr. Jose Bautista, Saint Louis University School of Law (Class of 1999), for his help in preparing the index.

Part I

Europe

Chapter 1

Protection of Human Rights by the Judiciary in Romania

MONICA MACOVEI

INTRODUCTION AND HISTORICAL BACKGROUND

Romania was a monarchy from the nineteenth century until 1947. Following the adoption of the 1866 and 1923 Constitutions, largely inspired by the Belgian model, the country developed a multiparty system within a constitutional monarchy. Political pluralism, separation of powers, independence of the judiciary and freedom of the press constituted the main foundations of the sociopolitical system. Free speech was supported by particularly strong guarantees. Censorship, government prior authorization and suspension and suppression of newspapers were constitutionally prohibited.[1] Pre-trial detention of journalists was also prohibited.[2]

Unfortunately, however, Romanian democracy was short-lived. Following World War II, Soviet-style communism was imposed. King Michael was forced to abdicate in 1947; a systematic and violent destruction of the old political, social, economic and cultural order ensued. Concentration camps were established for the extermination of real and alleged political enemies. Private property was virtually eliminated and replaced by state ownership of all major resources. Culture was tightly regimented.[3] Having seized control of all spheres of public and private life, the communists acted methodically with a sense of impunity secured by the Soviet military presence. Almost any form of behavior that could be construed as reflecting opposition to Communist Party policies was deemed criminal. The Party adopted the slogan, Who is not with us is against us. Although the communists claimed that their program embodied the finest of human virtues, in reality they had no respect for individual human rights. In order to be a good communist, one had to surrender one's integrity and honesty to the suprapersonal "Party."[4]

The entire legal structure immediately became the object of radical reforms. All pre-war judges were replaced with newcomers without any legal background. "Blue-collar" workers became "people's judges" overnight. For many years to come, they loyally served the supreme power of the state—the Party— by convicting and then imposing long prison sentences on intellectuals, members of banned political parties, former judges and all persons considered politically unreliable. Any attempt to detect the smallest hint of the rule of law, or of any due process elements or human rights protection within these trials, would be futile. The convictions were based on legislation that criminalized speech and actions inconsistent with communist ideology.

Two Constitutions were adopted (one in 1948 and the other in 1952) during the communist period. These documents proclaimed the unity of political power represented by the Communist Party.

Around 1960, in order to assert their own political independence from the Soviet Union, the Romanian communist leaders invoked the principle of non-interference into other communist countries' internal affairs. The process of rapid industrialization was to ensure the country's economic independence. As Romania was slowly departing from the Soviet model, communist leaders resorted to the instrument of nationalism. This new commitment to national values resulted in the rewriting of history books, rehabilitation of some pre-war intellectuals and the end of mandatory Russian-language instruction.[5] Nevertheless, the most essential features of the communist political system remained intact. In reality, the nationalistic dictatorship blindly followed the Soviet political pattern.

Nicolae Ceausescu became the Communist Party's Secretary General in 1965. He continued playing the same nationalistic card.[6] During his first years in power, the intellectual life of the country was not entirely under dogmatic constraints, although all political criticism was forbidden. Art of a political nature was tolerated, but it was always expected to express and support the nationalistic communist ideology. What in fact existed was a false feeling of freedom.

The political climate deteriorated a few years later when Ceausescu consolidated his power and boldly imposed numerous restrictions on individual rights. Soon thereafter, a highly centralized state developed. Uniformity became the order of the day, with the chief aim being the annihilation of intellectuals.[7] The nation was supposed to consist of a unified working people whose vocabulary would be composed of communist words.[8] This ideal was given more than mere lip service. Ceausescu and his repressive apparatus used brute force and threats in order to impose total conformity. Any individual opinions or actions were to be eliminated.

In 1965, a new Constitution was adopted. Like the previous basic laws, the document promoted the unity of state power and the supremacy of the Communist Party in all spheres of life. Workers were declared the ruling class. State property was the rule, and the state monopolized all trade. The duty to work was constitutionally proclaimed and was enforced by laws punishing those who could not provide proof that they were employed in state-sponsored gainful activity. On paper at least, the rights of citizens were protected by several constitutional provisions. However, these rights were not considered natural to the individual but were instead only privileges granted by the state. Therefore, no enforcement mechanism was established to protect them. In the area of civil liberties, the Constitution was a dead letter, as it was impossible to invoke its provisions in court or against a public authority. Judicial review did not exist.

In the 1980s, Ceausescu's personal dictatorship reached absurd dimensions. Any form of speech considered critical of the political system or the communist leaders, even if expressed through art or seemingly innocent jokes, was sanctioned with imprisonment. Fear ruled the country. The rights of individuals were unquestionably subordinated to the collective interest, as defined by the ruling party elite. Romania became a model of modern totalitarianism.

In fact, there was not even the appearance of the independence of the judicial branch. Instead, the judiciary had the constitutional duty to protect the communist system. The Supreme Tribunal was responsible to the National Assembly and, between its sessions, to the Council of State (an executive body), which in reality functioned under strict Party control.

All administrative positions within the judiciary, (e.g., court presidents) were occupied by those considered absolutely loyal to the Party. Acting through those administrators, the Party was able to influence the outcome of politically sensitive cases. The Party also supervised the process of promotions to appellate courts.

Heads of higher-level prosecutorial units and court administrators were members of the same Party cells. Understandably, there was a great deal of behind-the-scene interaction and cooperation between these two branches, viewed as parts of one communist power structure. Broadly defined anti-state offenses were transferred to the jurisdiction of military courts. In this way, the Party's control over most of the more important cases was fully assured.

Although judges were to serve until death or retirement, in fact, they could be removed from office as any other civil servants. Curiously enough, the tenure of Supreme Tribunal justices was limited to five years (with the possibility for re-appointments). It is clear that in this way the Party wanted to ensure the political reliability of the highest court of the land.

Individual rights were not protected from the power of the state. In particular, no effective enforcement mechanisms were provided for when individuals had their rights violated. The constitutional clauses referring to civil and political rights were included purely for propaganda purposes.

Since the revolutionary upheaval of December 1989, the country's legal framework has changed radically. Most of the communist dogma has been rejected. A new sociopolitical system was to be created, based on the principles of political pluralism, private property, separation of powers, the rule of law and the independence of the judiciary. The idea of strict observance of human rights was publicly supported by those in power. The new 1991 Constitution[9] gives binding international human rights treaties the status of domestic law, which, in turn, take precedent over regular legislation in cases of conflict.[10] However, the new constitutionally created institutions have not yet fully matured, and the old structures and attitudes still linger.

The parliamentary and presidential elections of November 1996 brought radical political changes and completed, from a political point of view, the 1989 anti-communist Revolution. Finally, after 60 years, the communists seem to have lost power. A coalition of three democratic groups, led by the Democratic Convention, was able to form a government. Emil Constantinescu, the Convention's leader, became President.

The transition from dictatorship to democracy is a difficult and often convoluted process. Since a complete and perfect revolution is probably not possible, especially when it is aimed at establishing a democratic order, the new desired system cannot be created overnight. The 1989 Romanian Revolution is in many ways still in progress.

One must bear in mind that most of the existing legislation and case law was adopted and developed under the former government, run by political figures with communist backgrounds. One of the major tasks of the democratic forces now in charge is thus to ensure an effective protection of individual rights. Identifying the most glaring shortcomings and pointing out issues that need correction are the main goals of this chapter.

THE INDEPENDENCE OF THE JUDICIARY

As a necessary check on the potential excesses of both the executive and legislative branches, only an independent and impartial judiciary may effectively guarantee the protection of human rights. For this reason, it should not be surprising to find that authoritarian governments traditionally limit the power of the judicial branch. In contrast, one of the distinctive features of a political system based on the principle of the separation of powers is the independent position occupied by the strong judiciary. The independence and impartiality of the Romanian judiciary is compromised by the unclear division of powers between judges and prosecutors, by the politicization of judicial appointments and by the power of the executive in manipulating judicial proceedings.

The Relationship between Judges and Prosecutors

Unfortunately, the current Romanian legal system does not strictly adhere to the principle of separation of powers. Ombudsman and the Constitutional Court have been added to the so-called state authorities, moving away from the classic power structure. Although the Constitution guarantees the irremovability, independence and impartiality of judges, the judiciary remains the least independent of the three governmental branches because it continued, until recently, to be the target of repeated assaults by the executive. The Constitution, the Law on

Reorganization of the Judiciary[11] and post-1989 case law are illustrative of this phenomenon.

By leaving the Public Ministry—the supervisory body over prosecutorial power—in a state of definitional ambiguity, the Constitution fails to limit prosecutorial power. On the one hand, the Constitution treats the Public Ministry, along with the courts, as part of the judicial branch, although many scholars claim that the Ministry should instead be a part of the executive. But constitutional provisions concerning the Ministry are included together with provisions applicable to the courts in a section entitled "Judicial Authority." Similarly, the Constitution classifies all prosecutors and judges as members of the judiciary.

However, when defining the nature and scope of prosecutorial power, the Constitution changes course, mandating that prosecutors carry out their activities not only in accord with the principles of legality and impartiality but also within the framework of hierarchical control in accordance with Article 131 of the Constitution. As provided in Article 32, paras. 3–4 of the 1992 Law on Reorganization of the Judiciary, the hierarchically superior prosecutor may issue binding orders to, and suspend or reject decisions of, subordinate prosecutors. Besides the lack of independence, prosecutors—unlike judges—do not enjoy the guarantee of irremovability.[12] Their status has been correctly formulated in terms of the executive power, and consequently, it doesn't fit the requirements of an independent judiciary. However, by combining within the same body judges who enjoy independence and irremovability and prosecutors who do not, the very core of the independence of the judiciary is endangered.

A large part of prosecutorial activities may not be reviewed by judges. For example, the prosecutorial decisions terminating criminal proceedings may not be appealed in the courts, even if an arrest or search warrants have been issued in those cases during criminal investigations. The principle of access to justice is also severely violated by an inability to appeal search and wiretap warrants to independent judges.

Moreover, Article 409 of the Criminal Procedure Code (as amended in 1993) gives the General Prosecutor exclusive authority to lodge so-called extraordinary appeals against final judicial verdicts passed in criminal cases. This power may be exercised on the official's own initiative or on motion of the Minister of Justice or a party to a criminal case. Ultimately, however, the General Prosecutor has unfettered discretionary power in this area.

The powerful role of prosecutors has also been retained in other respects. Article 31 of the Law on Judicial Reorganization provides for the power and duty of prosecutors to supervise the on-site compliance with law at pre-trial detention and prison facilities and to uphold their educational and safety standards. In fact, prosecutors themselves often do not comply with the legal requirements by failing to control pre-trial and prison facilities. Paradoxically, the internal rules concerning lockups are confidential to prosecutors. I personally experienced this when the General Inspectorate of the Police refused to hand me the internal rules for their lockup, although at that time I was employed at the Human Rights Department of the Office of General Prosecutor. I was not able to obtain them even using personal contacts. My request was officially put on hold; unofficially, I have been told that the rules are classified as "top secret."

Under the inquisitorial model typical for the civil law tradition, the Public Ministry supervises the activities of investigating prosecutors performing judicial functions such as issuing arrest warrants. Prosecutors have exclusive power to issue arrest warrants during criminal investigations; but these warrants are valid only for 30 days. Extensions are issued by judges at the request of prosecutors. However, if a detainee does not contest the legality of the warrant, then he or she will not be brought before a judge for the entire 30-day period. Searches to be conducted during the investigation period are authorized exclusively by prosecutors. Judges may order searches only after an indictment has been issued and the case has come before the Court (Articles 101, 102 of the Criminal Procedure Code). The search authorization does not have to specify the object of the search. Consequently, anything found during a search may be used in further proceedings against the suspect. This unprincipled assignment of power is a significant handicap to judicial independence, an independence that is then further weakened by the appointment process.

Judicial Appointments

Judges are appointed for an unlimited term (Article 133 of the Constitution) by the President at the recommendation of the Superior Council of Magistracy (prosecutors are appointed the same way). Supreme Court judges are appointed for only six years, with the possibility of renewal. Besides judges, prosecutors are also members of the Superior Council of Magistracy, which is composed of ten judges and five prosecutors. Therefore, acting through prosecutors, the executive is in a position to influence the judicial nomination process. The Council also acts as a judicial disciplinary body. As a result, the professional careers of judges depend on both judges and prosecutors. In contrast, prosecutors have their own disciplinary body composed exclusively of prosecutors. Justices of the Constitutional Court are appointed for nine years. The Chamber of Deputies, the Senate, and the President appoint three justices each.

The 1992 Judicial Reorganization Act

The 1992 Judicial Reorganization Law greatly improved the position and public perception of the judiciary. Nevertheless, it had its shortcomings. In particular, the Law allowed the executive to tinker with the independence of the judiciary. Article 19 of the Law provided for a strict control over judges exercised by the Minister of Justice through an inspectorate body composed of general inspectors and judges.[13] This provision also gave court presidents the same authority over their subordinates. Since general inspectors were civil servants and employees of the executive branch, the Law effectively subordinated the judiciary to executive branch officials.

Following Opinion No. 176/1993 (para. 7) of the Parliamentary Assembly of the Council of Europe, a group of deputies of the Democratic Party initiated in 1993 a motion to amend Article 19. In January 1994, the Juridical Commission of the Chamber of Deputies rejected the motion, reasoning that since the Minister of Justice may initiate extraordinary appeals, he must have the ability to review the substance of final judicial verdicts.

Finally, when defining "magistrates," Article 47 of the Judicial Reorganization Law also included, in addition to judges and prosecutors (following the constitutional provisions), high officials and civil servants.

These few examples demonstrate the unusually strong powers the 1992 Law gave to the Minister of Justice and other civil servants in relation to judicial activities. These powers clearly endangered the judiciary's independence and impartiality, which was already threatened by interference from the executive branch.

Conflicts with the Executive

The shortcomings of the Judicial Reorganization Law were exacerbated by the attitude and actions of the authorities, which, in several instances, blatantly violated existing legal provisions. On July 14, 1993, two weeks after the Law came into force, Petre Ninosu, then Minister of Justice, relieved Corneliu Turianu of his duties as president of the Bucharest Court without instituting formal disciplinary proceedings. Although the dismissal was officially justified by charges that Turianu politicized the judiciary, obstructed reforms, allowed for excessive media transparency and so forth, public rumors linked his dismissal to the previous Bucharest Court's decision to strike former President Ion Iliescu from a party slate of Senate candidates (where he had placed his name in case he lost the presidential race) just before the national elections held in September 1992. At that time, Corneliu Turianu headed the Bucharest Court, while Ninosu was Iliescu's lawyer. When Ninosu later became Minister of Justice, he dismissed Turianu out of revenge. The Ninosu case vividly illustrated the executive branch's brazen willingness—indeed, determination—to interfere with judicial decision making for purely political reasons.

Another demonstration of the executive branch's interference with the judiciary took place in May 1994, when President Iliescu publicly criticized the judicial branch for rendering decisions to return houses that had been nationalized under communist rule to their original private owners. The President characterized these decisions as "illegal" and called on local government officials responsible for carrying out the courts' rulings to refuse to do so because, as the President explained at the time, "Courts should not have been allowed to decide these cases in the absence of legal provisions."

Two important events followed this speech. First, the Constitutional Court, reviewing a parliamentary motion to suspend the President for infringing upon the independence of the judiciary and the right of private property, found that "no major violation" of the Constitution had taken place. As a result, the Court rejected the motion on the ground that although the President had indeed overstepped his bounds, he had not strayed so far as to warrant suspension.[14] Second, the General Prosecutor initiated extraordinary appeals by petitioning the Supreme Court to overturn most of the judicial decisions that were the subject of Iliescu's criticism. Notwithstanding the highly questionable legal basis for the challenged court rulings, the timing of the General Prosecutor's efforts to overturn these decisions speaks volumes about their political motivation. Even assuming that the Public Ministry (including the General Prosecutor's Office) belongs to the executive branch, such unabashed subservience to the political whims of a President seeking to exert pressure on the courts clearly poses a threat to the independence of the judiciary. In February 1995, the President got his wish. Acting on the petition of the Prosecutor General, the Supreme Court overturned lower court decisions concerning property ownership that had provoked the President's ire. Moreover, the Supreme Court essentially emasculated the power of the judicial branch in this area by ruling that, in the future, lower courts could not entertain claims concerning nationalized property until the question was resolved by Parliament.

Furthermore, former President Iliescu failed to appoint judges to tribunals and courts of first instance within the time limit set up by Article 129 of the Law on Judicial Reorganization. According to Articles 129 and 52, judges may not be removed once they are appointed and take the oath, and in accordance with Article 54, all acts undertaken by them before taking the oath must be considered null and void. Since the time limit expired in August 1994, and new judges had not been appointed, all judgments adopted during the following eighteen-month period were formally a nullity. However, as was widely expected, these judgments were considered valid, and nobody was held accountable for the judicial crisis.

The former President started appointing judges to the tribunals and courts of first instance only in December 1995, following strikes declared by some courts. However, he did not appoint those judges whose previous decisions were "inconvenient" to the executive branch. In the meantime, the Parliament, willing to validate the unlawful behavior of both the President and the Superior Council of Magistrates, retroactively extended the time limit for judicial appointments. Fortunately, such incidents are now relics of the past. The new government has not made any attempt to interfere with the smooth functioning of the judiciary.

The 1992 Judicial Reorganization Law was amended in 1997. The amendments have eliminated the most glaring shortcomings of the executive-judiciary relationship. First, one of the amendments clarified the relationship between the Minister of Justice and prosecutors. Although the 1991 Constitution stated that prosecutors perform their duties under the authority of the Minister (Article 131), a provision of the 1992 Law added the General Prosecutor as a necessary link between the Minister and prosecutors. This provision, which was intended to maintain the exclusive power of the Prosecutor General over the prosecutors, was eliminated by one of the 1997 amendments (Article 37, as amended). Second, the 1997 Law amended the long-criticized Article 19 of the 1992 Law, which, as discussed earlier, gave the Minister the power to exercise firm control over the everyday functioning of the judiciary. The current language guarantees the judiciary's full independence from the executive.

The continued maintenance of military prosecutors and courts as a parallel system of justice can be considered as the only present manifestation of the executive's interference with the judiciary. The military justice system handles all cases involving alleged police abuse or mistreatment in police lockups or prisons. Since the Ministry of Interior and the General Directorate of Prisons (belonging to the Ministry of Justice) are in fact part of the military, such cases are investigated and tried by military prosecutors and judges.

Law no. 34/1993 on Military Courts and Prosecutors' Offices declares that military prosecutors and military judges are appointed in the same manner as their civilian counterparts. At the same time, Article 30 of the Law provides for their active military status with all the accompanying rights and duties. Military judges are paid by the Ministry of Defense and enjoy all other military rights, but they may also be punished for violating military rules under the terms of the Disciplinary Military Statute (Article 31). Selection and training of military magistrates (judges and prosecutors) are regulated by both the Ministry of Justice and the Ministry of Defense (Article 41). There are no legal guarantees of the independence of military prosecutors and judges. Referring to this issue, the Council of Europe stated: "Although many assurances were given that the police were under civilian control, the problem remains that complaints against police officers may be brought only before military prosecutors who alone can decide to bring charges. Given the apparent reluctance to bring charges in a number of cases, this situation, too, gives rise to legitimate concern."[15]

Most importantly, the military prosecutors' decisions to terminate cases may not be appealed in a court. Victims of police abuse may thus complain only to the Military Section of the General Prosecutor's Office.

There are legal provisions pertaining to police abuses that demonstrate the lack of independence of those investigating such cases. Article 208 of the Criminal Procedure Code authorizes the police to self-investigate cases relating to their own abusive behavior. Most significantly, investigations may be carried out by an officer belonging to the same police station as the policeman suspected of abuse. Not surprisingly, no indictments are brought in such cases. The situation improved in 1994 when the General Prosecutor ordered military prosecutors to carry out such investigations. This rule was codified in November 1996 when several amendments were introduced to the Code of Criminal Procedure.

Interestingly, the salaries of police officers are higher than those of the judges and prosecutors. In addition, military prosecutors and judges receive higher salaries than their civilian counterparts. The pay disparity between police and judges and between military and civilian magistrates reflected the value placed by the former government on each respective part of the state apparatus. The August 1997 amendments to the 1992 Law on the Reorganization of the Judiciary have equalized the material situation of judges and prosecutors.

FREEDOM OF EXPRESSION

Although solemnly guaranteed by the Constitution, freedom of expression is subjected to severe limitations that dilute the substance of the right.[16] Specifically, freedom of expression "shall not be used to damage the dignity, honor, or private life of an individual or his right to his own image."[17] Moreover, a content-based limitation is provided by the constitutional prohibition of "any defamation of the country and the nation; incitement to war or aggression, and to ethical, racial, class or religious hatred; incitement to discrimination, territorial separatism, or public violence; and obscene conduct contrary to good morals."[18] Consistent with this hierarchy of values, courts are deprived of the power to apply the principle of proportionality in order to balance conflicting values in specific free speech cases. The notion of the "public interest" as a factor justifying a strong and broad protection of expression, primarily when the press is involved, is not yet part of the Romanian culture.

Ordinary legislation implemented the above-mentioned constitutional clauses. The Audiovisual Law provides prison sentences for disseminating programs whose content might defame the country or the nation.[19] The Criminal Code provides imprisonment for any "communication or dissemination, by any possible means, of false news, facts or information or forged documents which could impair the security of the State or its international relations"[20] (note that there is no "danger" requirement; the good faith of the media agent is irrelevant); any "public act committed with the intention to defame the country or the Romanian nation;"[21] or any "act which would be contemptuous to the national symbols . . . or to the symbols used by the public authorities."[22]

Besides restraining the content of free speech, the vague and ambiguous language of these provisions could result in the prosecution of persons solely for having exercised their universally recognized right to freedom of expression. Legitimate questions may be raised: Whose perspective shall be adopted when considering the falsity of information? Wouldn't the alleged concrete damage to the international relations of the country be "politically" established since the questions of external relations are the attribute of the ruling political party? Who or what is going to be considered a victim (an aggrieved party) since the country and nation are abstract notions? Would national minorities be covered by the term *nation*? and, Would political leaders personify the country and the nation? Although the judiciary shall certainly have the essential role in the interpretation and application of the law, the mere existence of such vaguely defined and politically related criminal prohibitions endangers the very essence of a pluralistic society whose cornerstone is freedom of expression, including the right to political speech.

The current legal provisions criminalizing defamation of public officials and civil servants constitute another barrier to the exercise of free speech in the public interest. The Criminal Code prohibits any "public insult directed at a person serving an important state or public function, if related to his official capacity, if this would prejudice the State's authority."[23] The penalty provided in this instance is imprisonment for up to five years. Similarly, a criminal provision exists in relation to civil servants. The penalty is increased to seven years' imprisonment if the alleged victims of defamatory speech are members of the judiciary or military.[24] The difference in the range of penalties is quite revealing.

The current legal provisions relating to the exercise of free speech, directed mainly at political discourse critical of the government, demonstrate that legislators reject the idea that defamation of political public figures is a necessary component of a democracy to keep those in power in check. The protection of those who govern is strengthened by two procedural rules applicable to crimes against public officials: (1) The state acts *ex officio*, considering itself the primary victim; however, by deciding to protect the civil servant's dignity (which is considered a harm of a secondary value), the judicial authorities move the concept of "dignity" from the ethical field to that of the legal field, inducing the false idea that a standard of the "offended person" exists; and (2) the proof of truth is not legally allowed, demonstrating once again that the criminal provisions blindly protect those in power.

Despite these constitutional and criminal law restrictions, the media, as well as many individuals, have expressed critical opinions about public figures.[25] Considering the large number of critical speeches directed at civil servants and political figures, it is clear that criminal provisions pertaining to such expression seldom have been enforced. Nevertheless, there have been cases where legal actions were initiated against both journalists and ordinary citizens who made insulting speeches critical of those in the executive branch. The charge of "offense against authority" was mostly used when the defamatory speech was directed at former President Iliescu. Among civil servants, police officers have long considered themselves victims and have responded by starting criminal proceedings. However, despite such official reactions, all forms of the media have not hesitated to perform their duty to inform people and carefully scrutinize public figures. Nevertheless, the mere existence of criminal prohibitions, as well as case law punishing criticism of public figures, is likely to discourage the media from performing its role as a supplier of information and public watchdog; it may also create fear in those individuals critical of the government (the "chilling effect").

As already mentioned, when the targets of insults or defamation are ordinary citizens, different provisions of the Criminal Code apply.[26] In such cases, the applicable penalties are lower than those provided for defamation of public figures but are still high when compared to other European countries. The sentences are up to two years' imprisonment or a fine, in the case of insult, and up to three years' imprisonment or a fine, in the case of libel, regardless of whether the defamatory speech is delivered through the media or directly to the victim. In everyday practice, courts usually impose fines or suspended sentences. Civil damages for moral harm may also be claimed by the victims of defamation. One may not, however, file a civil claim unless criminal liability has already been established in a criminal court.

The "proof of truth" defense is provided for under the criminal law in cases of insult and libel.[27] However, neither good faith nor acting in the public interest is a defense in such cases. The "proof of truth" defense is especially problematic when applied to cases of insult that usually involve value judgments. Whereas the existence of at least certain facts can be proven, the veracity of statements containing value judgments cannot be easily demonstrated. One can even argue that opinions and such are not, by their very nature, true or false. Opinions may be different because they are formulated by different persons.

Access to information, a part of the freedom of expression, is another important issue of concern, given the impact of information on the activities of citizens, non-governmental organizations, journalists and civil servants. Access to information depends on how the idea of transparency is incorporated in the legislation. Two basic statutes regulate access to information: the Law on the Protection of State Secrets, mainly having a restrictive function, and the Law on Free Access to Information.

Curiously enough, the 1971 communist-era Law on the Protection of State Secrets has not been explicitly abrogated. Nevertheless, given the new political realities, it has not been applied during the 1990s. In addition, access to information is guaranteed in the Constitution. Along with establishing a person's right of access to information of public interest, the constitutional provisions require the public authorities to provide correct information on matters of public affairs and of personal interest. Public and private media are also required to provide correct information to the public.[28]

Nevertheless, the generous constitutional framework is not fully functional owing to the existence of supplementary provisions restricting the access to information. In addition, decisions that violate these constitutional provisions may not be challenged in individual cases unless the inconsistency between a law and the Constitution is demonstrated. The failure of legislators to adopt laws on access to information makes it impossible to invoke constitutional provisions if the public authorities fail to satisfy the media's or citizens' request for information. Consequently, access to information still depends on the goodwill of the representatives of the public authorities.

In order to make the constitutional provisions and guarantees effective, it is necessary to adopt legislation imposing on the authorities a duty to supply information, to establish adequate procedures, to specify the penalties to be applied should these obligations be disregarded and to introduce some form of judicial supervision. The limitations on the exercise of this right must be specifically prescribed by law. Such limitations may be justified only when narrowly defined "national security interests" are at stake.

THE RIGHT TO LIFE AND TO PHYSICAL AND MENTAL INTEGRITY

The right to life and to physical and mental integrity are constitutionally protected.[29] For example, the death penalty is prohibited.[30] The criminal law does not prohibit taking life when it is done (1) in self-defense against unlawful aggression; (2) in order to execute a lawful arrest; or (3) to prevent the escape of a lawfully detained person. Prosecutors and judges are usually mindful of the narrow scope of these exceptions. In practice, the taking of life by those exercising state authority (as well as by any other individuals) is rarely recognized as lawful. In the few cases where it may be found to be lawful, one of the three above exceptions must be proven beyond any doubt.

To safeguard the physical and mental integrity of individuals, Article 22(2) of the Constitution guarantees the right to be free from torture and from inhuman or degrading treatment or punishment. The constitutional provisions prohibiting torture were strengthened in 1991 by the insertion of a new provision into the Romanian Criminal Code, punishing acts of torture with up to fifteen years' imprisonment.[31]

Inhumane or degrading treatment or punishment was also prohibited by old criminal law provisions, and those found guilty could receive sentences ranging between three months and five years.[32] Curiously enough, although penalties were increased for a large number of crimes by the Law on amending the Criminal Code adopted in November 1996,[33] criminal offenses relating to inhuman or degrading treatment or punishment were not among them. This is puzzling when one considers the fact that at the same time punishments for criminal offenses involving individuals who physically assault public servants were substantially increased.[34] Such an approach reflects the lack of concern for protecting the physical integrity of individuals when they are victimized by public authorities.

In most of the inhumane or degrading treatment cases, the alleged abuses are perpetrated by police officers during criminal investigations. Although reports of physical brutality have substantially declined in lockups and prisons in the past six years, the abuse still continues.[35] Unfortunately, the number of police officials prosecuted for brutality is surprisingly low when compared with the number of reported violations. Most of the reported cases relate to physical abuse of pre-trial detainees held in police lockups. Police agents engage in such practices for the purpose of obtaining confessions.

Since an aggrieved individual is unable to challenge police actions in the courts, the use of unlawful methods in the search for evidence continues. Under the rules of criminal procedure, written reports prepared by the police during the criminal investigation stage are presumed true, and police officers are not questioned by the court. Consequently, claims of police misconduct brought by the defense are not given a judicial hearing. Such claims are instead sent to military prosecutors for investigation, but the trial proceeds without waiting for the results of those investigations. A final conviction of a police officer is the only event that would compel judicial review of the case involving a victim of police abuse.

Another incentive to police misconduct is the rule that penal proceedings preclude any civil proceedings based on the same set of facts. Therefore, under the current case law, a victim of police abuse (actually, of any physical abuse) may not file a claim for damages unless a final guilty verdict against the officer has been obtained. In this context, it is important to consider that proving criminal liability is more difficult than proving civil liability. Although there are provisions in the Romanian Civil Code on the civil liability of employers for the conduct of their employees, these provisions have never been applied to cases of police abuse.

THE RIGHT TO PERSONAL LIBERTY AND SECURITY

The right to personal liberty and security is constitutionally guaranteed.[36] The power to deprive an individual of liberty rests with the magistrates (prosecutors and judges) and is strictly regulated by both the Constitution and the Code of Criminal Procedure. These laws regulate legal detention; time limits allowed for pre-trial detention; the right to appeal detention warrants; the right to apply for release under judicial supervision or on bail;[37] the obligation to provide publicly funded legal defense and translation (if necessary); and the right to mandatory release if the grounds for arrest or detention cease to exist. The police may detain a person without a warrant for up to 24 hours.[38] After a criminal charge has been prepared, the prosecutor may issue a detention warrant. The detainee must be promptly informed of the charges against him in a language he understands. The length of detention may not exceed 30 days.[39] Within this period, the detainee may file a complaint with the court challenging the legality of the warrant. The length of detention could be extended only by a court of law. Each extension is limited to a maximum of 30 days, but the number of extensions is unlimited. However, the total length of detention may not exceed half of the maximum length of imprisonment provided by law for the criminal offense.

The Code of Criminal Procedure allows victims to obtain compensation for unlawful detention. A civil claim may be brought following a judicial decision to acquit or a prosecutor's decision to terminate the case.

The constitutional presumption of innocence is reflected in the Code of Criminal Procedure and is protected by the judiciary. Citizens are considered innocent until proven guilty by a final court decision. Prosecutors bear the burden of proof; the accused has the right to remain silent. The presumption of innocence existed in previous criminal legislation, and the same legal guarantees were provided. However, even to this day once charges have been filed, conviction is almost certain. This is especially true when the suspect is held in pre-trial detention. Under these circumstances the presumption of innocence is nothing but a fiction.

Under international standards, an investigating authority should not have the power to issue a detention warrant because this body is not impartial. Unfortunately, in Romania the prosecutor is empowered both to detain suspects and to conduct investigations. Moreover, the same prosecutor usually handles the case from the moment of charging and issuance of the warrant until the end of the investigation, when the case is terminated or sent to court.

Also subject to criticism is the right to complain to the court about the legality of the warrant only once during a 30-day period of detention. This means that for a substantial time (e.g., 20 days) a detainee might not be brought before a judge. If one doesn't complain about the legality of a warrant, he is not brought before the court for the entire period of 30 days specified in the warrant. This is a consequence of the inquisitorial system, which allows prosecutors to perform certain judicial functions.

Generally speaking, the above-mentioned legal requirements are observed by practitioners. It should be noted that judges are conscious of their independence, releasing many of those detained by the prosecutors. Previously, they were less likely to do so, although the law provided them with the releasing power when they were requested to extend the period of pre-trial detention.

THE RIGHT TO PRIVACY

The rights to respect for one's home and correspondence, as components of the right to privacy, are guaranteed by the Constitution (Articles 27 and 28).[40] The exemptions are specified by the Code of Criminal Procedure and the Law on National Security. Searches must be authorized by judges or prosecutors, whereas it is enough if wiretapping is authorized only by a prosecutor. Under current law, no appeal against decisions authorizing searches is provided. However, when searches are ordered by prosecutors, complaints may be filed with the General Prosecutor's Office. This right is based on the common proceedings of complaining against any investigatory action. It is important to stress that search and wiretapping warrants may not be appealed in court. The Code of Criminal Procedure and the Law on National Security provide that prosecutors' decisions to issue wiretapping warrants are to be reviewed by supervisory personnel within the prosecutors' office. This means that the same agency issues warrants and oversees their legality; such a situation is obviously unacceptable. Moreover, warrants need not specify the object of search or wiretapping nor the conditions under which these activities may be carried out. All telephone conversations of the targeted person may thus be recorded, and everything found during a search may be used against that person. With respect to the duration of wiretapping, the law provides warrants valid for up to a maximum of 30 days, but the number of subsequent warrants is unlimited. Night searches are constitutionally prohibited, except when they follow a flagrant offense.

Violation of legal provisions relating to the enjoyment of these rights may result in criminal liability.[41] No enhanced punishment is provided in cases where a perpetrator committed a crime while executing official duties. It seems that enhanced sentences should be available if a state representative illegally interferes with an individual's exercise of rights to privacy or correspondence. First, the state, rather than ordinary citizens, is more likely to violate the secrecy of private communications. Second, the state's technological resources pose a greater danger for individuals, especially when the violations are performed repeatedly and for a longer period of time. Despite the absence of specific provisions providing for different degrees of criminal liability, judges still may choose from a fairly wide range of penalties.

Protection of sexual life, another component of the right to privacy, is guaranteed by the Constitution.[42] The Criminal Code, as amended in 1996, criminalizes homosexual relations between consenting adults "if the act was committed in public or has produced public scandal."[43] Under current case law, the "public scandal" requirement may be met even if the "scandal" occurs after the homosexual act (e.g., if others hear about it and feel indignant). The wide and ill-defined range of situations covered by the term "public scandal" raises concern that these provisions could lead to the prosecution of adults solely for engaging in private, consensual homosexual relations.

It is also an offense punishable by a sentence of one to five years' imprisonment "to entice or seduce a person to practice same sex acts, as well as propaganda, association or any other forms of proselytizing with the same aim."[44] These provisions could lead to the imprisonment of individuals solely for exercising their constitutionally protected rights of freedom of expression and freedom of assembly and association. This explains why gays and lesbians may not set up private organizations, nor may they issue publications concerning homosexual subject matters. As a result, they often use human rights nongovernmental organizations as an umbrella.

THE RIGHT TO A FAIR AND PUBLIC HEARING WITHIN A REASONABLE TIME BY AN INDEPENDENT AND IMPARTIAL TRIBUNAL

The right to a fair and public hearing within a reasonable time by an independent and impartial tribunal established by law (due process) in both civil and criminal cases is provided by the provisions of the Criminal and Civil Procedure Codes. The same principle applies to administrative courts that are empowered to review administrative decisions. Specifically, administrative courts deal with challenges to discretionary decisions of public authorities that adversely affect an individual's rights or interests. The claimant is entitled to bring his case before an administrative court to have questions of law and facts reviewed.

Impartiality

Due process requires that the tribunal meet the requirements of independence and impartiality. The issue of independence has been previously discussed (the manner of appointment, terms of office and the protection against outside pressures).

The issue of impartiality merits further discussion. The personal impartiality of tribunal members is presumed unless there is proof to the contrary. As a safeguard, both criminal and civil procedure laws provide for changing the composition of a tribunal if the impartiality of any of its members is questioned. In practice, courts are not reluctant to apply these provisions. Therefore, even the appearance of impartiality (the consideration that justice shall not only be done but also be perceived to be done) seems to be effectively ensured. Further, trial prosecutors do not take part in judicial deliberations. Judges who might previously have been involved in the prosecution of the accused do not sit in the criminal case involving the same person. Nevertheless, doubts may still arise. In particular, judges who previously extended the pre-trial detention must have assumed that the accused had committed a crime, but they are later allowed to sit in the criminal case involving the same individual. It is questionable whether judges in this situation may be truly impartial when determining the defendant's guilt or innocence.

The way in which court proceedings are recorded may also raise legitimate concerns. Neither tape recording nor written notes are utilized. Instead, a court clerk simply writes down what the judge dictates. Therefore, the court transcripts are not authentic records of the proceedings. They are merely a reflection of the judge's utterances based on his understanding and reproducing capacity. Sometimes judges simply summarize the defendants' and witnesses' statements, and the clerk writes the summary down.

Doubts about the manner in which justice is done may also arise from the procedural rule preventing trial prosecutors and defense attorneys from questioning defendants and witnesses directly. Defendants and witnesses may be interrogated only through judges. Historically, this practice was justified by the desire to protect those giving testimony in court from being influenced or subjected to psychological pressures. However, the rule may also be viewed as a specific feature of the inquisitorial system, providing the judge with absolute power and an active role during the proceedings.

Right to Public Hearing and Judgment

A public hearing and a judgment, as means by which confidence in courts can be maintained, is constitutionally guaranteed[45] and enforced by the judiciary. Some exceptions, such as in cases involving juveniles, public order, national security and the protection of privacy considerations, are permitted under conditions defined by law. Judgments are pronounced publicly, even where the case proceedings are closed to the public. However, problems may arise with regard to the judicial functions of the public prosecutors. Because they are considered members of the judiciary, their failure to comply with the requirement of "openness" of proceedings and the decision-making process to the public is obvious.

Reasonable Time Requirement

The requirement that the hearing be held within a reasonable time is provided for neither by the Constitution nor by the procedural laws. The Code of Criminal Procedure calls for speedy proceedings in cases involving detained persons, but this is a somewhat different matter. Internal guidelines provide some time limits for criminal investigations and civil and criminal trials. However, owing to the large number of cases, the guidelines are rarely complied with by police officers, prosecutors and judges. Other factors contribute to delays, such as complications in preparing and sending experts' reports to court. Generally, however, criminal cases are handled with little delay.

THE RIGHT TO PRIVATE PROPERTY

The right to private property is guaranteed by the Constitution and enforced by the judiciary.[46] Expropriation on grounds of public interest is strictly regulated and allowed only if just compensation is paid in advance. If the parties do not agree upon compensation, the courts shall decide the matter.

Returning property to legitimate owners has raised several difficult legal and social policy issues. Since communist-era expropriations were based on a properly promulgated statute, the judiciary lacked adequate legal measures to return property to previous owners in the absence of new statutory regulations. In 1991 the Law on Land Return was passed. Under the Law, courts may determine the size and place of the land to be returned if a special commission created fails to reach a decision.

In view of the enormous housing problem, returning buildings to legitimate owners has proven to be a most difficult issue. As a consequence, in November 1995 the Parliament adopted a law providing for reparation. Unfortunately, property rights were not restored, save in a few cases.[47] Moreover, the Law gives tenants the opportunity to buy the houses they live in. The then parliamentary opposition characterized this Law as "the second nationalization" and voted against it. Nevertheless, the bill was passed, and at the time of this writing the Law was being implemented.

In July 1997, one of the now-ruling parties drafted a bill returning all houses to their former owners. The draft will probably reach the Parliament in the near future. Although the draft envisages welcome restitution to the victims of the nationalization process, it may be seen as violating one of the basic principles of the law of contracts that prohibits the nullification of legally executed contracts. This problem is especially difficult regarding these contracts between tenants and the state that were concluded in the very recent past. The difficulty is that these contracts were concluded on behalf of the new democratic government. The principles of non-retroactivity of legal provisions may also turn out to be another stumbling block. The Parliament will have to deal carefully with these sensitive matters.

One may note that courts ruled in favor of former owners where expropriation was unlawfully executed, that is, when it took place in violation of the laws then in existence. However, such cases are not covered by the 1995 Law. Neither are cases of expropriation in the public interest, which took place during the last ten years of Ceausescu's rule. However, courts will decide such cases applying the general rules governing civil claims.

A legitimate concern is raised by the return of the property of the Greek Catholic Church. Although the legal status of the Church has been re-established, its property was not statutorily restored.[48] Courts have been asked to decide a few cases involving this issue. In one case the Greek Catholic Cathedral from Blaj has been returned to the Church. Another case, concerning a Bucharest church owned by the Greek Catholics for more than 100 years, is not yet final. The court of first instance ruled that although the right to the property belongs to the Greek Catholics, the use of the Church may not be taken from the Orthodox Church, since more Orthodox followers live in the neighborhood. In Bucharest, a city of 2.5 million, there are officially 11,000 Greek Catholics (unofficially there are 50,000 of them), but it is impossible to get a Greek Catholic majority living in the vicinity of one church. The court's reasoning might result in denying Greek Catholics the right to use any of the Bucharest worship places that used to belong to their Church. Certain Greek Catholic followers have thus declared that this decision amounts to an impermissible judicial obstacle to the right to practice their religion. It is quite likely that the new legislation will correct the injustice. A bill providing for the return of the Greek Catholic churches is currently under consideration in the Parliament.

CONCLUDING REMARKS

The change of the institutional system, the adoption of the new Constitution, the reinstatement of the multiparty system and local and national free elections are all reflective of a political life with unquestionable democratic dimensions.

Several years have passed since the December 1989 Revolution, and Romanian society is undergoing a continuing change of attitudes, mentalities and behaviors. The experience of accumulating rights and the methods by which these rights are exercised and protected have had a profound impact on individuals. Important segments of the population are involved in the emerging free press, in the process of reorganizing local communities and in building the civil society. A significant step has been taken by establishing numerous non-governmental organizations that are active in civic education, the protection of human rights and the internal evolution of democratic structures.

The legislative process is gradually becoming more sensitive to the international human rights standards. Non-governmental organizations are allowed and even encouraged to take part in the activities of parliamentary commissions when drafts directly involving or having an impact on human rights issues are debated. Nevertheless, some of the newly adopted legislation, particularly involving the judiciary and criminal law issues, does not comply with internationally established human rights standards. Many reforms have not been fully implemented, or they disguise deep structural obstacles to the full protection of human rights. Although the independence of the judiciary was publicly supported by those in power, it was not, at least until recently, fully observed in practice.

The newly elected government declared itself committed to the protection of human rights. Although only time will tell, the slowly developing changes aimed at installing and maintaining democracy are here to stay. Romania's progress toward liberal democracy has reached the point of no return.

NOTES

1. Rom. Const. art. 24 (1886); Rom. Const. art. 25 (1923).

2. Rom. Const. art. 26, para. 5 (1923).

3. Vladimir Tismaneanu, *Reinventing Politics—Eastern Europe from Stalin to Havel* (New York: Free Press, 1993), 18–24.

4. *Id.* at 24.

5. *Id.* at 83.

6. *Id.* at 223, 228, 234.

7. *Id.* at 116.

8. *Id.* at 84.

9. The Constitution of Romania was adopted in the Constituent Assembly Session of Nov. 21, 1991, and became operative pursuant to its approval by the National Referendum of Dec. 8, 1991. The English-language version may be found in Albert P. Blaustein and Gisbert H. Flanz, eds., *Constitutions of the Countries of the World*, Vol. XVI (Dobbs Ferry, NY: Oceana Publications, 1992), 5–31.

10. Rom. Const. art. 11, 20 (1991).

11. Law no. 92/1992, amended in Aug. 1997. The new statute became operational on Aug. 14, 1997.

12. Article 75 of the Law on the Reorganization of the Judiciary provides for stability.

13. The process of deliberation in judicial chambers was exempted from hierarchical control, but once a decision had been made, the inspectorate was authorized to review it and evaluate the work of the judges from the point of the substance of their decisions.

14. The Decision of July 5, 1994, of the Romanian Constitutional Court.

15. Frederick König, rapporteur for the Political Affairs Committee of the Council of Europe, "Preliminary Draft Report on the Application by the Republic of Romania for Membership of the Council of Europe," Doc. AS/pol(44)62, Strasbourg, May 7, 1993, at 9. This same issue was mentioned in the 1995 Report on Romania, adopted in May 1995 by the Committee on Legal Affairs and Human Rights of the Council of Europe.

16. Rom. Const. art. 30, paras. 1–4 (1991).

17. Rom. Const. art. 30, para. 6 (1991).

18. Rom. Const. art. 30, para. 7 (1991).

19. Law no. 48/1992, art. 39 (a–d).

20. Article 168/1 of the Criminal Code. It is a new prohibition, introduced by the November 1996 Law on Amending the Criminal Code.

21. Article 236/1 of the Criminal Code. This also is a new criminal prohibition, introduced by the November 1996 Law on Amending the Criminal Code.

22. Article 236 of the Criminal Code. It has been kept in force without any modifications since 1969 when the current Criminal Code came into force.

23. Article 238, para. 1 of the Criminal Code. The November 1996 Law on Amending the Criminal Code retained the crime and increased the punishment.

24. Article 239, paras. 1 and 3 of the Criminal Code. The text of the provisions and the range of penalties have been modified by the November 1996 Law on Amending the Criminal Code.

25. The overwhelming majority of printed, audiovisual and electronic media is in private hands.

26. Articles 205 and 206 provide for crimes of "insult" and "defamation."

27. Article 207 of the Criminal Code.

28. Rom. Const. art. 31 (1991).

29. Romania has ratified both the European Convention of Human Rights and Fundamental Freedoms and the European Convention for the Prevention of Torture and Inhuman and Degrading Treatment or Punishment.

30. Rom. Const. art. 22(3) (1991).

31. The Romanian Criminal Code was adopted in 1968 and came into force in 1969. It has since been amended many times.

32. Article 250: Abusive Treatment; Article 266: Abusive Investigation; Article 267: Exposure to Abusive Treatment.

33. Law no. 140 was adopted on Nov. 5, 1996, and came into force on Nov. 14, 1996. It was one of the last pieces of legislation adopted by the former Parliament.

34. Up to seven years, up to twelve years if serious harm occurs and—if the victim is a high official or a member of the police or magistracy—up to fifteen years regardless of the severity of damage.

35. See *Amnesty International Report* (Alameda, CA, 1995).

36. Rom. Const. art. 22 (1991).

37. These rights were not provided by the previous Code of Criminal Procedure.

38. Detention ends either when a conviction or an acquittal is entered by the court or when a non-indictment decision is taken by the prosecutor. Thus, within the meaning of the law, preventive detention also encompasses pre-trial detention.

39. Previous criminal legislation allowed the prosecutor to issue four warrants, each one month in duration, before bringing the detained person before a judge. At the end of the four months the prosecutor had to ask for the extension of the preventive detention if investigations had not been completed.

40. "Correspondence" encompasses postal communication, telephone, telegraph and all other means of short- or long-distance communication.

41. Article 192 of the Criminal Code ("Violation of Domicile") provides for sentences up to three years of imprisonment or a fine and up to seven years if the crime is perpetrated by an armed person, by more people acting in concert, during nighttime or

by using a ruse. Article 195 of the Code ("Violation of the Secrecy of Correspondence") provides for sentences of up to three years of imprisonment.

42. Rom. Const. art. 26 (1991).

43. Article 200, para. 1 of the Criminal Code.

44. Article 200, para. 5 of the Criminal Code.

45. Rom. Const. art. 26 (1991).

46. Rom. Const. art. 41 (1991).

47. If the former owners or their heirs live as tenants in the houses that had been nationalized—but only with respect to the apartment they live in.

48. The Greek Catholic Church was declared illegal and its property confiscated by Decree No. 358/1948. Since Dec. 1989, the Greek Catholics have been free to practice their religion. The property issue was left (by the Decree No. 126/1990) to special commissions formed by Orthodox (owning now the former Greek Catholic places of worship) and Greek Catholic representatives. In most cases, the Greek Catholics did not recover their churches.

Chapter 2

The Judicial Protection of the Constitutional Rights and Freedoms in Russia: Myths and Reality

IGOR PETRUKHIN

A HUMAN BEING IS THE SUPREME VALUE

According to communist ideology, if there is a conflict between social and private interests, preference must be given to the former. Lenin's phrase "We recognize nothing private" captured well the essence of this approach. The dominance of the public interest was obvious in every area of life. As a result, a human being as a separate and unique entity decreased in value. Such an attitude was adopted to justify the cruelty of the Bolshevik Revolution and the Civil War, as well as such subsequent phenomena as forced labor, forcible collectivization and mass repressions of the "enemies of the people."

Many generations of Soviet people were raised in a society that embraced the spirit of Machiavelli: The end justifies the means. This principle meant, in particular, that in the struggle against crime all means were acceptable. Violence and torture were justifiable methods of obtaining confessions. The age-old conflict between "control over crime" and "human rights" was resolved, and is still resolved, in favor of the use of tough measures in the prevention of crime even if it results in the violation of human rights. Even today, the authorities have the illusion that criminality can be controlled by harsh punishments. Many law enforcement agents still reason that "it is better to convict 10 innocent persons than to acquit one guilty person." The discovery of the truth, until now, was the chief goal of criminal proceedings, whereas the protection of individual rights was at best only a means of its achievement.

The democratic traditions, which had started developing in Russia after the abolition of serfdom in 1861 and the radical judicial reform of 1864, were discredited and consigned to oblivion after the 1917 Bolshevik Revolution. Presumption of innocence and other democratic principles of justice were declared "dogmas of the bourgeois law." The judiciary became an obedient tool of the Communist Party. Human rights were recognized on paper, but in practice they were often gravely violated. The official line was that rights and freedoms were a myth in the bourgeois countries and the reality in the communist ones.[1]

There was no constitution in a contemporary sense. The instrument that was called the constitution was just the text that did not reflect the real life of the society and the functioning of the state. A highly abstract mode of analysis dominated the legal scholarship. Authors had first to provide spacious citations from the documents of the Party's congresses and speeches of "the leaders" before they could express their own ideas. A strict censorship of all publications was part of the communist power system.

During the 1953–1964 Khrushchev "thaw" and the 1964–1985 Brezhnev "stagnation," the first cautious steps were made toward democratization of social political life. The more crucial reforms, however, started when the country entered the period of Gorbachev's "perestroika" (1985–1991). They gained fresh impetus after the suppression of the August 1991 coup and the victory of democratic forces allied with Yeltsin. In particular, the ideal of a state governed by the "Rule of Law," in which the fundamental value is the individual and in which the basic guarantees of individual rights and freedoms are protected by the judiciary, has been accepted by, and secured in, the 1993 Constitution of the Russian Federation.

The comprehensive judicial reform of a truly democratic nature began in 1991 shortly after the proclamation of independence by Russia and other former republics of the Soviet Union. "The Blueprint for Judicial Reform in the Russian Federation" was then presented to the Parliament by the President.

The basic trends of judicial and legal reform outlined in the document are the following: creating a strong and independent judicial branch; developing constitutional review; creating a court system consistent with the country's administrative structure; ensuring the leading position of the judiciary functioning independently outside the system of law enforcement bodies; expanding judicial protection of constitutional and other individual rights, including judicial supervision over preliminary investigations in criminal matters and over the course of implementing court sentences; expanding the system of jury trials; transforming the Soviet-style procuracy into an organ of public prosecution, devoid of supervisory functions; strengthening the prestige of the bar and its role in the protection of individual rights; and humanizing criminal policy, in particular, the system of sanctions.

The "Blueprint" is based on the assumption that it should be up to the judiciary to guarantee the observance of rights and legally protected interests of citizens vis-à-vis the state authority. The individual and the state must be equal parties. It is the court that should level off the inequality between the powerful machine of governmental authority and the "little guy."

The judiciary should become the primary protector of individual rights and freedoms and of civil peace and harmony. Constitutional provisions on human rights and freedoms shall be applied directly, thereby determining the meaning and content of the laws and ensuring justice (Article 18 of the Constitution). This indicates that rights and freedoms are not conferred by the basic law but only recognized by it.

Over the centuries, the idea that the court was a repressive body designed to punish or impose harsh sanctions was deeply ingrained in the consciousness of the nation. Andrey Vyshinsky, the leading jurist of the Stalinist era, long before the widespread repressions of the 1930s, claimed that "criminal procedure . . . is a system of coercive norms, which are established by governmental power."[2] Somewhat later, he expressed this idea even more categorically: "Suppression and coercion are an expression of the uniform policy of the Soviet court."[3] The image of a "policeman-court" ("executioner-court") is still present in the social consciousness. Currently, however, the court assumes a completely different role: It exercises control over the legality of the methods of the struggle against crime, protecting the citizen from arbitrariness and lawlessness.

One considerable achievement of judicial reform was the establishment in 1991 of the Constitutional Court of the Russian Federation. Unfortunately, the Court failed to pass a decision banning the Communist Party (its primary cells continued to exist, and the central bodies of the renewed Communist Party, which currently constitutes the left-wing parliamentary opposition, were later rebuilt on the basis of these cells) as well as failed to avoid becoming entangled in the political and armed conflict between the Supreme Soviet and the President in the fall of 1993. This resulted in the suspension of the Court's operation for about a year. Having resumed its work, the Court concentrated on the protection of citizens' fundamental rights and freedoms. Its activity in this sphere has proved rather effective. The Constitutional Court has decided over 70 cases, mainly involving various individual rights. For example, the Court ruled that the dismissal of an employee who reached retirement age was unconstitutional and that the Penal Code's section providing punishment for refusal to return from abroad was in conflict with the Constitution. The Court also ruled that a lawyer should be allowed to participate freely in a case involving classified data without the necessity of obtaining a clearance to state secrets.

Other achievements of judicial-legal reform should also be noted. Judicial supervision over detention during the preliminary investigation was introduced in 1992 (Article 220[1], 220[2] of the RSFSR Code of Criminal Procedure). The new market-oriented Civil Code was adopted in 1996, and the new Penal Code took effect on January 1, 1997. The idea of humanization of punishments has been partly reflected in the new Correctional Code of the Russian Federation, which was adopted by the Duma on December 18, 1996. The new Family Code, Water Code, Land Code and Arbitral Procedure Code have also been promulgated. Unfortunately, the new Code of Criminal Procedure has not yet been adopted. There are serious controversies among the drafters over several versions of the code: there is also considerable diversity of opinion among the Duma factions on issues such as jury trial, the relationship between prosecutorial and judicial supervision over the preliminary investigation and the necessity of making the preliminary investigation adversarial.

After a long debate, the Federal Law on the Court System of the Russian Federation was finally adopted by the Duma on October 23, 1996. This piece of legislation is more a framework, as it presupposes the adoption of statutes on separate branches of the court system.

THE PROTECTION OF THE INDIVIDUAL AS THE GOAL OF THE SYSTEM OF CRIMINAL JUSTICE

The protection of individual rights in the process of the search for the truth has become the separate and vital goal of the criminal justice system. The legislature has finally recognized that a certain number of crimes will always remain undiscovered and that, in some cases, the truth will never be established or will be established only at a great social cost. Consequently, in many instances the legislature gives preference to the protection of individual rights and legal interests. Thus, the law protects the victim's personal interests in the case of rape (Article 131 [1] of the Penal Code), since the proceedings may start only upon the victim's complaint. If the victim does not want the inquiry, the criminal investigation must stop.

Similarly, crimes such as insult, slander, libel and infliction of minor bodily injuries may not be investigated (nor even recorded) without the victim's complaint or if the defendant and the victim have reconciled prior to the commencement of deliberations in the judge's chamber (Article 27 of the RSFSR Code of Criminal Procedure). According to the Russian Federation Law of 15 December 1996 on the Changes and Amendments to the RSFSR Code of Criminal Procedure, a criminal case may be dismissed on the motion of an "aggrieved party" if the latter and the accused have reconciled, assuming that the crime is minor, the suspect has no criminal record and the harm caused has been redressed (Article 9 of the Code of Criminal Procedure). In such cases, the state, abandoning the search for the truth, gives priority to the private interests of the parties (unless the public prosecutor decides to intervene due to the important public interest involved).

The removal of physical evidence (e.g., a bullet) from the human body without the clearly expressed consent of an individual is prohibited (Article 32 of the Fundamental Legislation of the Russian Federation [RF] on the Protection of Citizens' Health). Obviously, the lack of consent may hinder the discovery of truth. Yet, in such cases, the interests of the individual are deemed more important.

In some instances it might be desirable to establish the mental condition of the victim or witnesses in an institutional setting in order to properly evaluate their testimony. However, neither the victim nor witnesses may be placed into a psychiatric institution without their consent. The law provides for involuntary commitment only with respect to the suspect (Article 188 of the Code of Criminal Procedure).

To secure the right to appeal, and to safeguard the protection of the accused's right to a defense, the law prohibits appellate courts from setting aside judicial mistakes that worked in the defendant's favor if appellate proceedings were initiated only by the defendant or his defense attorney. Thus, the defendant's right to appeal is considered more important than the correction of certain mistakes discovered by an appellate court in considering a defendant's appeal.

The current law requires the courts to establish whether the crime has been committed and to identify the guilty (Article 2 of the Code of Criminal Procedure). This is not in conformity with the ideal of a state governed by the Rule of Law. This task should belong to the investigatory bodies, that is, the investigators and public prosecutors. Judges have their own specific duties, that is, to determine whether the accusation has been proven, whether a violation of the law has taken place during the preliminary investigation and whether the interests of citizens and society have not been infringed upon during the proceedings.

In a number of cases, despite best efforts, it is impossible to ascertain whether it was the defendant who committed the crime. The presumption of innocence then takes effect, and the defendant must be unconditionally acquitted. In view of such an outcome, it would, nevertheless, be a mistake to claim that, having failed to establish the truth, the court has not fulfilled its duty.

Another prevalent erroneous view is that one of the tasks of the judiciary is to combat and eradicate criminality.[4] It is obvious that the struggle against crime is the task of the entire society. Law enforcement bodies are unable to eliminate crime, which is rooted primarily in the conditions of material and spiritual life. Therefore, law enforcement agencies and the judiciary can, at best, only reduce crime through crude means of repression. In reality, the level of criminality in a given society depends only to a limited extent on the activities of law enforcement agencies.

THE RIGHT OF A CITIZEN TO APPEAL TO A JUDGE FOR PROTECTION

Usually, the citizen's rights are exercised without difficulty, and obligations are performed voluntarily. However, in some situations the implementation of rights is hindered. The intervention of the court is then necessary for the restoration of legal order. Each person is guaranteed the judicial protection of his rights (Article 46 of the Constitution).

Five forms of court proceedings may be distinguished as follows: (1) civil proceedings; (2) criminal proceedings; (3) administrative proceedings (if the case concerns administrative violations falling under the jurisdiction of the court); (4) arbitral proceedings; and (5) constitutional adjudication.

The right to petition for judicial protection belongs to all citizens on an equal basis. However, the court may deny a complaint or motion for review in cases specifically provided for by the law (Article 129 of the Code of Civil Procedure). In practice, though, the victim is often deprived of judicial protection. In many instances law enforcement bodies, in violation of existing regulations, do not even register crime reports. Moreover, they do not proceed with a case unless there is certainty that a crime will be successfully discovered. They also do not prosecute in other situations (e.g., when either the accused or the offense he had committed have been found to be no longer socially dangerous). Generally speaking, law enforcement agencies do not send weak cases to the court for fear that the accused may be acquitted or the case returned to them for additional investigation. In 1996 alone, 400,000 criminal cases did not reach the court; they were discontinued at an investigatory stage without a conclusive determination of the suspect's responsibility. The root of this problem is the inability of the investigatory apparatus to ensure the discovery of crimes and its desire to conceal this shortcoming by terminating cases without a final determination of responsibility.

The frequency of citizen petitions to the court for the protection of rights depends on a variety of social and legal factors. The current revival in various areas of social life, the economic acceleration, the intensification of business contacts—all result in a large number of petitions to the courts. However, the frequency of judicial miscarriages of justice turns citizens away from the judiciary, giving rise to a hostile public attitude toward it.

The right of citizens to petition for judicial protection is secured by the institution of "citizens' judges." Article 47, chapter 1 of the Constitution proclaims, "No one may be deprived of the right to the consideration of his case in the court and with the judge under the jurisdiction of which the case belongs by law."

This provision requires, first, that jurisdiction must be specifically established by law and, second, that it may not be changed arbitrarily. The delineation of the jurisdiction defines boundaries of the citizen's subjective right to have his case heard before a "legitimate" court ("his/her" court). Every person should know in advance which court or which judge will consider his or her case. This formula reflects the manifestations of the principle of equality before the law and before the court. The right to a "legitimate" court appeared for the first time in Russian constitutional legislation in 1993.

However, under the current legal regime, a higher-level court may, on the defendant's motion, take over any criminal case from a lower court and try it as a court of first instance. A higher-level court may also take over any civil case and try it as a first instance court even in the absence of a defendant's motion (Article 40 of the Code of Criminal Procedure; Articles 114–116 of the Code of Civil Procedure).

In addition, the law permits the transfer of criminal and civil cases from a court under whose jurisdiction they fall to another similar court of the same level. This decision may be taken by a chairman of a higher court "for the purpose of the quickest, fullest and most objective consideration of the case" (Article 44 of the Code of Criminal Procedure). As a result, the right of the citizen to the consideration of his case by "his/her" judge is flouted.

The right to a "citizen's judge" in civil cases operates in favor of the defendant (according to the general rule, all legal documents are served at the defendant's place of residence). Only in special instances, where it is essential to protect the interests of certain categories of citizens, may a lawsuit be heard by the court at the plaintiff's residence (e.g., in cases concerning alimony or paternity—Article 118 of the Code of Civil Procedure) or at the location of a disputed property or parcel of land (Article 119 of the Code of Civil Procedure).

Another provision of the Code of Criminal Procedure (Article 41) is also in conflict with Article 47 of the Constitution. When it is impossible to ascertain the place of commission of the crime, then the case will be heard by a court of the district in which the preliminary investigation was concluded. However, the preliminary investigation may be conducted in the place where the crime was discovered, in the place where the suspect was detained or in the place where the majority of witnesses reside (Article 132 of the Code of Criminal Procedure). In such cases the defendant is deprived of the right to "his/her" judge and must appear before the court of a "foreign" republic, region or district. However, the right to a citizen's judge is protected by the rule that mandates the reversal of a court's decision that has been handed down in violation of jurisdictional rules; the case then will be transferred for consideration to the appropriate court.

THE APPEAL TO A COURT AGAINST ILLEGAL ACTIONS AND ACTS

Article 46 of the Russian Constitution states:

1. Everyone shall be guaranteed protection of his or her rights and liberties in a court of law.
2. The decisions and actions (or inaction) of state organs, organs of local self-government, public associations and officials may be appealed against in a court of law.
3. In conformity with the international treaties of the Russian Federation, everyone shall have the right to turn to interstate organs concerned with the protection of human rights and liberties when all the means of legal protection available within the State have been exhausted.

One must note that not only fundamental constitutional rights but other rights and freedoms are also under judicial protection. In other words, one may petition a court for the protection of rights that are granted to the citizen not only by the Constitution or statutory law but also by other normative acts.

The right to judicial protection belongs to every person, including incompetent ones. In such situations, these rights may be exercised through a representative, in particular, a lawyer.

One may appeal legal decisions and official actions or inactions. In particular, one may appeal the decrees of the Russian President, decrees of the Council of

Ministers of the Russian Federation (RF) and various acts of ministries and other governmental agencies. These appeals may take place only if a given normative act or an official action or inaction in the opinion of the citizen violates in a concrete situation his rights and freedoms. One may also appeal orders, sentences and other decisions handed down by courts or law enforcement agencies. Decisions of collective bodies (e.g., the decision of a university admission committee or a committee for the distribution of humanitarian aid) may also be appealed to a court.

Actions (decisions) may be appealed to a court in a situation where (1) the citizen's rights and freedoms have been violated; (2) obstacles in the realization of rights and freedoms have been created; (3) a duty has been improperly imposed on a citizen (e.g., a military duty has been imposed despite a citizen's request based on religious convictions); or (4) a citizen is held liable in the absence of a legal basis. The complaint must indicate the nature of the alleged erroneous decision or action involved in a particular case.

Appeal may be directed against the decisions or actions of official bodies and persons from all three branches of government—legislative, executive and judicial. These include the decisions or actions of local self-government, public associations and other government employees.

The Federal Law of 15 November 1995 On Changes and Additions to the RF Law on the Appeal to the Court against Actions and Decisions Violating Citizens' Rights and Freedoms provides for the liability not only of officials but of all government and municipal employees if they violate the law or fail to protect citizens' rights. Officials and government employees whose actions and decisions are appealed have the burden of proving the legality of their decisions and actions. This reflects the principle that a citizen's complaint is presumed to be justified. All the citizen has to prove is that a violation of his or her rights and freedoms has taken place.

An appeal by way of civil legal proceedings may not be directed against (1) actions (decisions) whose review belongs to the exclusive jurisdiction of the Constitutional Court (e.g., international treaties that have not yet entered into force, treaties between the Russian Federation and its subjects) and (2) actions (decisions) for which the legislature has provided for other forms (or procedures) of judicial appeal (Article 3 of the Law of 27 April 1993 On Appeals against Actions and Decisions Violating Citizens' Rights and Freedoms).

Unfortunately, Article 46 of the Constitution and Article 3, Section 3 of the Law of 27 April 1993 are substantially undermined by the Law of 28 April 1993 modifying certain rules of civil procedure.[5] The Law provides for no appeals against normative acts (and decisions handed down in the implementation of these acts) that concern the protection of the national defense (the management of military units, the organization of combat duty, the securing of combat readiness) or the state security of the Russian Federation. If these acts may not be appealed in accordance with the Code of Civil Procedure, then they generally are not subject to appeal. It is difficult, however, to imagine defense and security

interests of such magnitude that could ever justify the removal from the jurisdiction of the court of a person's complaint involving the violation of a person's
rights by official persons and bodies of the Ministry of Defense, the federal
counterintelligence services and other governmental departments.

The Law of 27 April 1993 provides that the right to appeal also extends to
private corporations and joint-stock companies. Article 1 does not distinguish
between these bodies and governmental institutions and corporations. This is
consistent with Article 46, Section 1 of the Constitution, which guarantees the
judicial defense of rights and liberties to every person regardless of the nature
of his or her employment.

Almost 10,000 complaints against actions of officials and government agencies were filed in 1992; 12,526 in 1993; 27,767 in 1994; and 34,685 in 1995.
About 70 percent of these complaints have been decided in favor of complainants. Although the number of complaints has increased considerably, it is still
very small considering that the country's population exceeds 150 million. This
relatively small number reflects judicial bureaucratic delays as well as the high
court fees involved in appealing a case.

A citizen also has the right to seek redress from the Russian Constitutional
Court by filing a complaint alleging the unconstitutionality of a law that has
been applied in his case. The Court, having considered the complaint, may
declare unconstitutional any law that has been applied in that case.

What should be done if a law that is applied by a court in a specific case is
violative of the Constitution? In the author's view, in such a situation the court
should suspend the proceedings and refer the case to the Constitutional Court
for a decision as to the constitutionality of the relevant legal provision (Article
125, paragraph 4 of the Constitution). After the Constitutional Court's verdict,
the court should resume the proceedings and render a decision consistent with
the Court's ruling. However, the Russian Supreme Court has given a different
answer to this question—namely, that a court should simply refuse to apply an
unconstitutional law and render the decision based only on those legal provisions
that are consistent with the Constitution.[6]

In my view, the implementation of this ruling leads to undesirable consequences. Every judge would thereby be authorized to evaluate the conformity
of laws with the Constitution. Laws that judges deemed unfit for application
would be, in the words of Joseph Stalin, "put off to the side," though they will
not have been formally repealed. Chaos and arbitrariness would set in. Moreover, the unconstitutional law would still be effective since not all judicial decisions are published in Russia. In my opinion, the repeal of such a law may
be accomplished only by the Constitutional Court. There is no need for us to
adopt the American system of judicial review. Our legal system (as are all the
systems of Continental Europe) is based on statutory law, with a Constitution
at the very top. Under this system, there exists a hierarchy of legal norms to be
strictly observed by the courts. If a norm appears to violate the Constitution,

then the Constitutional Court should first take action to clarify and remedy the problem.

According to the Law of 27 April 1993, a complaint is to be filed, at the option of the citizen, either directly to a court or to a governmental body that is higher than the agency whose actions or decisions is being appealed. The citizen has an option to file a complaint to the court located in his place of residence or to the court where the agency whose action is being appealed is located. Having received the complaint, the court may suspend the implementation of the decision being appealed. Soldiers also have the right to appeal to military courts against the actions and decisions of military managerial bodies, commanders and superiors.

Under the 1993 Law, complaints are to be handled in accordance with procedural rules governing civil proceedings. At the citizen's request, a case may be considered by a single judge rather than by a judicial panel. The court (or the judge) may declare an appealed action or decision illegal, to force governmental agencies to satisfy the demands of the citizen or to rescind legal measures applied to a citizen on the basis of the invalidated action. The decision of the court is binding on all governmental organs and officials.

Article 46 of the Constitution permits the appeal to a court against decisions and actions of all law enforcement bodies—public prosecutors, investigators, bodies of inquiry, heads of investigative departments, corrective-labor institutions, operative-investigative bodies, the external intelligence services, counter-intelligence services, tax authorities and customs officials. Until recently, the decisions and actions of these bodies and official entities could be appealed only to the public prosecutor's office, which was considered to be the primary supervisory and monitoring body. Now, the monitoring function of the public prosecutor is gradually being transferred to the courts. However, it does not make sense to have two monitoring bodies with identical functions.

Unfortunately, several legislative acts adopted in the 1992–1995 period contradict Article 46 of the Constitution. These acts do not mention the right of a citizen to appeal illegal actions and decisions to a court. These include the Law on Militia (as amended in 1993); Law on the Institutions and Bodies Implementing the Criminal Punishment in the Form of the Deprivation of Liberty (1993); On the Protection of Highest Bodies of State Power in the Russian Federation and Their Officials (1993); On the Interior Troops of the Ministry of the Interior Affairs of the Russian Federation (1996); On Federal Bodies of Governmental Communications (1993); On Private Detective and Protective Activities in the Russian Federation (1992); and On Federal Bodies of the Tax Authority (1993). These acts generally state that supervision from the point of view of legality in the above-mentioned areas of state activity will be exercised by the public prosecutor. Similarly, the Law of 5 July 1995 on Operational Investigatory Activities does not provide for judicial review.

Finally, the federal Law On the Federal Security Service Bodies (1995) provides for the right to appeal to the court against the actions of the Federal

Security Service Bodies (FSB). However, at the option of the citizen, a complaint may be filed to a higher-level FSB official or to a public prosecutor (Article 6).

Despite these limitations, in the past several years the scope of judicial review has gradually been expanded. The Law of 23 May 1992, amending certain rules of criminal procedure, permits an appeal to a court in cases of pre-trial arrest.[7] Complaints to a court by citizens are permitted concerning unlawful actions undertaken by physicians (Article 69 of the Fundamental Legislation of the RF on the Protection of the Health of Citizens; Articles 47–49 of the Law of the RF on Psychiatric Aid and Guarantees of the Rights of Citizens Under Its Provision). The decision of a labor dispute commission may be appealed directly to a court (Articles 201, 209, 210 of the Labor Code of the RSFSR).

But there are still areas of law in which the prosecutor's supervision dominates. The law of corrections is one of those areas. Although under Article 46 of the RF Constitution courts may review complaints of the convicted against the illegal actions of the officials of the correctional institutions, the new Correctional Code (1996) does not mention the right to turn directly to the court without applying first to the administration.

Judicial decisions may be appealed to a higher-level court. A complaint results in appellate review. A regrettable exception is the lack of appeal of the decisions of the Russian Supreme Court when it acts as a court of first instance. This is in violation of Article 46 and Article 50, paragraph 3 of the Constitution. It is absolutely necessary to provide for an appellate procedure in such cases. In my view, an appellate panel of the Supreme Court should be created for this purpose.

Other prohibitions against the appeal of certain decisions (e.g., the refusal to exempt an individual from serving a punishment due to illness [Article 362] or the transfer of a case to another court [Articles 43, 44]) rendered by a court of first instance also violate Article 46 of the Constitution.

The right of each person to an appeal to supranational bodies remains dormant because Russia has yet to recognize the jurisdiction of such bodies. In March 1996 Russia was admitted to the Council of Europe. By a Decree issued on 16 May 1996 On Gradual Reduction of Death Penalty with Regard to Russia's Accession to the Council of Europe, President Yeltsin instructed the government to prepare a draft law on Russia's accession to Protocol No. 6 of the European Convention on Human Rights, providing for the abolition of the death penalty.

THE COURT AND THE RIGHT TO LIFE

Article 20 of the Russian Constitution declares:

1. Everyone shall have the right to life.
2. Capital punishment may, until its abolition, be instituted by the federal law as an exceptional punishment for especially grave crimes against life, with the accused having the right to have his case considered in a law court by jury.

The death penalty is a punishment of an exceptional nature, to be applied only on the basis of a court verdict. It may be handed down for a limited number of crimes enumerated in Article 21 of the Criminal Code. The intention to abolish the death penalty is expressed in the above-mentioned provision of the Constitution.

It should be noted that capital punishment had been abolished on three occasions in Russia (1917, 1920 and 1947–1950), but each time it has been restored. Arguably, the legal consciousness of the nation was not ready for such a liberal step. Such factors as the rise in crime, the application of more severe, barbarian methods for the commission of some crimes (e.g., murder), the appearance of organized crime and sloppy investigatory activities contributed to the restoration of the death penalty. In the 1960s and 1970s, the number of capital crimes rose to 22 (including embezzlement on a particularly large scale, large-scale bribery, the disruption of the operations of correctional institutions and so forth).

However, since the end of the 1980s, there has been a reduction in the number of crimes for which the death penalty could be imposed. In particular, the death penalty was abolished for economic crimes. By 1993, the number of capital crimes was reduced to six (excluding military crimes). Life imprisonment may always be imposed in lieu of the death penalty. In the 1991 Russian Declaration of Rights and Liberties of Man and Citizen, the death penalty is characterized as an exceptional punishment to be imposed for "particularly grave crimes" (Article 7). Under the Constitution, the scope of the death penalty should be limited to particularly grave crimes "against life." Under the 1996 Criminal Code, the following offenses are capital: aggravated murder (Article 105, paragraph 2); murder of a government or public official (Article 277); murder of an official administering justice or conducting an investigation (Article 295); and murder of a law enforcement officer (Article 317).

During the 1993–1994 period, only a handful of death sentences were carried out in Russia. In contrast, in 1995 the number rose to 78. This may be attributed to the general "brutalizing" of the criminal policy due to the sharp rise in crime.

In 1996 the President introduced a moratorium on the use of the death penalty, which has been observed since then. Nevertheless, death sentences are still being imposed.

Under Article 59 of the Criminal Code, individuals under 18 years of age at the time of committing a crime, women and men over age 65 at the time of receiving their sentence may not be sentenced to death.

According to established practice, the file of a criminal case in which a death sentence has been imposed is submitted to the Supreme Court of the Russian Federation for review, even in the absence of a complaint by the convicted person. After judicial review of the sentence, a person awaiting execution may be pardoned by the President of the Russian Federation (Article 89, paragraph "c" of the Constitution). Until the presidential decision has been taken, the death sentence may not be carried out. In 1990, 28 of the 571 persons sentenced to death in the USSR were pardoned. No one was pardoned in the Russian Federation in 1996.

A death sentence is carried out by a firing squad (Article 23 of the Criminal Code). Public executions are not permitted.

A defendant charged with a capital crime has the right to a trial by jury (Article 20, Section 2 of the Constitution).

According to the Law of 16 July 1993, juries decide only the question of the defendant's guilt, whereas it is up to the judge to impose the punishment, including the death penalty. It hardly seems just that juries take no part in the decision concerning the death penalty.

If the defendant agrees that his case be heard by the panel of three professional judges in one of the nine regions in which the jury trial has been introduced, the defendant may be sentenced to death by the panel.

JUDICIAL PROTECTION OF THE HONOR AND DIGNITY OF THE INDIVIDUAL

Article 21, Section 1 of the Constitution provides for the protection of the dignity of the individual. It also guarantees protection of children and the mentally ill. Further, the statutory law forbids the humiliation of the dignity and honor of all persons who are subject to examination in connection with criminal proceedings (Article 181 of the Code of Criminal Procedure) and persons brought in to participate in an investigative experiment (Article 183 of the Code of Criminal Procedure).

Under Article 21, violation of human dignity is never justified. This is particularly true with respect to those sentenced to imprisonment, those in poverty that forces them to ask for assistance and those suffering from disgraceful (by conventional notions) illnesses, such as mental illness, syphilis or AIDS. In fact, the individual who has been limited in his rights, or is dependent on other persons, requires more respect for his dignity.

The Russian Federation is bound by obligations embodied in the 1984 United Nations Convention against Torture and Other Cruel, Inhuman or Degrading Treatment or Punishment, and other international documents. An individual who believes that he has been subjected to torture or ill-treatment has the right to turn to a court with a complaint.

The 1996 Criminal Code provides, consistently with Article 21 of the Constitution, criminal responsibility for actions that are characterized by cruelty and violence or that infringe upon the honor and dignity of the person. Civil law protection measures are also available (e.g., filing for compensation for a moral injury that is caused by the dissemination of defamatory information [Article 151 of the Civil Code; Article 62 of the Law of 27 December 1991 On Mass Media]). The burden of proof with respect to the veracity of the information is placed on the person who disseminated it. If defamatory information was brought to the public attention, then it must be publicly retracted. The amount of monetary compensation for a moral injury is determined by the court rather arbitrarily, as there are no clear legal guidelines for the calculation of damages. Financial responsibility is incurred both by the editor (publishing house) and by the author.

The illegal deprivation of freedom amounts to torture (Article 127 of the Criminal Code). Long-term detention pending trial may also be considered torture. In the past, with the approval of the Presidium of the Supreme Soviet of the USSR, excessively long pre-trial detentions (up to three or even five years) were not uncommon. This practice has been discontinued. Nowadays the Prosecutor General may extend the term of the pre-trial detention for up to eighteen months. Until recently, the period during which the accused and his or her defense attorney familiarize themselves with the case materials was not considered as the detention time (Article 97, paragraph 5 of the Code of Criminal Procedure). The Constitutional Court has declared this provision unconstitutional as violative of the accused's right to counsel and right to freedom and dignity.[8] This issue has now been settled by law: Not later than five days before the expiration of the maximum term of the pre-trial detention (eighteen months), the Prosecutor General must apply to the judge with a motion for extension for a period of up to six months, until the accused and his or her defense attorney familiarize themselves with the case materials or until the end of the inquiry initiated on the motion of the accused or his or her defense attorney (Article 1 of the Law of 11 December 1996 On the Changes and Additions to Articles 26, 27 and 133 of the RSFSR Code of Criminal Procedure).

No upper limit for pre-trial detention has been established regarding detention during a trial stage of proceedings. This is troubling since judicial proceedings may take years.

Over 40 percent of those charged are placed in pre-trial detention. This contradicts Article 21 of the RF Constitution and Article 9, paragraph 3 of the International Covenant of the Civil and Political Rights, which declare that pre-trial detention should be used sparingly.

Unfortunately, the conditions for those in prisons, pre-trial detention centers and corrective labor camps meet neither international nor constitutional standards (e.g., inadequate food, overcrowded cells, the brutality of prison personnel, beatings and psychological pressure on detainees by correctional personnel). Recently, measures have been taken to improve the situation (the Law of 15 July 1995 On Holding in Custody of Those Suspected of and Charged with the Commission of Crime[9] and the implementing regulations [The Regulations for the Ministry of Internal Affairs Pretrial Detention Centers registered with the Ministry of Justice on 31 January 1996]).[10] The Regulations of the Ministry of Internal Affairs Detention Centers, registered with the Ministry of Justice on 11 January 1996, specify in detail the rights and obligations of detainees and convicts in greater detail.[11]

JUDICIAL PROTECTION OF THE FREEDOM AND INDIVIDUAL INVIOLABILITY OF CITIZENS

Article 22 of the Constitution states:

1. Everyone shall have the right to freedom and personal inviolability.
2. Arrest, detention and keeping in custody shall be allowed only by an order of a court of law. No person may be detained for more than 48 hours without an order of a court of law.

The right to freedom and the inviolability of the individual belongs to every person. In all cases in which this right is violated, an individual may demand its vindication by the Court (Article 46 of the Constitution).

These rights are legally protected. The protection consists of the impermissibility, prevention and punishment of infringements on (1) life, health, bodily inviolability and sexual freedom (physical inviolability); (2) honor, dignity and moral freedom (moral inviolability—Article 21 of the Constitution); (3) the normal course of psychological processes (psychological inviolability); and (4) the freedom of the individual that is expressed in granting him the opportunity to do what he wishes in his free time, permitting him to choose his place of residence freely and refraining from placing him under supervision (individual security).

The Constitution has introduced judicial control over the legality and soundness of measures that limit the freedom of the individual, namely, arrest and detention. Two basic forms of arrest may be distinguished: arrest as a penal measure and arrest as a preventive (detention) measure. The former may have the following forms: (1) administrative arrest, that is, punishment imposed for a period of up to 15 days (in the state of emergency up to 30 days) by a court or a judge (Article 32 of the Code on Administrative Violations); (2) arrest as a criminal punishment (i.e., holding of the convicted in isolation for a period of up to six months (Article 45 of the Criminal Code); and (3) disciplinary arrest, which is a military disciplinary penalty imposed by military superiors. Under Article 22 of the Constitution, an arrest is allowed only following a judicial decision. This rule, however, does not apply to disciplinary arrest in view of the fact that this punishment is imposed only for military violations.

Arrest as a preventive measure (detention) is used in criminal proceedings (Articles 89, 96 of the Code of Criminal Procedure), and it requires judicial approval. A judicial decision is a decision (order) of an individual judge to whom an investigator or a prosecutor has applied with a motion to detain. A judicial decision within the meaning of Article 22, Section 2 of the Constitution is also a decision concerning the detention of the accused that is rendered by a judge at the trial stage of criminal proceedings. A judicial decision is also necessary, either for the extension of the detention or establishing the time limit of the defendant's stay in custody when the case is being handled by the court. The change or recision of this preventive measure is also possible but only on the basis of a judicial decision.

In addition, one may also distinguish detention in the form of a short confinement without a judicial warrant or a prosecutor's approval. This form of detention is permitted in connection with criminal proceedings only for a period of 48 hours (until the adoption of the provisions implementing Article 22, Section 2 of the Constitution, the length is still 72 hours [Article 122 of the Code of Criminal Procedure]).

Administrative detention may last longer than 48 hours. Those who violate the border-area regulations may be detained for identification and for inquiry into the circumstances of the violation for a period of up to 3 days; if they cannot be identified, they may be detained for a period of up to 10 days. Vagrants or minors may be placed in Centers for Social Rehabilitation for a period of up to 30 days. However, in accordance with Article 22, Section 2 of the Constitution, which has been brought into conformity with Article 9, Section 3 of the International Covenant of Civil and Political Rights, a judicial decision is required if the length of detention is to exceed 48 hours. The implementing legislation, however, has not been issued so far.

The Concluding and Transitional provisions of the Constitution state that "until the procedural rules of the Russian Federation has been harmonized with the provisions of the present Constitution, the previous rules remain in force." This means that for the time being Article 22, Section 2 of the Constitution remains merely a declaration of intentions. In particular, the decisions to detain and to extend the period of detention are still in the hands of the public prosecutors. This is in conflict with Article 5 of the International Covenant of Civil and Political Rights, under which such decisions should be made by agencies of a judicial nature. The Russian public prosecutor is certainly not one of them. Since the transitional provision mentioned above concerns only criminal procedure rules, all administrative detentions exceeding 48 hours must be approved by a judge.

Until the entry into force of Article 22, under which arrests should be authorized by a court, the Law of 23 May 1992 has temporarily introduced an alternative in the form of judicial control over the legality and validity of pre-trial detention orders made by an investigator and approved by the public prosecutor.[12] It is important to emphasize that what is being tested by the court are not only the formal (procedural) prerequisites for the detention but also the sufficiency of the factual basis. As a consequence, the investigators and the public prosecutor are required to present to the court evidence that substantiates the legality and necessity of extending its length.

Judicial supervision of the legality and soundness of a detention order, and in particular the extension of the length of detention, is performed by a single judge no later than three days after the receipt of a complaint and the file of the case. The participation of the public prosecutor is mandatory. A detainee and his defense attorney have the right to participate in the proceedings and to familiarize themselves with the materials that have been presented by the investigator and the public prosecutor. The judge renders either a written decision concerning the rescision or notice of no change in the preventive measure. The decision must contain a statement of reasons. If the evidence on which the detention order has been based has not been submitted, the order must be annulled.

The judge who has reviewed the legality and validity of the detention order must be excluded from further proceedings in the case to ensure impartiality.

The coercive placement of a suspect (accused) in a psychiatric institution is considered a form of detention. Consequently, a judicial decision to that effect is required. The length of confinement is considered the period of detention (Article 188 of the Code of Criminal Procedure).

Criminal measures such as ordering a soldier to serve in a disciplinary battalion (Article 55 of the Penal Code) are also considered a detention within the meaning of Article 22 of the Constitution. Other measures restricting citizens' freedoms include coercive medical treatment of the mentally ill who represent a danger to themselves and others (they may be placed in a hospital with the subsequent judicial approval for compulsory treatment—Articles 32–36 of the Law On Psychiatric Aid and the Guarantees of Citizens Rights); the temporary isolation and treatment of sick persons suffering from serious infectious diseases (leprosy, syphilis, etc.); and the placement of juveniles in special schools, dormitories and so forth, on the basis of a decision by a commission for the affairs of minors. The coercive limitation of freedom in all of these cases may be accomplished only through a judicial decision.

THE JUDICIAL PROTECTION OF PRIVACY

Article 23 of the Russian Constitution states:

1. Everyone shall have the right to privacy, to personal and family secrets, and to the protection of one's honor and good name.
2. Everyone shall have the right to privacy of correspondence, telephone communications, mail, cable and other communications. Any restriction of this right shall be allowed only under an order of a court of law.

The concept of "private life" includes the functioning of the individual in the special areas of family, social, personal and intimate relations, which should not be subject to control by the government, public organizations or other citizens; the freedom of solitude, reflection and entering into contacts with other people or abstaining from such contact; the freedom of expression and the freedom to engage in legitimate activities outside the sphere of official relations; the privacy of the dwelling, diaries, personal notes, correspondences and other items of mail, cable, telephone or other forms of communication; the privacy associated with child adoption; and the certainty of entrusting one's personal and family secrets with the clergy, a doctor, a lawyer or a notary public without fear of divulgence.

One should distinguish secrets that are exclusively personal (that are entrusted to no one) from professional secrets (personal secrets that are entrusted to those engaged in various professions, e.g., doctors, lawyers, notary publics or the clergy). The recipients of professional secrets are responsible for their divulgence. However, not everything that a person conveys to a doctor, lawyer or notary public is a secret.

Mandatory disclosure of personal and family secrets, and of information about the private life of a citizen, arises primarily in three areas: (1) in the anti-crime context; (2) in the health care context; and (3) under the declaration of a state of emergency or war.

The rule of criminal procedure, which prohibits the disclosure of only the intimate side of the lives of persons participating in the case (Article 18 of the Code of Criminal Procedure), does not conform to Article 23, Section 1 of the Constitution. The Constitution speaks of the preservation of private—not intimate—secrets and thus has a broader scope. In addition, the divulgence of this information is prohibited with respect to all persons and not only those participants in the trial.

One's private life, together with personal and family secrets, is protected by the judiciary. The 1996 Criminal Code provides criminal responsibility for the disclosure of the secret concerning adoption against the will of the adoptee (Article 155); the disclosure of facts pertaining to a preliminary investigation or inquiry, including cases where the investigator or the public prosecutor warned the participants of a trial not to disclose facts about the private lives of citizens (Article 310 of the Criminal Code); a violation of the privacy of correspondence, telephone conversations, mail, cable and other communications (Article 138 of the Criminal Code); and a violation of the inviolability of a dwelling (an illegal search or illegal eviction) and other violations of this right (Article 139 of the Criminal Code).

The disclosure during criminal proceedings of information about the private lives of citizens obtained during the interrogation of a witness (including a doctor) or the victim is permitted only if this information is necessary to establish the circumstances relevant to the charge to be proven (however, no one may be compelled to testify against himself, his spouse or close relatives— Article 51 of the Constitution).

Regrettably, the Law On Operational Investigatory Activities of 5 July 1995 permits significant encroachment by governmental bodies into the private lives of citizens.[13] The Law authorizes ''non-procedural'' (secret intelligence) methods, even in the absence of facts substantiating the commission of a crime, such as the surveillance of persons, the control over postal items, the bugging of telephone and other conversations and the collection of information transmitted through other channels of communication. The Law authorizes the use of audio, photo, film surveying and other technical means. Such highly invasive methods may be used by the investigatory bodies of the Ministry of Internal Affairs, the Federal Security Service, the External Intelligence Service of the Republic, the Federal Tax Authority, the Security Service of the President, the Federal Defense Service, agencies and bodies charged with the execution of criminal punishment, the Border Service and the Customs Service.

Unfortunately, the Law does not clearly specify the categories of individuals about which the gathering of the information is permitted. From this point of view, the above-mentioned statute violates Article 23 of the Constitution protecting the right to inviolability of private life. No one has ever lodged a complaint to the Constitutional Court challenging the July 1995 Law, probably due to the fact that people do not know whether they are being investigated. In addition, many citizens are not very well acquainted with their rights. There are also people who say: "Let them bug. I have nothing to hide." It must be emphasized, however, that for the first time in the history of Russia a provision requiring a judicial order to inquire into the private lives of citizens has been included in a law dealing with the operational investigatory activities of law enforcement agencies.

The Law On the Federal Tax Authorities (Article 11, paragraph 20) grants to tax collection agencies the power to offer an award to private citizens who assist in uncovering unreported income (up to 10 percent of the unreported amount of money to a person who has provided useful information). This provision encourages significant interference with citizens' private lives and is seemingly violative of Article 23 of the Constitution.

The Law of 11 March 1992 On the Private Detective and Protective Activities in the Russian Federation prohibits the collection of information regarding citizens' private lives (Article 7, paragraph 3).[14] At the same time, the law permits "the surveillance aimed at obtaining the necessary information" by means of video recording, audio recording, filming and taking photos (Article 5). This passage may be interpreted as contradicting Article 23 of the Constitution because "surveillance" may include both "external surveillance" and "electronic shadowing."

Article 23 of the Constitution protects the secrecy of "information" in the broad sense of the word. "Information" includes not only correspondence, telephone conversations and mail and telegraph communications but also other information such as messages transmitted by fax, telex, satellite links and other modern methods of communication. In most cases, the information that people exchange with each other does not contain any personal or family secrets. Nevertheless, even then it is not subject to a disclosure. The protection also extends to letters addressed to a private person but sent to his or her business address. Government officials and government employees (e.g., postal and telegraph workers, investigators, prosecutors and experts) may be held liable for disclosing the content of the correspondence. Liability is also provided for disclosure of yet unmailed correspondence. Not only state officials but any other person who deals with the correspondence (e.g., a private person involved in the mailing activity) shall be liable for such a violation (Article 138 of the Criminal Code).

Article 23 applies also to persons who are conducting an inquiry or a preliminary investigation (operational investigatory activities have already been mentioned above). These persons may conduct an examination and collection of postal-telegraph correspondence, and tap telephone conversations, but only on the basis of a judicial decision. This rule went into effect on the day the new Russian Constitution was published, December 26, 1993. It follows, then, that Article 174 of the Code of Criminal Procedure, which does not provide for judicial involvement at this stage of criminal proceedings, although it has not been formally repealed, is no longer effective. The same applies to the USSR Law of 12 June 1990 On the Changes and Additions to the Fundamentals of the Criminal Procedure.

THE COURT AS THE PROTECTOR OF THE INVIOLABILITY OF THE HOME

Article 25 of the Constitution declares: "The home shall be inviolable. No one shall have the right to enter a home against the will of persons residing in it, except in cases stipulated by federal law or on the basis of a judicial decision."

Within the meaning of Article 25, "home" is, first, any dwelling designed or adapted for the permanent or temporary residence of people. In addition, "home" also covers rooms, places of common use (in apartments shared by two or more families), basements, kitchens, annexes, outbuildings used for household purposes, hotel rooms, rooms in rest homes, single rooms in hospitals, tents, hunting lodges or garden homes. Any means of transportation located on private property or in the possession or use of citizens, regardless of their location, such as separate compartments in trains or cabins on boats, must also be considered "homes." Similarly, lots of land adjacent to the house (if clearly separated from the surrounding area) and business quarters that are temporarily converted into living quarters fall under the heading of "home" irrespective of their legal status (municipal, private, cooperative, etc.). A broad definition of the "home" best secures the rights of citizens by permitting penetration into the home only in exceptional circumstances and under the strict observance of special rules. Unfortunately, there is no legal definition of the "home," which fosters inconsistency and uncertainty in everyday practice.

The prohibition on penetration into the home includes not only the ban on entering the home, contrary to the will of the persons residing therein, but also other forms of obtaining household information. In particular, the use of modern technical means for "bugging" household conversations and visual surveillance of the home are prohibited. The following activities are therefore proscribed: installation of micro-audio recording devices and video equipment, the installation of audio-visual equipment that records everything that occurs inside the home and surveillance of the home from a long distance. Such actions are permitted only on the basis of, and through, procedures established by law.

Entering a home without a judicial warrant is not unlawful in two situations: (1) under unforeseen emergency circumstances and (2) for the protection of legal order. Entry into the home without the consent of those living within is allowed in the absence of judicial decision during fires, earthquakes, floods, landslides and indoor plumbing and sewage accidents; to prevent damage to electrical wiring, heat and gas supplies; and to verify well-being if it is suspected that the owner of the premises has died or is in great distress. The basis and procedures for entry into the home in these instances are regulated by different departmental instructions. Article 25 of the Constitution alone is no longer sufficient; the promulgation of a comprehensive federal statute that would specify the basis and procedure on entering into the home is necessary.

Entry into the home without the consent of the inhabitants is also authorized on the basis of a judicial decision for the purpose of (1) discovering a crime and establishing the facts; (2) obtaining information concerning a crime and persons suspected of committing it through the operational investigative activities and (3) implementing sentences and other judicial decisions.

Until the adoption of the new code of criminal procedure, a warrantless entry into the home by an investigator, a prosecutor accompanying a witness or even an expert is authorized if the entry is for the purpose of carrying out a search or seizure or an examination of the scene of a crime. The law requires the approval of the prosecutor only in conducting a search; in other cases the investigator's approval is sufficient. Moreover, under exigent circumstances a search is allowed even without the prosecutor's approval.

The Law of 5 July 1995 On Operational Investigatory Activities states that all investigatory bodies must obtain a judicial warrant to conduct activities resulting in the limitation of the rights to the inviolability of the home. However, in urgent cases when a grave crime might be committed, as well as when there is information that state, military, economic or environmental security might be in danger, the operational activities may be undertaken without the judicial warrant; in such cases, however, a subsequent notification of a judge within 24 hours is required. These rules apply not only to entries into the home without the consent of the inhabitants but also to phone taps, other forms of communication interception and examination of postal-telegraph correspondence. Unfortunately, the circumstances under which such activities are authorized without a judicial warrant are not clearly defined. As a result, warrantless investigatory activities have become the rule rather than the exception.

The 1995 Law establishes the basis and procedures for judicial handling of materials that serve to support an authorization of entry into the home without the consent of the inhabitants. The Law further offers guidelines on the necessity of telephone tapping and examination of postal-telegraph correspondence. A head of the investigatory agency prepares a written order concerning the operational investigatory activities and presents it to a judge. The order must contain a statement of reasons. On the judge's request, other materials that demonstrate the necessity of such activities may be presented, except data regarding secret agents and persons collaborating on a confidential basis, as well as information about the organization and the tactics of the operational investigatory activities (Article 9). The judge may issue a warrant for a period of six months (unless otherwise stated in the order) on the basis of the order of the head of the agency. If the judge does not approve the order, then the head of the agency may appeal to a higher-level court. The Law does not specify the procedure to be applied in such instances. In particular, it is not clear whether a hearing is to take place.

Unfortunately, the Federal Law of 22 February 1995 On the Federal Security Service in the Russian Federation is not consistent with the July 1995 Law with respect to entering premises if agents have received information that supports a belief that a crime is being or has been committed or if the agents are pursuing persons suspected of committing the crime (Article 13). In such cases neither judicial warrants for entry into the home nor subsequent judicial supervision is envisaged. Neither is there prosecutorial supervision over such actions because the prosecutor is only notified within a 24-hour period of when the actions have taken place. Thus, the search of a home in connection with operational investigatory activities is permitted before any crime has been committed or a criminal investigation has been initiated, without any witnesses and without any procedural formalities.

Finally, bailiffs have the right to enter the home of a citizen to attach property or to implement judicial decisions related to forfeiture of property (Articles 350–354 of the Code of Civil Procedure).

An unlawful entry into a home without the inhabitants' consent is a crime (Article 139 of the Criminal Code).

Regrettably, Article 25 of the Constitution is internally inconsistent. On the one hand, entry into a home is permitted either in cases specified by law or when a judicial warrant has been issued. It might thus appear that the warrant is only necessary in cases other than those specified by law. It seems, though, that the idea behind Article 25 was that the law should specify all instances of authorized entries into the home but that in certain situations a judicial warrant would also be necessary. Unfortunately, Article 25 did not specify the instances in which a judicial warrant must be obtained. As a result, the requirement of a judicial warrant for entry into a home is usually not followed. Obviously, it is imperative to provide, by ordinary legislation, all the grounds and procedures for entry into the home and to define those instances in which a judicial warrant is required.

THE PROTECTION OF THE RIGHTS OF THE INDIVIDUAL TO A TRIAL BY JURY

Article 47, Section 2 of the Constitution protects the right of a defendant to have his case decided with the participation of a jury in instances specified by federal law. The constituent subjects of the Russian Federation are not entitled to introduce any changes to the law. A trial by jury has already been introduced by the Law of 16 July 1993 On the Introduction of Changes and Additions to the Law of the RSFSR on the Court System of the RSFSR, to the Code of Criminal Procedure of the RSFSR, to the RF Criminal Code and to the Code of the RSFSR on Administrative Violations.[15]

Since November 1, 1993, the law has been applied in the territory of the Moscow, Saratov, Ryazan and Ivanov Oblasts and the Stavropol *Krai* and, beginning on January 1, 1994, in the territory of the Ulianovsk and Rostov-on-Don Oblasts and the Altai and Krasnodar *Krays*. Thus, trial by jury is being introduced in stages (as happened in Russia during the second half of the nineteenth century).

Under the 1993 law, twelve jurors, in addition to the judge, decide the question of the defendant's guilt. The judge presides over and supervises the trial proceedings and, on the basis of a jury verdict, either acquits the defendant or hands down a guilty verdict. The judge then imposes punishment. This is precisely the model of trial by jury that existed in Russia until October 1917.

Under the law, two alternate jurors should be present in the courtroom to replace any member of the jury in case of sickness or death or other unforeseen circumstances. The jurors are selected by lot from voters between the ages of 25 and 70 years. They are summoned to serve for ten days, once a year. Each party may peremptorily challenge two jurors.

Jury trials are empaneled to try the most dangerous crimes (aggravated murder, treason, etc.) and a few lesser offenses subject to the jurisdiction of the Regional Courts. The defendant has a right to choose between a jury trial, a trial before a panel of three professional judges or a trial before a panel of one professional judge and two lay assessors. The admission or denial of guilt does not affect the determination of whether or not a case will be tried by a jury. Even if the public prosecutor decides to reduce a charge during the trial, the jurors will continue to hear the case unless the victim or his or her legal representative objects.

Under the 1993 law, the primary features of a jury trial in Russia are the following:

- A preliminary hearing, preceding the consideration of the case, is conducted by the trial judge with the participation of the parties; the judge may terminate the case, return it for additional investigation, change the jurisdiction, change the venue or put the defendant on trial. In practice, this phase is reduced to the review of the petitions of the parties and does not include the submission and examination of the evidence.

- In an adversarial trial, the judge remains mostly passive while the parties are gathering and submitting the evidence and, in particular, conducting questioning and cross-examination.

- The participation of both a public prosecutor and a defense attorney is mandatory.

- The refusal of the public prosecutor to pursue a charge results in a termination of the case, if the victim or victim's representative does not object.

- Jurors and judges have the right to take part in assessing the evidence, but they are the last to ask questions; if the judge finds that a given piece of evidence was obtained in violation of the law, such evidence is inadmissible.

- After the closing arguments by the parties the judge sets before the jury questions pertaining to whether the crime has taken place, whether the defendant committed the crime, whether the defendant is guilty and if he is guilty, whether mitigating circumstances are present.

- The judge delivers a summation to the jury in which he relates the charge against the defendant, explains the applicable law, reminds them of the evidence that has been examined, explains the rules for assessing the evidence and the meaning of the presumption of innocence and explains the procedures to be followed during jury deliberations (Article 451 of the Code of Criminal Procedure).

- The jurors deliberate secretly; a guilty verdict may be rendered if there are at least seven votes in favor of conviction.

- The verdict of the jury does not have to include reasons.

- A verdict of "not guilty" results in the immediate release of the defendant, although it may be appealed by a prosecutor.

- The judge may not agree with the guilty verdict and may order a new trial with new jurors.

- If a guilty verdict has been rendered, then the judge, without the participation of the jury, examines evidence relevant to the individual defendant, after which he renders a sentence prescribing the punishment. The judge may also pass a sentence exempting the defendant from punishment on certain grounds (e.g., the statute of limitations has run out, an amnesty law has been passed).

The fundamental task of judicial reform in Russia is to create a court that is just, independent and truly a people's court. Justice for the people and through the people—that is our main objective. A trial by jury is the best way of achieving this goal. Famous Russian jurist I. Ya. Foynitzkiy wrote many years ago that the jury trial has become "a world-wide judicial institution that is characteristic of civilized nations, . . . the central junction of a new judicial system, its best ornament and its most solid support basis."[16]

What are the advantages of a trial by jury?

First and foremost is its collective nature. A body of twelve is well suited to review all of the circumstances of a case and secure a sound decision. In this way, the state function of administering justice is vested in the people. A jury is an intermediary in legal disputes between the state and defendants. The state has at its disposal a powerful apparatus, prisons and technology. Therefore, the power of the state and the power of the defendant are unequal. The essence of a jury trial is to create a buffer zone between the strong state apparatus and the defendant to equalize the two sides. In a police state the principle "Where there is power, there is law'' is celebrated. By contrast, in a law-governed state the fundamental principle is "Where there is law, there is power."

Jurors may be truly independent because they are immune to external pressures. A trial by jury fosters citizens' sense of social involvement and a feeling of responsibility.

As a doctor becomes accustomed to the sick and dying, so a professional judge becomes accustomed to harsh sentences, tears and the suffering of people. Five years of imprisonment is a trifle for many judges. A judge knows from experience the kind of evidence that is generally sufficient for a conviction. If the evidence is present, then a guilty verdict automatically follows. Stereotypes develop that convert the judiciary into something resembling a bureaucratic organization. A judge who, day in and day out, is preoccupied with deciding cases acquires a one-sided view. He does not know real life in all of its manifestations. Jurors can compensate for this deficiency by contributing their everyday experiences, knowledge and human compassion. Free of stereotypes and routine, they can render just decisions.

Finally, the jury trial also enhances the prestige of lawyers. It is a celebration of justice, and it generally wins the support of the public.

At present, a jury trial is used in relatively few cases. However, it is important that any person accused of committing a grave crime (a felony) has the right to have his case heard by a jury (although jury trials are often unwieldy, complicated and expensive).

Opponents of jury trials claim that juries have insufficient legal knowledge to evaluate evidence in complex cases. In response, one can point out that the judge and the parties may summon experts to facilitate the jury's task. Other critics of the jury system claim that it is very difficult for jurors to distinguish between factual and legal matters (e.g., someone has been killed, but is it murder or manslaughter?). In reality, these two matters may not be neatly separated. It is necessary to establish not whether there was a loss of funds but whether there has been embezzlement; not whether someone has been killed but whether there has been a murder; not whether money has changed hands but whether a bribe has been given; and so forth. In answering the question of whether or not a person is guilty, the jurors will try to attach a legal label to the established facts. To avoid mistakes, in his instructions the judge must explain the meaning of the legal rules as they relate to the facts of the particular case.

Several attributes of a trial by jury make it a significant guarantee of individual rights. First and foremost is the requirement of the unanimity or qualified majority for a guilty verdict. It is sometimes suggested that jurors are more rigorous than the judges themselves. This a groundless fear! In many countries, and also in Russia, most studies have demonstrated that the "people's judges" are more humane and kinder than the "crown's judges."

The development of the trial by jury in Russia is the reality. In 1994, petitions for a jury trial (in those regions where the trial by jury functions) were filed in 20.4 percent of cases that fall under the jurisdiction of the regional and *krai* courts. In 1995, the number rose to 31; in the first nine months of 1996, petitions were filed in 37 percent of the cases. Jury trials handled 173 cases involving 241 persons in 1994, 305 cases involving 544 persons in 1995, and 307 cases involving 622 persons in the nine months of 1996.[17]

CONCLUDING REMARKS

The 1993 Russian Constitution is a good basis for the democratization of justice and the protection of citizens' rights. Many important laws have been adopted in its implementation. These laws govern various aspects of the market economy, they allow the authorities to fight crime more effectively and they also protect citizens' rights and freedoms. But the process of legal reform is far from over. Moreover, there exists the real danger of regression due to the country's difficult socioeconomic situation, the fear of rising crime rates and the desire of the powerful bureaucracies to restrict glasnost and to restore "law and order." In some instances, the gap between outwardly liberal legislation and its application in practice is quite considerable. Many citizens, fearing growing criminality, do not object to restrictions of their rights. Not all of them realize that what is declared today as a means of restraining crime may be used tomorrow to oppress political opposition.

The judicial profession has become less attractive. The courts are badly financed, receiving only about one third of the funds allocated to them by the state. In some regions, one may speak of the virtual paralysis of justice. Owing to high court costs, many people cannot afford to turn to the judiciary to vindicate their rights. The judiciary is generally distrusted. Defense attorneys have found themselves in a difficult situation because most of them handle 50 percent of their cases free of charge or for a low payment from the government while acting as appointed defense attorneys.

The judiciary is still under pressure from prosecutors, the Ministry of Internal Affairs and the Federal Security Service. These agencies are dissatisfied with the number of not-guilty verdicts (although they amount to only 0.5 percent of the verdicts), with the judicial supervision over pre-trial detention and with the remand by the judiciary of many cases for additional investigation. Finally, a series of laws on operational investigatory activities have legalized highly questionable methods and techniques typical of oppressive political regimes. All of these phenomena raise serious concerns regarding the future of judicial legal reform in Russia.

NOTES

1. For example, the book *International Human Rights Covenants and the Socialist Legislation* (Moscow, 1976) was published with the stamp "For Official Use Only." The book on miscarriages of justice that its authors were forced to call *The Effectiveness*

of Justice and the Problem of Elimination of Miscarriages of Justice (V. N. Kudryavtzev, ed., Moscow, 1975) was also "For Official Use Only."

2. A. Y. Vyshinsky, *Kurs Ugolovnogo Protzessa* (1927), 13.

3. A. Y. Vyshinsky and V. S. Undrevich, *Kurs Ugolovnogo Protzessa* (1934), 25.

4. J. Severin, "Kontzeptziya effectivosti ugolovnogo pravosudiya dolzhna sluzhit yevo perestroike," *Sovogospravo*, No. 4, (1988), at 4.

5. The Law of 28 April 1993 on Changes and Additions to the Code of Civil Procedure of the RFSFR, *Rossiyskaia Gazyeta*, June 3, 1993.

6. Para. 2 of the Ruling No. 8 of 31 October 1995 of the Plenary Session of the Supreme Court of the Russian Federation on Some Issues of the Implementation of the RF Constitution by the Courts.

7. On Changes and Additions to the Code of Criminal Procedure, *Rossiyskaia Gazyeta*, June 17, 1992.

8. The Court's Ruling of 13 June 1996 in (*re V. V. Shelukhin*).

9. *Rossiyskaya Gazyeta*, July 20, 1995.

10. *Rossiyskiye Vyesti*, Apr. 11, 1996.

11. *Rossiyskiye Vyesti*, Mar. 14, 21, 1996.

12. The Law On the Appeal to the Court against Illegal Arrests, *Rossiyskaia Gazyeta*, June 17, 1992.

13. *Rossiyskaia Gazyeta*, Aug. 18, 1995.

14. *Rossiyskaya Gazyeta*, Apr. 30, 1992.

15. For an in-depth analysis of the Russian jury law and its application in the first year of trials, see S. Thaman, "The Resurrection of Trial by Jury in Russia," 31 *Stanford Journal of International Law* (1995), 61–274.

16. I. Ya. Foynitzkiy, *Kurs Ugolovnogo Sudoproizvodstva*, 4th ed. (1912), 382.

17. A. Shurygin, "Novoi formy sudoproizvodstva—tri goda," *Rossiyskaya Justitziya*, No. 12 (1996), at 1.

Part II

Israel and the Occupied Territories

Chapter 3

The Protection of Human Rights by Judges: The Israeli Experience

STEPHEN GOLDSTEIN

HISTORICAL INTRODUCTION

Until quite recently, human rights in Israel have been protected almost exclusively by judge-made law. Indeed, almost uniquely in the world, Israeli courts have fashioned the law of human rights out of whole cloth.

The situation is the result of a number of factors. First is the fact that Israel is one of the few states that lacks a formal constitution in the sense of one written, unified document. That this situation was not the original intention of the founders of the State of Israel is clear. Indeed, the Declaration of Independence of May 14, 1948, expressly stated that the permanent and elected governmental organs of the state would be established under a constitution to be determined by an elected constituent assembly. However, even before the election of a constituent assembly, there began a vigorous public debate in Israel as to whether the time was ripe for the young state to adopt such a formal, written constitution.

The constituent assembly was, indeed, duly elected despite this debate. However, it never really operated as a constituent assembly but was, instead, transformed into the first Israeli Parliament, known as the Knesset. This Knesset accepted a compromise as to the proposed constitution, a compromise commonly known as the Harari Resolution.

According to this resolution, a constitution would not be written and adopted immediately. Nor would the task of creating a constitution be completely postponed to some later date. Rather, a Constitution would be adopted piecemeal in a series of "Basic Laws" by the Knesset, that is, the regular Parliament. Following the completion of these individual Basic Laws, they would be unified in one doctrine that would then constitute the Constitution of the state. As of this writing, the following Basic Laws have been adopted: The Knesset, The President, The Government, The Army, Economy, State Lands, Jerusalem, Judiciary, State Comptroller, Freedom of Occupation, and Human Dignity and Freedom.

These last two (i.e., Freedom of Occupation and Human Dignity and Freedom) were adopted only in March 1992.[1] Prior to that time, the Basic Laws had little relevance to the protection of human rights but were concerned almost exclusively with the organization of the state's governmental organs. And indeed, in 1996, the Israel Supreme Court, in its version of *Marbury v. Madison*, held that these Basic Laws have normative supremacy over ordinary laws and that the Court, therefore, may invalidate ordinary laws that are in conflict with them.[2]

Thus, Israel now may be entering a new era of protection of human rights by judicial power stemming from the Basic Laws. On the other hand, for purposes of this chapter, it is important to emphasize that for 44 years—that is, from the inception of the State of Israel in 1948 until the adoption of these two Basic Laws in the spring of 1992—Israeli judges fashioned laws on human rights in a constitutional, and indeed, legislative vacuum in terms of the protection of human rights.

Moreover, particularly at the beginning of the state, the judges were operating not only in a vacuum in terms of affirmative protection of human rights but also against a background of factors that were in opposition to the legal protection of human rights. At the independence of the state, Israel incorporated into its law the pre-existing British mandatory law, which had become based almost entirely on English law during the almost 30 years of British rule.

As in England itself, British mandatory law was very underdeveloped in public law, as compared with the highly developed system of private law. This underdevelopment meant, *inter alia*, the almost nonexistence of strong public law principles protecting human rights.

Even worse for the legal protection of human rights was the existence on the statute books of the Mandatory Government of the Emergency Regulations—1945. Despite the terminology, these Emergency "Regulations" have the status of primary legislation. They gave draconian powers to the Mandatory Government in its attempts to deal with the growing opposition of the Jewish population to British rule, including such things as press censorship, administration detention and the confiscation or destruction of buildings that were used in the course of terrorist activities.

Pursuant to the basic principle that the mandatory law in force on the eve of Israel's independence continued in force in the independent State of Israel unless and until altered by the appropriate state organ, the draconian provision of these 1945 Emergency Regulations continued in force in the State of Israel. Such was the primary legacy of British mandatory law to the legal "protection" of human rights in the fledgling State of Israel.

Moreover, neither were the other two primary ideological sources of Israeli legal development—Jewish law and socialism—particularly receptive to the development of a libertarian-based law of human rights. Jewish law, for reasons that we cannot go into in this chapter, is primarily duty oriented rather than rights oriented. Socialism is, of course, primarily communal rather than individualistically oriented.

Thus, the newly independent State of Israel was born into legal and ideological climates that were not favorable to the development of the legal protection of human rights. Moreover, neither was the political climate.

The new state was faced immediately with war and thereafter continual hostility from its Arab neighbors. Thus, defense considerations were of uppermost importance. Moreover, at the same time, Israel was faced with the enormous challenges of absorbing massive numbers of immigrants, a task that required enormous governmental intervention in the society. Finally, in this regard, the first prime minister, David Ben-Gurion, a tremendously powerful figure who rightly could be described as the "father of his country," was himself a socialist and not a proponent of a libertarian-oriented and human rights–protecting legal structure. Thus, the development of human rights by judges at the beginning of the state was indeed a very creative and courageous undertaking.

However, we should point out two legacies of the British legal heritage that did contribute affirmatively to the accomplishment of this undertaking. The first is the concept of English public law, where everyone, including the government, is subject to the law. Related to that concept is the principle that no governmental official may act against an individual unless he has been so empowered to act by the legislature, the sovereign body of the state; there is no inherent administrative or governmental authority. All authority must come from the sovereign legislature.

As we shall see, Israeli judges have far exceeded their English counterparts—and judges of other legal systems that are based on the English Common law, in exploiting these principles in order to create a very extensive system of legal protection of human rights. On the other hand, the inheritance of those principles from the British mandatory law was an important factor in this creative development.

Equally, if not more important, was an institution derived from mandatory law: the Israeli Supreme Court sitting as the High Court of Justice.

In addition to its appellate jurisdiction over other courts, the Israeli Supreme Court also sits as a court of first instance as the High Court of Justice, having jurisdiction in administrative and constitutional matters. The jurisdiction of the High Court of Justice is set forth as follows in the Basic Law: Judiciary:

(a) The Supreme Court sitting as a High Court of Justice shall deal with matters in which it deems it necessary to grant relief in the interests of justice and which are not within the jurisdiction of any other court or tribunal.

(b) Without prejudice to the generality of the provisions of subsection (a), the Supreme Court sitting as the High Court of Justice shall be competent . . .

(2) to order State authorities . . . and such other bodies and individuals as exercise any

public functions by virtue of law to do or refrain from doing any act in the lawful exercise of their functions or, if they have been unlawfully elected or appointed, to refrain from acting.

Pursuant to this authority, the High Court of Justice has the power to issue orders in the nature of the British prerogative writs (*habeas corpus, mandamus, prohibition, certiorari,* and *quo warranto*), along with injunctions and declaratory judgments. It thus serves as the basic administrative and constitutional tribunal in the Israeli system.

It is in its capacity as High Court of Justice that the Israeli Supreme Court has shaped, developed and enforced the protection of human rights. The importance of the fact that in Israel legal actions challenging governmental policy are brought originally in the Supreme Court cannot be overemphasized. The result is that the highest court in the country is placed in the position of determining issues of major political and social consequence, particularly concerning the validity of actions of government ministries, while these subjects are timely, thus enhancing its power to have a major impact on social and political matters. In addition, the fact that the development of the law of human rights has been concentrated in one court has also aided such development.

Finally, in this regard, the High Court is very "accessible." The filing fees for High Court of Justice actions are nominal, and the proceedings are simplified and relatively swift. Unlike regular Israeli procedure, both civil and criminal, which is based on the British model and thus emphasizes oral testimony and cross-examination, the procedure before the High Court of Justice is based on written presentations—documents and affidavits—generally without cross-examination.[3]

The institution of the High Court of Justice in Israel is a result of a political decision of the British mandatory period. Lower court judges in mandatory Palestine were local people. On the other hand, the Supreme Court consisted almost exclusively of English judges who spent a tour of duty in mandatory Palestine. For obvious political reasons, the mandatory government wanted actions brought against it and its agencies only before a court that was staffed with English judges—namely, the mandatory Supreme Court. This system was inherited by the State of Israel.

PROTECTION OF HUMAN RIGHTS

The First Period

In the first few years after the establishment of the state, the creative and courageous judges of the Supreme Court sitting as the High Court of Justice laid down the basic principles for the legal protection of human rights in Israel.

Thus, in a 1949 case concerning administrative detentions under the 1945

Defense Regulations, during the time when the fledgling state was in a highly dangerous security situation, the Court stated:

The authorities are subject to the law like every citizen of the state. And rule of law is one of the greatest foundations of the whole state. There would be grave damage to the public and to the state altogether, if the authorities could use the power conferred by the legislator, even temporarily, in utter disregard of the restrictions placed by the legislator on the manner in which this power is to be exercised. It is true that the security of the state, which requires the detention of a person, is no less important than the need to protect the citizen's right, but when it is possible to accomplish both purposes together, one cannot disregard one or the other.[4]

In the same year, the Court also held:

It is a fundamental rule, that every person is endowed with a natural right to engage in work or in manual labor, of his own choice, so long as the engagement in work or manual labor is not prohibited by the law.[5]

But perhaps the most important of these early cases along this line was the 1951 decision *Sheib v. The Minister of Defense*[6] in which the High Court of Justice ordered Prime Minister David Ben-Gurion, who then was serving also as Minister of Defense, to retract his prior intervention and not to intervene in the future in the hiring of the petitioner, well known as an extreme right-wing political activist, as a teacher in a private high school.

The Court so ordered since no then-existing legislation empowered the Minister of Education, let alone the Minister of Defense, to intervene in the hiring decisions of private educational institutions. In the absence of such legislation, any such governmental intervention was illegal.

In these cases and subsequent ones, the High Court of Justice developed the basic doctrine of judicial protection of human rights in Israel. This doctrine states that no government official may act against an individual unless he has been empowered to do so by primary legislation. That is, the individual is free to do as he pleases except insofar as the legislation has deprived him of, or restricted, such freedom.

The operative effect of this doctrine is that the courts should not interpret vague or ambiguous Knesset legislation as restraining individual liberty but rather should construe such legislation as not doing so. If the legislature wants to restrict individual liberty, it must do so in clear language. Furthermore, general delegation of power from the Knesset to the government ministries to enact regulations, that is, secondary legislation, should not be interpreted as delegating the power to enact restrictions on individual liberty. In other words, ministry regulations that restrict individual liberty should be invalidated in the courts unless they are supported by explicit Knesset-empowering legislation.

Of course, the use of this judicial power is limited by the need to interpret concepts of individual freedom in the context of specific primary and secondary legislation and the situation under adjudication. Yet the fact that so much of Israeli "law" is not Knesset legislation, but rather secondary legislation enacted by government ministries that can, therefore, be invalidated by the Supreme Court if considered contrary to fundamental concepts of individual liberty and without the requisite support in explicit Knesset legislation, created a *de facto* system of judicial review in Israel that is quite similar to that employed by courts possessing the power to review primary legislation.

Yet it must be emphasized that the theoretical basis of this power is much different than that of the power to invalidate primary legislation. Its basis is the preservation of legislative supremacy over administrative and other governmental organs that are subordinate to the legislature.

Unlike a judicial decision that a statute or course of administrative action is unconstitutional, a decision that can only be overturned by a constitutional amendment, a decision that administrative action or secondary legislation is invalid since it is not supported by sufficiently specific primary legislation can be corrected by the legislature's enacting the requisite specific legislation. Thus, this type of decision does not have the anti-majoritarian (or as some would say, the anti-democratic) consequences of constitutional invalidation of the legislative will. On the contrary, it represents a doctrine based on the importance of the legislative will. It requires that in situations concerning the curtailment of individual liberties the legislature express its will clearly. Thus, it is a doctrine designed to promote legislative responsibility rather than to derogate from it.

This doctrine was further expanded by the landmark 1953 judgment of Justice Simon Agranat in the *Kol Ha'am* case,[7] generally considered to be the most important constitutional decision in Israeli law, at least until the 1966 decision in the *United Bank Mizrachi* case concerning judicial review of primary legislation.

The case involved the authority of the Minister of the Interior, under the 1945 Emergency Regulations, to suspend any newspaper that has published material that "in his opinion" is "likely to endanger public peace." In this instance the communist newspaper *Kol Ha'am* (Voice of the People) had criticized the government for allegedly agreeing to send troops to fight in Korea on behalf of the UN forces. These allegations were, however, false, as the government had not so agreed. In response, the Minister of the Interior suspended the newspaper for ten days.

The High Court of Justice, on petition of the newspaper, invalidated the suspension. On the face of the legislation it would appear that the Minister of Interior's action was legal. Indeed, it was argued that since the legislation referred to the "discretion" of the Minister of the Interior, his action was not subject to judicial review at all or, at most, to review as to bad faith.

These arguments were rejected by the Court in an opinion written by Justice Agranat. He held that since the action involved the fundamental human right of freedom of speech, the legislation was to be interpreted so as to infringe on freedom of speech as little as possible. If the legislature wished to infringe further on such a fundamental human right, it had to do so *very* explicitly.

More specifically in this case, Justice Agranat reviewed the American First Amendment doctrine of freedom of speech; while rejecting the specifics of the "clear and present danger" test as inappropriate in Israel, he "interpreted" the legislation as incorporating a similar test as to the authority of the Minister of the Interior, that of "a near certainty of danger." Absent a determination, ultimately made by the Court, that the publication constituted "a near certainty" of endangering public peace, the action of the Minister is invalid.

There is no doubt that in this opinion Justice Agranat effectively incorporated American First Amendment doctrines as an integral part of Israeli law as to judicial review of governmental action and interpretation of primary legislation. This was done purposefully and explicitly, despite the fact that Israel had nothing comparable to the American First Amendment, neither in a constitutional document nor even in ordinary legislation.

However, the Court, through Justice Agranat, held that principles of freedom of speech, on the American model, were derived from the fact that Israel was a democratic country. It should be noted that Justice Agranat was born and raised in the United States, having graduated from the Law School of the University of Chicago prior to immigrating to mandatory Palestine as a young lawyer. This, of course, helps to explain the influence of American constitutional law principles, both judicial and academic, on his legal thinking.

However, it should be emphasized that the influence of American constitutional law principles, particularly those of the First Amendment, on the development of the legal protection of human rights in Israel has remained strong—and may, indeed, even have been strengthened—well after the retirement of Justice Agranat from the Supreme Court.

Kol Ha'am, and its incorporation of American First Amendment principles of freedom of speech, has also strongly influenced the development of Israeli law in areas not related to the press and national security. Thus, laws regarding freedom of assembly and demonstration have developed along lines quite similar to those in the United States.[8] Similarly, free speech interests have strongly influenced the interpretation of laws authorizing censorship of plays and films as well as laws concerning military censorship.[9]

As noted earlier, in *Kol Ha'am* the Court found the basis of the protection of the fundamental human right of freedom of speech primarily in the democratic nature of the State of Israel. However, it also held that Israel's Declaration of Independence, while not a binding legal document, is an additional source from which the protection of human rights may be derived, since it embodies the principles on which the state was founded.

The Declaration of the Establishment of the State of Israel, which was declared on May 14, 1948, provides in the third operative paragraph:

The State of Israel will be open for Jewish immigration and for the Ingathering of the Exiles; it *will foster the development of the country for the benefit of all its inhabitants; it will be based on freedom, justice and peace as envisaged by the prophets of Israel; it will ensure complete equality of social and political rights to all its inhabitants irrespective of religion, race, or sex; it will guarantee freedom of religion, conscience, language, education and culture*; it will safeguard the Holy Places of all religions; and it will be faithful to the principles of the Charter of the United Nations. (Emphasis added)

Thus, subject to express primary legislation to the contrary, the structure was laid for the basic concept of equality to all of Israel's inhabitants, for the rejection of discrimination based on religion, race or sex and for the guarantees of freedom of religion, conscience, language, education and culture.

Later Developments

As is true in other states, the degree of activism of the High Court of Justice can and does vary from time to time. We have thus far concentrated on the first years of the state, which, indeed, were the most important in laying the foundations for judicial protection of human rights in Israel.

In the last few years or so, the High Court of Justice has also been in an activist phase. In part, this phase has been a continuation of the earlier period in terms of the even more expanded protection of human rights. This is true, particularly with regard to freedom of speech, press and association.

A most important aspect of this expanded protection of human rights has been the increasing willingness of the High Court of Justice to challenge the factual and legal correctness of governmental assertions of "security interests" as grounds for restricting such human rights. On the other hand, other aspects of this recent activism reflect not continuation but, rather, a significant change in approach from that of the first period discussed earlier. Despite the very strong judicial activism of the first period, the High Court of Justice did not depart from traditional procedural restrictions of judicial intervention in the activities of other branches of government found in the doctrines of standing, justiciability and political question.

While there remain some differences of opinion among the justices on some of these points, the recent period of judicial activism has been characterized by the abolishment, or virtual abolishment, of these procedural restrictions on judicial intervention in the activities of other branches of government.[10] Thus, today there are virtually no procedural restrictions on the authority of the High Court of Justice to intervene in, and invalidate, the activities of other governmental agencies. This development is part of a more fundamental shift in the High Court of Justice's perception of its role. This shift is one from protecting human rights to safeguarding the "Rule of Law."

In 1971, in defending the requirement that a petitioner to the High Court of Justice have personal standing, Justice Yoel Sussman stated:

We will not hear the petition of a man complaining that the authority acted illegally, if he cannot show why he and no one else should request the correction of the irregularity. For it must be emphasized that the Court is not competent to stand guard over the observance of the law and the prevention of injustice in general. This is not the task of the judge.[11]

Again, while there is not unanimity among all the justices of the Supreme Court, a dominant theme of the recent activism of the High Court of Justice is that it is, indeed, "the task of the judges" "to stand guard over the observance of the law." In this view the law is both omnipotent and omnipresent, and it is for the judge, and only the judge, to determine its precise meaning and to ensure adherence to this judicial interpretation. Moreover, in enforcing the Rule of Law for all government officials, from the highest to the lowest, the Court not only enforces the prescriptions of statutory law but also enforces a Court-created principle that all governmental action must conform to the Court's determination of "reasonableness."

This view has led to the unprecedented intervention of the High Court of Justice in such matters as the internal decision-making processes of the Parliament, the validity of agreements among political parties, the prosecutorial discretion of the Attorney General and even the reasonableness of the government's appointment of a specific individual to be the director general of a government ministry.

In the view of this writer the recent shift from the protection of human rights to the protection of the Rule of Law, with its attendant virtual abolishment of procedural restrictions on the Court's intervening in the activities of other governmental bodies, is clearly a wrongheaded, regrettable development.[12] Moreover, this new type of activism has produced a significant side effect: increased pressure on the workload of the Supreme Court.

THE WORKLOAD OF THE COURT

There is no doubt that the Israeli Supreme Court is one of the most overloaded in the world. An extensive discussion of the problems of its overextensive jurisdiction would go well beyond the scope of this chapter. Moreover, we have recently discussed these problems at length in another context.[13] Thus, we will discuss here these issues very briefly and only insofar as they relate to the subject of this chapter.

The Israel Supreme Court basically has three types of jurisdiction: (1) original High Court of Justice jurisdiction, as discussed above; (2) mandatory appellate jurisdiction, both civil and criminal, over cases that begin in the higher-level first instance courts—the District Courts; and (3) discretionary appellate jurisdiction over cases that begin in the lower first instance courts—the Magistrates' Courts—from which there is a first appeal as of right to the District Courts and a second appeal with leave to the Supreme Court. In 1995, 1,361 cases were filed in the original High Court of Justice jurisdiction of the Court; 1,636 in its mandatory appellate jurisdiction; and 1,187 petitions for discretionary appellate review.

In terms of the treatment by the Court of these different types of cases, there is no doubt that a clear preference is given to the High Court of Justice cases at the expense of the mandatory jurisdiction cases. This is shown by the fact that, as of 1992, the last year for which there are comprehensive statistics, the median time for the determination of these mandatory appeals was 23.9 months, and 21.8 percent of them took more than 37 months for their determination. In contrast, in the same year the median time for determination of High Court of Justice petitions was only 4 months.

Moreover, 45 percent of these mandatory appeals cases were withdrawn or compromised. This reflects, in part, the parties' awareness of the questionable merits. It also represents, however, the great pressure exerted by the justices of the Supreme Court on the parties to withdraw or settle these appeals and thereby reduce their impact on the workload of the Court. And indeed, despite the clear preference given to High Court of Justice actions at the expense of the Supreme Court's appellate jurisdiction, the ever-increasing number of High Court of Justice actions has forced the Supreme Court to change its treatment of these actions.

Under the influence of the English tradition regarding prerogative writs, High Court of Justice actions are initiated in the Supreme Court by a petition for a rule nisi directing the public authority respondent to show cause as to why the requested relief should not be granted. Such a petition is brought before a single justice of the Court who may either grant it, with or without hearing the petitioner orally, or transfer it to a panel of three justices. A three-justice panel may do one of three things: (1) grant the order; (2) hear the petitioner orally; or (3) deny the request summarily; but the last may be done only if the panel believes that the petition does not state on its face a cause of action. In addition, the rules provide that if the panel decides to hear the petitioner orally, such a hearing is generally *ex parte*. However, if the respondent is a body who is represented in such proceedings by the Attorney General, the Court may, but is not obliged to, invite the Attorney General to the oral hearing.

The object of this procedure is quite clear. A single justice may grant, but may not deny, the order nisi. A denial may only be done by a three-justice panel. Such a denial generally requires hearing the petitioner, which hearing is generally *ex parte*. All these provisions attest to the fact that the granting of the rule nisi was viewed as a matter to be done as a matter of course, without generally involving an in-depth examination of the chances of the petitioner's success on the merits. Indeed, this was traditionally the case. That is, a request for a rule nisi was granted virtually automatically by a single justice and was viewed merely as a historic, technical means of initiating the action. Consideration of the merits of the petition was reserved to the later hearing of the merits.

However, in the last fifteen years or so, there has been an increasing tendency to transfer petitions for rules nisi to three-justice panels who then invite oral argument with both sides represented. Thus, the decision as to the granting of a rule to show cause becomes a form of preliminary determination of the issues involved. As of this writing, the Court has not addressed itself to this growing tendency, neither to acknowledge its existence expressly nor to explain or to justify it.

Yet, in my view, this tendency is a clear response to the ever-growing number of High Court of Justice cases filed as a result, at least in part, of the change in policy of the Court as described earlier. In light of this increase, the Court has resorted to the use of a decision on a rule nisi as a screening device. The need for such a screening device is accentuated by the fact that the granting of a rule to show cause has, at times, been the subject of misleading publicity. More than once, in politically sensitive issues, the virtually automatic granting of the rule nisi has been portrayed in the press as a victory for the petitioner, which seemed to indicate, at least primarily, Court disapproval of the action of the public body respondent. Of course, while the holding of hearings prior to the granting of rules nisi may be viewed as a defense against such distortions, it, paradoxically, adds weight to the victory claims of the petitioner if the rule is granted after such a hearing.

Moreover, if the rule is granted, the holding of this extra hearing increases the already too heavy burden on the Court. However, if the rule is not granted after such a hearing, there has been a significant saving to the Court. First, this hearing is generally considerably shorter than would be a full hearing on the merits following the granting of a rule nisi. Second, and no less important, the Court does not write an opinion explaining its failure to grant a rule nisi even if this occurs after a rather extensive hearing. This is a very substantial saving in judicial time, as the justices of the Israel Supreme Court generally write very long and time-consuming opinions in cases determined on the merits.

Finally, the statistics clearly indicate that today in the vast majority of cases rules nisi are not granted. Thus, for example, in 1992, of the 969 petitions filed, 819 (85 percent) were dismissed or withdrawn without a rule nisi having been granted. The statistics are similar for other recent years. It is impossible to tell from the available statistics, where rules nisi are not granted, the percentage of cases denied as frivolous without a hearing, the percentage of cases denied after hearings or, indeed, the percentage of cases where the petition was withdrawn or settled pursuant to the same type of judicial pressure described above regarding mandatory appeals, a pressure also exerted in these cases. Our impression is that the great number of cases in which rules nisi are not granted reflects all three types of situations.

CONCLUSIONS

Despite our criticism of some recent developments as set forth at the end of the last section, there is no doubt that, overall, Israeli judges, particularly those of the Supreme Court sitting as the High Court of Justice, have been very successful in protecting human rights even without a formal, written constitution. Moreover, despite the excessive interference by the High Court of Justice in recent years in domestic political matters, it has carefully refrained from interfering in matters of foreign policy. In particular, it has not interfered, though often requested to do so, in governmental policies involving the peace process in general and Israeli/Palestinian relations in particular.

However, the continuing intervention of the High Court of Justice to preserve the Rule of Law in highly charged political and social matters, particularly concerning religion, along with its recent assertion of judicial review of primary legislation, has led to charges by some sections of the Israeli public, particularly the religious and ultra-religious Jewish sectors,[14] that the High Court of Justice is acting pursuant to the particular social, religious and political ideology of the justices. This view has been reinforced by the rhetoric of a number of the Supreme Court justices, both in their opinions and in their out-of-court statements in books, articles and lectures.

These charges have led, *inter alia*, to a demand to review the method of selecting Israeli judges in general and Supreme Court justices in particular. There is no doubt that the current selection system of the Supreme Court justices, which is done on a professional and not on a political basis,[15] has produced judges with a relatively uniform background and ideology: secular and liberal, with the lone exception of one "reserved" seat for a religious justice.

Thus, the non-secular, non-liberal elements in the Israeli social-political system, particularly the religious parties, have begun to demand changes in the selection process so that the Supreme Court will more closely reflect the total Israeli society. As of this writing, this campaign has not borne fruit and, indeed, has been resisted strenuously by the Israeli secular, liberal establishment. Only time will tell if it will succeed, at least in part, in "democratizing" the judicial selection process.

The opposition to the recent trend of decision of the High Court of Justice concerning highly sensitive domestic political issues has also led to proposals that the High Court of Justice itself be eliminated as an institution and that actions against public bodies be brought in the regular lower courts and reach the Supreme Court only on appeal. Under this view, the concentration of power in the High Court of Justice as the first, and last, instance in such cases is undesirable. In addition, the President of the Israel Bar Association has argued that the concentration of the Supreme Court justices on High Court of Justice cases has been to the great detriment of the other cases on its docket, particularly the appeals as of right from the District Courts. Moreover, in his view the procedure of the High Court of Justice, that is, primarily written rather than oral, is inconsistent with the basic English-based Israeli procedural system.

It is very clear to us that the jurisdiction of the Israel Supreme Court must be reformed. We have long advocated restructuring the Israel court system so as, *inter alia*, to eliminate appeals as of right to the Supreme Court.[16] If this were done, without a doubt the Supreme Court could handle both its discretionary appellate jurisdiction and its jurisdiction as the High Court of Justice. Thus, if the latter jurisdiction were to be removed from the Supreme Court, it would be not on the basis of workload but rather on the merits—that is, these cases would better be heard in the regular first instance courts and reach the Supreme Court only on appeal.

As we have already noted, the concentration of actions against public authorities in the Supreme Court as a matter of original, and therefore immediate, jurisdiction has been most important in allowing that Court to develop Israeli public law, particularly in the formative years of the state. On the other hand, the fact that major political controversies may be adjudicated immediately—for example, when they are very alive and the subject of hot debate—in the Supreme Court has often enmeshed that Court, undesirably, in political thickets. Moreover, there is the problem of the procedure used by the High Court of Justice.[17]

Thus, we would probably not advocate creating such jurisdiction if it did not already exist. Yet, it does exist and indeed has existed since before the creation of the state. Moreover, despite the criticism of the High Court of Justice by certain sectors of the Israeli public, there is no doubt that this most important institution in the Israeli governmental-judicial structure still enjoys the trust and confidence of the great bulk of the Israeli population. Given these facts, we would not recommend abolishing it.

NOTES

1. For an English translation of these Basic Laws and a commentary on them, see D. Kretzmer, "The New Basic Laws on Human Rights: A Mini-Revolution in Israeli Constitutional Law?" 26 *Israel Law Review* (1992), 238.

2. United Mizrachi Bank v. Migdal Co-operative Village, 49(4) P.D. 222 (1995). Technically the important determinations of this case are dictum, since the Court held that the statute in question did not violate the Basic Law. On the other hand, this dictum was assented to by eight of the nine judges who sat on this especially large panel, and there is no doubt that it represents Israeli law.

3. For further discussion of the High Court of Justice in this regard, see S. Goldstein, "Judicial Protection of Human Rights without a Formal Written Constitution," in: *II Papers, Judicial Protection of Human Rights at the National and International Level*, International Congress on Procedural Law for the Ninth Centenary of the University of Bologna (1988), 75; S. Goldstein, "Regional Report: Common Law Countries," for the International Association of Procedural Law, International Colloquium, Thessaloniki (May 1997), 21–25 (hereinafter "Regional Report," Thessaloniki Colloquium).

4. Al-Karbuteli v. Minister of Defense, 2 P.D. (1949) 5, 14. See generally D. Kretzmer, "Forty Years of Public Law," 24 *Israel Law Review* (1989), 341 at 353.

5. Berjano v. Minister of Police, 2 P.D. (1949) 80.

6. 5 P.D. (1951) 395.

7. 7 P.D. (1953) 871.

8. See generally D. Kretzmer, "Demonstrations and the Law," 19 *Israel Law Review* (1984), 47.

9. See generally Z. Segal, "A Constitution without a Constitution: The Israel Experience and the American Impact," 21 *Capital University Law Review* (1992), 1 at 25–26.

10. See generally Goldstein, "Judicial Protection of Human Rights without a Formal Written Constitution," *supra* note 3; Goldstein, "Regional Report," Thessaloniki Colloquium, *supra* note 3.

11. Association of Life Insurance Companies Ltd. v. Minister of Finance, 26 (1) P.D. 230, 234.

12. For a debate on this issue, see Kretzmer, *supra* note 4; and I. Zamir, "Administrative Law: Revolution or Evolution (In Response to Prof. D. Kretzmer)," *id.* at 356. See also Goldstein, "Regional Report," Thessaloniki Colloquium, *supra* note 3.

13. Goldstein, "Regional Report," Thessaloniki Colloquium, *supra* note 3, which contains further and more detailed discussion of all the issues discussed in the remainder of this section.

14. For a general discussion of the diversity of Israel in terms of religion and the role of religion in the political and social life of the state, see S. Goldstein, "Israel: A Secular or a Religious State?" 36 *St. Louis University Law Journal* (1991), 145.

15. See generally S. Goldstein, "Contrasting Views of Adjudication: An American/Israeli Comparison," in: D. Liepold, W. Luke and Sh. Yoshino, eds., *Gedachtnisshrift für Peter Arens* (Munich 1993); Goldstein, "Regional Report," Thessaloniki Colloquium, *supra* note 3.

16. See Goldstein, "Regional Report," Thessaloniki Colloquium, *supra* note 3, and sources cited therein.

17. But see S. Goldstein, "Towards a New Israeli Civil Procedure: Away from the Worst of Both Worlds," in: A. M. Rabello, ed., *Essays on European Law and Israel* (Jerusalem, 1996), 719–731.

Chapter 4

Judicial Protection in Israeli-Occupied Territories

JOHN QUIGLEY

Judicial protection of human rights presents particular problems in a situation of belligerent occupation. *Belligerent occupation* refers to the control of a piece of territory not by the state that enjoys sovereignty there but by a state that has come into temporary possession as a result of military hostilities. Unlike the ordinary situation in which a state possessing sovereignty also controls a territory, with belligerent occupation there is a split between *de jure* and *de facto* authority. The displaced sovereign has its institutions, and it continues to claim the right to rule. Moreover, international law backs its position, viewing it as still the lawful authority in the territory. At the same time, the belligerent occupant exercises day-to-day control, imposing certain institutions, primarily those of a military nature, and they control certain aspects of life in the territory.

Under the international norms that regulate belligerent occupation, an occupant must preserve, to the extent feasible, the institutions of the displaced sovereign. Thus, the courts of the displaced sovereign are to be allowed to function and to exercise civil and criminal jurisdiction over the population. However, the population also requires protection against the institutions of the occupant, and these are not likely to be subject to the authority of the courts of the displaced sovereign.

These problems have manifested themselves in Israel's occupation of the Arab territories it captured during the 1967 Middle East War, namely, the Gaza Strip on the eastern Mediterranean coast and the West Bank of the Jordan River. The administrative actions against which the Palestinian population needs judicial protection are those of the Israeli military government, which is not subject to the jurisdiction of the indigenous courts. In addition, the Israeli military government has extended its functions well beyond those normally exercised by a belligerent occupant. In violation of the rules of military occupation, it assumed numerous administrative functions from the indigenous institutions. A Palestinian who seeks redress against the military administration may not approach the indigenous courts. The Israeli military government, by assuming control over many aspects of life, has marginalized the courts of the displaced sovereign.

Because the Israeli military government has assumed broad functions, and because it is not subject to the indigenous courts, Palestinians are left with no judicial protection within the existing framework of government. Into this gap, however, stepped the Supreme Court of Israel, which does have jurisdiction over the Israeli military government, as it does over any branch of the Israeli administration. Early in the occupation, the Supreme Court of Israel decided that if a Palestinian complained to it against an act of the Israeli military government, it would entertain the case.

The protection that the Supreme Court of Israel came to provide, however, was limited. The Supreme Court is a court of the same government whose actions were the object of complaint. The Palestinian complainants were not citizens of the state under which that government functioned. Nor were they loyal to it. Indeed, most were hostile to it, because it was a government that illegally occupied their territory. In such a situation, judicial protection is strained to the maximum. In a normal situation of undivided sovereignty and control, a citizen approaches a court for redress against a government act as a loyal citizen of that government. He claims rights due him as a citizen. A resident of occupied territory is not in this position when approaching a court of the occupant. He is likely to be viewed with less than equanimity by the court's judges.

The judges of the Supreme Court of Israel share the values of the Israeli military government, not the values of the Palestinian population. The longtime chief justice of the Supreme Court of Israel, Meir Shamgar, was in his youth a guerrilla fighter for a Jewish military organization that was widely viewed as terrorist for its killings of Palestinian civilians. Even apart from the particular political position of the individual judges, the Supreme Court as a whole supports the Israeli government in its view that Israel is surrounded by enemy Arab states and that the Palestinians are more loyal to them than they are to Israel. There is nothing peculiar about this perception on the part of the Israeli judges. In any country, judges share the dominant values of the society. The problem is that in a belligerent occupation, these judges make rulings on the lives of persons who are presumptively hostile to the order represented by the judge.

On the critical issue of military necessity, which is often raised by the Israeli military government to justify an action against a Palestinian, the judges of the Supreme Court of Israel have shown that they are disposed to believe that a breach of order in the Gaza Strip or West Bank was a threat to Israel's continued occupation. In most instances the judges have accepted the rationale offered by the Israeli military government for its actions, and only rarely have they allowed a Palestinian complainant to prevail.

The frailty of the judicial protection of rights for the Palestinian population of the Gaza Strip and West Bank has led to calls at the United Nations for international protection for the Palestinians. The UN General Assembly established a special three-nation committee to monitor Israel's human rights practices, called the Special Committee to Investigate Israeli Practices Affecting the Human Rights of the Population of the Occupied Territories.[1] Each year the committee reports massive abuses by Israel. The General Assembly annually adopts resolutions condemning Israel for human rights violations against the Palestinians.

The issue of judicial protection is of crucial importance for the Palestinians because the Israeli military government violates their rights in many ways. The context for these violations is that the Israeli military government has sought not merely to hold the Gaza Strip and West Bank, pending its return to Jordan or Egypt, or to a Palestinian governing authority. Rather, it has attempted to change the character of the territories by seizing Palestinian-owned land and installing its own inhabitants in settlements there and by restricting the types of economic activity in which Palestinians might engage. These efforts have continued even as the government of Israel negotiated with the Palestine Liberation Organization over the fate of the Gaza Strip and West Bank in the wake of their 1993 Declaration of Principles and 1995 Interim Agreement.

The military government's efforts to assume ever greater control led the Palestinians to object and resist, both by seeking judicial protection for rights and by acts of violence that in turn brought repressive measures by the military government, measures often out of proportion to the acts that engendered them.

These repressive measures reached their height during the *intifadah*, or uprising, by the Palestinian population that began in December 1987 as a manifestation of accumulated grievances over the military government's efforts at a takeover of land and livelihood. These repressive measures violated the rights of the Palestinians as those rights are found in human rights law and in the special body of law that regulates belligerent occupation, called humanitarian law.

In 1990, as rights abuses increased, and the General Assembly's resolutions went unheeded, the UN Security Council adopted Resolution 681, which asked all states party to the Geneva Civilians Convention of 1949, the principal treaty that governs belligerent occupation, to protect the Palestinian population. After that call proved fruitless, the Security Council in 1994, by Resolution 904, called for a UN presence in the Gaza Strip and West Bank to monitor Israel's protection of Palestinian rights. Thus, the issue of protection for the Palestinian population has been recognized as one requiring international attention because the institutions of Israel have not provided it.

LAND CONFISCATION AND SETTLEMENTS

The issue of land confiscations has been extensively litigated by Palestinians seeking to protect land being taken by the military government. Few Palestinians have succeeded, even though the confiscations are all illegal. Through confiscation, the Israeli government has acquired over half the land area of the Gaza Strip and West Bank.[2] Much of this land the government has turned over to Israeli civilians for settlement. The confiscations are illegal under a treaty called the Hague Regulations of 1907,[3] which reflects the customary international law accepted by all states of the world as binding.[4] Article 46 of the Hague Regulations prohibits the confiscation of private property by an occupant. Much of the land confiscated in the West Bank and Gaza Strip is privately owned.

However, the Israeli government, and particularly the Likud Party, which formed Israel's government for most of the 1980s, declared as a matter of political principle that the West Bank is Israel's, and it set about establishing settlements to make Israel's control an on-the-ground reality. Prime Minister Itzhak Shamir called settlement in the West Bank "holy work."[5] During the 1980s the government allocated $300 million annually for settlement construction and maintenance.[6] In 1983, the Likud government prepared a "master plan" for Israeli settlement in the West Bank, envisaging the eventual incorporation of the West Bank into Israel and aiming "to disperse maximally large Jewish population in areas of high settlement priority, . . . and in a relatively short period by using the settlement potential of the West Bank to achieve the incorporation [of the West Bank] into the [Israeli] national system."[7]

When Palestinian landowners petitioned the Supreme Court of Israel for redress, the government justified its overriding of property interests not on the basis of expanding the Israeli state but on the theory that the settlements protected Israel's security in the Gaza Strip and West Bank.

In one court case over its right to take private land to build a settlement, the government said in an affidavit that the establishment of the projected settlement was "part of the security conception of the Government which bases the security system *inter alia* on Jewish settlements. In accordance with this concept all Israeli settlements in the territories occupied by the IDF [Israeli Defense Force] constitute part of the IDF's regional defense system," it said. "In times of calm these settlements mainly serve the purpose of presence and control of vital areas, maintaining observation, and the like. The importance of these settlements is enhanced in particular in time of war when the regular army forces are shifted, in the main, from their bases for purposes of operational activity and the said settlements constitute the principal component of presence and security control in the areas in which they are located."[8]

The Supreme Court has accepted this rationale and has ruled in favor of the government in all but a handful of cases. The Court upheld one confiscation of a tract of privately owned land, for example, after the Ministry of Defense said that the purpose was to form a defensive line of three settlements to protect the Tel Aviv airport.[9]

In one instance the Supreme Court ruled illegal the construction of a projected West Bank settlement, to be called Elon Moreh, on private land that was being confiscated for that purpose. The military government, supporting the planned construction, argued that the settlement would promote security. The settlers themselves, however, told the Court that their purpose in establishing the settlement was to assert a territorial claim to the West Bank. This objective of the settlers belied the security claim of the military government, and as a result the Court ruled the planned settlement illegal.[10]

With its security rationale for taking private land revealed as a makeweight, the military government shifted to confiscating land that was nominally state-owned. Much of the land of the West Bank was held under a tenure system that was in a technical sense state ownership, although individual families had occupied the land for generations and, as long as they paid taxes on it, were considered its owners.[11]

Whatever the rationale, land confiscation for settlement was illegal under the Geneva Civilians Convention, whose Article 49 states that an occupant may not "transfer parts of its own civilian population into the territory it occupies." An occupant must serve as a custodian for occupied territory pending a resolution of the military conflict that gave rise to the occupation. It thus may not change the character of the territory while it is in occupation. By rejecting the petitions of Palestinian landowners, the Supreme Court of Israel allowed their lawful interests to be overridden.

TORTURE

Criminal charges have been brought against many Palestinians on security-related offenses. These cases are tried before an Israeli military court whose judges are military officers. This composition of the courts has been problematic in terms of rights protection, for Israeli military judges are officers in the army attempting to suppress Palestinian resistance.

Typically in these cases the prosecution holds little evidence beyond a confession that the suspect has made to Israeli interrogators.[12] These confessions are usually written in Hebrew, which suggests that the Palestinian suspect may not have understood precisely what the confession contained.

The suspects have often alleged that they confessed under torture. An inquiry by the U.S. embassy in Jerusalem arrived at the conclusion that many of these allegations were valid.[13] Yet the Supreme Court never ruled a Palestinian's confession to be coerced. Its record on this issue was so uniform that attorneys representing Palestinians declined to raise the torture issue in Court, because their experience with the military courts led them to conclude that the plea would be rejected and that mentioning torture would lead the Court to impose a higher sentence.

A commission headed by a former chief justice of the Supreme Court of Israel conducted a special inquiry into torture by Israeli interrogators. The *Report of the Commission of Inquiry into the Methods of Interrogation of the General Security Service Regarding Hostile Terrorist Activity* concluded that torture was routine practice.[14] Instead, however, of calling for an end to torture, the Commission condoned torture on the ground that Palestinians were otherwise unlikely to cooperate with Israeli interrogators. To be sure, the Commission said that the only force that might lawfully be used against Palestinians was "moderate physical force," which the Commission distinguished from torture. Under internationally accepted definitions of torture, however, the level of force that the Commission authorized would constitute torture, since any physical force aimed at producing a confession is torture. The Israeli government approved the Commission's recommendation condoning moderate physical force, thus making the use of torture official policy for the Israeli government.[15]

DEPORTATION

The Israeli military government deported Palestinians it found to be active in resistance to the occupation, particularly during the uprising that began in 1987.[16] A deportee was permitted to approach an appeals board, and then the Supreme Court, to challenge the deportation order.[17] However, the deportee had no right to see the evidence on which the deportation order was based.[18] Deportees frequently approached the High Court, but it always accepted the government's rationale and never ruled a deportation order invalid.[19]

Nonetheless, all these deportations are illegal. Article 49 of the Geneva Civilians Convention states: "Individual or mass forcible transfers, as well as deportations of protected persons from occupied territory to the territory of the Occupying Power or to that of any other country, occupied or not, are prohibited, regardless of their motive."[20] The Supreme Court has avoided the mandate of Article 49 by construing it to prohibit only mass deportations for purposes of forced labor or extermination.[21]

The Court's narrow interpretation of Article 49 has been rejected by the international community.[22] A number of the deportations have been protested as violations of Article 49 by the United States,[23] by the European Economic Community[24] and by the United Nations Security Council.[25] The United States, explaining its vote in the Security Council in condemnation of certain deportations, said that Article 49 prohibits all deportations from occupied territory, whether or not the purpose was to send the person to forced labor or extermination.[26]

DEMOLITION OF HOUSES

As a penal measure in the West Bank and Gaza Strip, the Israeli military government demolishes the houses of Palestinians it arrests on security-related charges, typically carrying out the demolition shortly after arrest.[27] This practice is illegal under the law of belligerent occupation and under human rights law, and Palestinians have petitioned the Supreme Court of Israel to stop pending demolitions. The Court has asked the government to explain its rationale and for that purpose has on occasion delayed demolitions, but it has never ordered the government not to carry one out.[28]

Demolitions as practiced by the Israeli military government are illegal on a number of grounds. As a punishment, they are unlawful since that are carried out prior to a determination of guilt, thus violating the presumption of innocence and the right to a trial before punishment is imposed. The Geneva Civilians Convention, Article 53, prohibits property destruction by the occupant unless it is rendered "absolutely necessary by military operations." The demolitions as practiced by the military government are outside the context of military operations.

The United Nations General Assembly has condemned the demolitions as a violation of Palestinian rights.[29] The U.S. Department of State has stated, "In violation of the Geneva Convention, houses of individuals believed to have been involved in terrorism have been demolished."[30]

In some cases it has been discovered after a demolition that the suspect was innocent.[31] Moreover, since the punishment typically affects persons in addition to the suspect, it is a collective penalty and unlawful on that score as well.[32] Under the Geneva Civilians Convention, Article 33, no person "may be punished for an offence he or she has not personally committed."

Chief Justice Shamgar, while earlier serving as Attorney General of Israel, justified the demolitions as necessary "to destroy the physical base for military action when persons in the commission of a hostile military act are discovered. The house from which hand grenades are thrown," he stated, "is a military base." Shamgar also justified the demolitions as a deterrent against terrorists.[33]

The Supreme Court has upheld the demolitions on the rationale that they serve as a deterrent to acts of violence. It has said that the deterrent effect "should naturally apply not only to the terrorist himself, but to those surrounding him, and certainly to family members living with him. He should know that his criminal acts will not only hurt him but are apt to cause great suffering to his family."[34] This ruling violates the norm that punishment must be imposed only on a person who has been found guilty.

ADMINISTRATIVE DETENTION

The Supreme Court of Israel has approved another illegal practice of the Israeli military government, the detention of Palestinian suspects without a charge or a trial. The Court has found such detention lawful on the rationale that it is not punishment for past acts but is aimed at averting future acts.[35] Detention without trial allows the Israeli military government to detain persons it believes to be dangerous without amassing evidence sufficient to convict them in court. The military government has detained thousands of Palestinians in this fashion, often for extended periods of time.

When Israel occupied the West Bank and Gaza Strip in 1967, the military government adopted an order permitting detention without trial.[36] In 1980 the military government amended the order to allow limited judicial review. A detainee was to be brought before a military judge within 96 hours. The judge was to quash the detention if he found that the order was not issued for objective reasons of security. The judge was to review a detention order every three months.[37]

A limitation on judicial review by the military judge was the identity of the judge as a military officer. A second limitation was that the detainee had no right to learn the grounds for suspicion, which was typically deemed classified intelligence information.[38] Nonetheless, the detainee bore the burden of proving that the reasons leading to the order "were not objective reasons of state security."

Appeal could be taken to the Supreme Court of Israel.[39] However, the Court decided that it should accept the reasons offered by the military government unless those reasons were in an objective sense not reasons of state security or unless it appeared that the detention was motivated by bad faith.[40]

During the post-1987 Palestinian uprising, the Israeli military government increased its use of administrative detention and eased the procedural requirements for its application. Under prior provisions, the detention had to be authorized at the highest level of government, but in 1988 the military government authorized any military officer above the rank of colonel to order detention.[41]

The same amendment also revoked the 1980 regulation that had called for review of the detention by a military court. The purpose was "to ease the heavy burden on the military courts and the military prosecutor resulting from the large number of administrative detention orders issued in the last three months." However, a detainee was given a right to appeal to a newly established Military Appeals Committee composed of a military judge and two other military officers.[42] Under an amendment adopted later in 1988, appeal to a single judge was substituted for appeal to a three-judge panel.[43]

The Israeli practice of administrative detention falls short of the international standards for incarceration because it does not require prompt notification to the detainee of the reasons for the detention. It also violates the international requirement that a detained person have access to a court with the power to order release if the detention is not lawful.[44] Although such access is provided in form, the concealment of the reasons for the detention effectively deprives the detainee of the opportunity to challenge the lawfulness of the detention.

RETURN OF DISPLACED PALESTINIANS

The Supreme Court of Israel has permitted another blatant illegal action by the Israeli military government, namely, its continuing exclusion of the thousands of Gaza Strip and West Bank Palestinians who were rendered refugees by the 1967 war. When it captured the Gaza Strip and West Bank in 1967, one-quarter million Palestinians were displaced.[45] Israel declared that the exodus was voluntary and that the departing Palestinians "were not war-time refugees."[46] In a note to the UN Secretary General, it stated, "Any allegation that Israel has been expelling residents from their homes and thus creating a new refugee problem is untrue."[47]

UN officials, however, found a pattern of expulsion by Israeli forces.[48] In three Palestinian refugee camps near the West Bank town of Jericho, aerial bombardment by Israel's air force made 35,000 Palestinian civilians flee to Jordan.[49] The U.S. embassy in Jordan reported that the Israeli air force hit numerous civilian targets on the West Bank with no military significance.[50]

The UN Security Council demanded that Israel "facilitate the return of those inhabitants who have fled the areas since the outbreak of hostilities."[51] The General Assembly echoed the demand.[52] Under this pressure, Israel agreed to entertain applications for return under a program it denominated "family reunion,"[53] and in Jordan, applications were filed covering 170,000 Palestinian refugees.[54] Of this number, however, Israel permitted only 14,000 to return.[55]

Beyond those Palestinians forced out during the hostilities, many others were temporarily out of the country for schooling or on business or pleasure trips. The Red Cross dealt with the many families who found themselves separated "because a member was outside the territory when the war broke out."[56] Israel did not recognize these Palestinians as having a right to return, and they remained stranded abroad.[57] In September 1967, the military government conducted a census, which resulted in about 1 million persons being identified as residents.[58] To these persons, Israel issued identification cards.[59] Palestinians displaced or absent during the hostilities were not included in the census and hence were not deemed residents and thus, according to the Israeli government, had no right to return to their homes.

In addition, after 1967, many Gaza Strip and West Bank Palestinians went abroad to attend universities or to search for employment. This phenomenon led to a third category of Palestinians with repatriation problems, because the military government deemed a Palestinian absent for more than a short time to have lost residency rights.[60] Israel maintained that it was not required to recognize the residency rights of Gaza Strip or West Bank Palestinians following extended residence abroad.[61] To regain residency rights, these Palestinians were required to apply under Israel's family reunification program. In the 1980s, many of these persons applied, but Israel admitted few of them. In this way, thousands more Gaza Strip and West Bank Palestinians became refugees.[62]

The Supreme Court of Israel entertained petitions from Palestinians who were refused repatriation. The Court backed the government, refusing to order the reentry of Palestinians excluded by the government. The Court said that persons born in the West Bank or Gaza Strip who resided abroad for extended periods forfeited their residency rights. The Court upheld, for example, the exclusion of a Palestinian man born in the West Bank who left in 1958 and lived in Venezuela. He married a Venezuelan woman, and four children were born to them there. In 1975, all six entered the West Bank on a temporary tourist visa and overstayed, whereupon the military government ordered them to leave.[63]

In another case, a woman born in the West Bank resided there with her parents until 1968, when, at age sixteen, she left for Jordan, where she married. From Jordan, she and her husband moved to Kuwait. In 1972 she returned to the West Bank on a temporary visa and applied for permanent residence for herself, her husband, and their children. The military government refused. The Supreme Court upheld the refusal, finding that the woman had left the West Bank voluntarily, thereby forfeiting her residency right.[64]

The only instance in which the Supreme Court of Israel has intervened was one in which the military government acted arbitrarily in dealing with an applicant. A native West Banker left in 1962 to work in West Germany. In 1968, while on a visit to the West Bank, he married a woman from his native village, and on the basis of the marriage he applied for permanent residency. In 1970, the military government approved the man's application, but by then he was hospitalized in West Germany and could not travel. He applied again in 1973, but this time was refused, apparently on national security grounds. The Supreme Court said that the refusal was arbitrary, since the man had previously been granted permanent residency.[65]

Under international standards, a person has a right to return to his native country following a period abroad. A person does not sever his tie with his native country simply by living abroad. The Universal Declaration of Human Rights states, "Everyone has the right to leave any country, including his own, and to return to his country."[66] The International Covenant on Civil and Political Rights similarly states that "no one shall be arbitrarily deprived of the right to enter his own country."[67] The Supreme Court of Israel, however, subverts this right by agreeing with the military government that West Bank and Gaza Strip Palestinians enjoy only a defeasible right of residency.

THE SUPREME COURT'S THEORY OF THE APPLICABLE LAW

The Supreme Court of Israel arrived at its strongly pro-government positions only after holding that a variety of international norms are not binding on it in deciding Palestinians' petitions. This position on the law allowed it to uphold government action that was in violation of international standards.

A body of law has developed over several centuries to regulate the treatment of an occupied population by an occupying power. Called humanitarian law, this body of rules requires humane treatment of the population of territory occupied during military hostilities. These rules apply to Israel in the Gaza Strip and West Bank because it came into control of these territories during hostilities. Humanitarian law gives the belligerent occupant the right to maintain order. At the same time it protects the occupied population against abuses. It also is aimed at ensuring that the belligerent occupant does not irrevocably alter the territory in terms of population or resources, because the notion is that the occupant should return the territory intact upon a final peace settlement. Humanitarian law presupposes a temporary status; it applies pending the return of occupied territory to its lawful sovereign.[68]

Humanitarian law is found in norms of customary international law and in multilateral treaties. The most recent treaty on belligerent occupation is the 1949 Convention Relative to the Treatment of Civilian Persons in Time of War.[69] Israel and the other states involved in the 1967 hostilities are parties.

Israel disputes the applicability of the Geneva Civilians Convention to its occupation of the Gaza Strip and West Bank, however. It argues that the Convention applies only to the occupation of territory legitimately belonging to a state party to the Convention.[70] It contends that Jordan, from which it took the West Bank, did not have good title there and that Egypt, from which it took the Gaza Strip, did not have good title there.[71]

The Israeli government asserts, however, that it applies in a *de facto* sense those provisions of the Convention it deems "humanitarian."[72] The Supreme Court of Israel has followed that position, applying certain provisions of the Convention but not others.[73] The courts have not indicated precisely which provisions are to be applied.

The Israeli view on the non-applicability of the Geneva Civilians Convention is rejected by other states because the Convention by its terms applies "in all circumstances" (Article 1) and "to all cases of declared war or of any other armed conflict" (Article 2). The strong international consensus is that the Convention applies to Israel's occupation of the Gaza Strip and West Bank.[74]

As a further limitation on the applicability of treaties to Israel's occupation, the Supreme Court of Israel has relied on a notion that Israel adopted from the British law on treaties, namely, that a court will not deem a treaty to operate as domestic law unless the Parliament adopts legislation to transform the treaty into domestic law.[75] Israel's Parliament has not transformed the Geneva Civilians Convention, or human rights treaties, into domestic law.

Despite its restrictive view on treaties, the Supreme Court of Israel does find customary humanitarian law to apply to Israel's occupation of the Gaza Strip and West Bank.[76] Customary humanitarian law is found by the Court, as it is found by other authorities, to be reflected in the norms contained in the 1907 Hague Regulations.

The Hague Regulations contain the important basic proposition that an occupant must protect the "community life" of the occupied territory, preserving existing laws and institutions to the extent possible. The Supreme Court applied this norm in a case that raised the issue of associational rights. A group of lawyers in the West Bank organized a professional association for lawyers there, but the Israeli military governor issued an order retaining for himself the right to appoint the members of the union's executive committee and prohibiting independent financing of the union. The lawyers challenged the order in the Supreme Court. The Court found the military governor's order invalid. It ruled that the lawyers had a right to elect their own executive committee and to fund the union. To reach this result, the Court cited the "community life" provision of the Hague Regulations. The Court said that since the late twentieth century normal "community life" includes the free operation of professional unions. Thus, normal "community life" meant that professional groups should be allowed to maintain their associations without government interference.[77]

The Supreme Court has, however, ignored other provisions of the Hague Regulations, like those prohibiting house demolitions. The fact that the Supreme Court denies the applicability of the Geneva Civilians Convention has led it to uphold most of the illegal actions of the military government. The Convention, as mentioned above, prohibits deportation of members of the occupied population, as well as detention without charge.

Both the Hague Regulations and the Geneva Civilians Convention require an occupant to maintain in force the laws of the displaced sovereign. Thus, an occupant is not free to impose its own legislation. It must apply the law in force in the territory it occupies. The Hague Regulations state in this regard, in Article 43, that the occupant must "respect, unless absolutely prevented, the law in force in the country." The Geneva Civilians Convention states, in Article 64, that the penal laws of the occupied territory "shall remain in force" but that the occupant may "subject the population of the occupied territory to provisions which are essential" to enable it to "maintain the orderly government of the territory, and to ensure the security of the Occupying Power." Thus, while the occupant is given limited scope to enact new laws, it may not do so in a wholesale fashion.

Israel has violated this standard by importing its own legislation. The military government has enacted hundreds of legislative-style orders that regulate many aspects of community life. It has also applied a set of provisions called the Defense (Emergency) Regulations, which were put in force in Palestine by Great Britain when it controlled Palestine in the 1930s. These were provisions designed to deal with a civil war that occurred in Palestine in the 1930s, and they allowed for extraordinary governmental remedies, such as the power to deport individuals, the power to detain without charge and the power to demolish houses as a penalty. The military government in the Gaza Strip and West Bank has followed these regulations to authorize these practices, even though they are prohibited by humanitarian law. Israel's government argued that Jordan applied the Defense (Emergency) Regulations when it controlled the West Bank. In fact, Jordan did not deem the Regulations to be in force and did not apply them. Thus, they constituted new law when Israel applied them starting in 1967, and their use violated the Hague Regulations and the Geneva Civilians Convention.

The Supreme Court has also declined to apply international human rights norms in assessing the military government's treatment of the Gaza Strip and West Bank Palestinians. This position has freed the military government from a number of norms that would restrict its activity.

Israel's government has asserted that human rights treaties are not applicable on the ground that applying a human rights treaty implies sovereignty in a territory. Israel is a party to the Convention against Torture, which, in Article

2, requires a state party to prevent torture "in any territory under its jurisdiction."[78] Israel's foreign ministry has said, however, that the Torture Convention does not apply in the occupied territories because its application would contradict the Israeli government's view that the status of the territories remains to be determined. The ministry's rationale was that if it applied the Torture Convention in the territories, it would be making a claim to sovereignty.[79]

However, the International Court of Justice has indicated in a related context that rights treaties must be applied even absent sovereignty. The Court said that South Africa's control over Namibia was unlawful but that South Africa must nonetheless observe "general conventions such as those of a humanitarian character, the non-performance of which may adversely affect the people of Namibia."[80]

Israel is a party to the International Covenant on Civil and Political Rights, the major civil rights treaty in the world today. However, it does not deem the Covenant to apply to its conduct in the Gaza Strip and West Bank. The general view in the international community, however, is that human rights law applies to Israel's occupation. The U.S. Department of State, in its annual reports on rights in the occupied territories, assesses Israel's conduct under the same human rights standards it uses to assess the conduct of states within their own territory.[81] The Human Rights Commission has referred to the International Covenant on Civil and Political Rights in assessing Israel's conduct in the Gaza Strip and West Bank.[82]

Judicial protection for the rights of the population of Israel's occupied territory is available in the sense that the Supreme Court of Israel entertains petitions and has the power to order the military government to desist from unlawful action. However, the Supreme Court has found violations so rarely as to render its protection of rights ineffectual. By agreeing with suspect rationales advanced by Israel's government, and by limiting the kinds of norms that apply, the Court has allowed the military government to violate the rights of the Palestinian population of the Gaza Strip and West Bank. The experience of judicial protection in the Gaza Strip and West Bank points up the need for additional international mechanisms to protect a population under belligerent occupation, particularly where the occupation continues for an extended period.

NOTES

1. G.A. Res. 2443, 23 U.N. GAOR, *Resolutions* at 50, U.N. Doc. A/7218 (1969).

2. W. Lehn, *The Jewish National Fund* (London, 1988), 183.

3. Convention Respecting the Laws and Customs of War on Land, Oct. 18, 1907, Annex: Regulations Respecting the Laws and Customs of War on Land, Art. 43, 36 *Statutes at Large* (1910), at 2277 (hereinafter Hague Regulations).

4. E. Cohen, *Human Rights in the Israeli-Occupied Territories 1967–1982* (Manchester, 1985), 43.

5. D. Hirst, *The Gun and Olive Branch: The Roots of Violence in the Middle East* (London, 1984), 453.

6. G. Aronson, *Creating Facts: Israel, Palestinians and the West Bank* (Washington, DC, 1987), 268.

7. M. Benvenisti, *The West Bank Data Project: A Survey of Israel's Policies* (Washington, DC, 1984), 19–28.

8. Ayoub v. Minister of Defense, High Court No. 302/72, 27(2) *Piskei Din* (1972), in Raja Shehadeh, *Occupier's Law: Israel and the West Bank* (Washington, DC, 1985), 109.

9. Amira et al. v. Minister of Defense et al., High Court of Justice 258/79, 34(1) *Piskei Din* (1980) 90, summarized in 10 *Israel Yearbook on Human Rights* (Tel Aviv, 1980), 331 at 332.

10. Mustafa Dweikat et al. v. Government of Israel et al. (Elon Moreh Case), High Court No. 390/79, 34(1) *Piskei Din* (1980) 1, in M. Shamgar, ed., *Military Government in the Territories Administered by Israel 1967–1980: The Legal Aspects*, vol. 1 (Jerusalem, 1982), 404–441; excerpted in 9 *Israel Yearbook on Human Rights* (Jerusalem, 1979), 345–350.

11. Shehadeh, *supra* note 8 at 22.

12. *Report and Recommendations of an Amnesty International Mission to the Government of the State of Israel, 3–7 June 1979, including the Government's Response and Amnesty International Comments* (London, 1980), 35–37.

13. Cable titled "Jerusalem 1500" sent by U.S. Consulate, East Jerusalem, to U.S. Dept. of State, May 31, 1978, excerpted in "Allegations of Torture: Excerpts from State Department Cable," *Christian Science Monitor*, Apr. 4, 1979, 26.

14. Excerpted in *Jerusalem Post* (daily ed.), Nov. 1, 1987.

15. "Cabinet Adopts Inquiry Finding: Shin Bet Perjury Report Draws Mixed Reaction," *Jerusalem Post* (international ed.), week ending Nov. 14, 1987, 1.

16. J. Brinkley, "U.S. Criticism Sets Off a Furor in Israel," *New York Times*, Aug. 25, 1988, A3; "Israeli Sends Four Palestinians into Exile in Lebanon," *Al-Fajr*, Aug. 21, 1988, 1.

17. Cohen, *supra* note 4 at 107.

18. J. R. Hiltermann, "Israel's Deportation Policy in the Occupied West Bank and Gaza," 3 *Palestine Year Book of International Law* (Nicosia, Cyprus, 1986), 154 at 182–183; U.S. Dept. of State, *Country Reports on Human Rights Practices for 1988* (Washington, DC, 1989), 1379.

19. Cohen, *supra* note 4 at 107.

20. P. J. Morgan, "Recent Israeli Security Measures under the Fourth Geneva Convention," 3 *Connecticut Journal of International Law* (1988), 485 at 492–495.

21. Abu Awad vs. IDF Commander of Judea and Samaria, High Court of Justice 97/79, 33(3) *Piskei Din* (1979) 309, quoted in Hiltermann, *supra* note 18 at 171.

22. Cohen, *supra* note 4 at 110.

23. U.S. Dept. of State, *supra* note 18 at 1379.

24. "U.S. Criticizes Israeli Expulsion Policy," *Al-Fajr*, Aug. 28, 1988, 4.

25. S.C. Res. 607, Jan. 5, 1988, U.N. Doc. S/INF/607 (1988); S.C. Res. 608, Jan. 14, 1988, U.N. Doc. S/INF/608 (1988); P. Lewis, "U.N. Councils Again Asks Israelis to Stop Deporting Palestinians," *New York Times*, Jan. 15, 1988, A9.

26. Security Council, *Provisional Verbatim Record*, Jan. 5, 1988, 11, U.N. Doc. S/PV.2780 (1988).

27. C. V. Reicin, "Preventive Detention, Curfews, Demolition of Houses, and De-

portations: An Analysis of Measures Employed by Israel in the Administered Territories,'' 8 *Cardozo Law Review* (1987), 515 at 547.

28. U. Halabi, ''Demolition and Sealing of Houses in the Israeli Occupied Territories: A Critical Legal Analysis,'' 5 *Temple International & Comparative Law Review* (1991), 251 at 265.

29. See, e.g., G.A. Res. 41/63D, 41 U.N. GAOR, Supp. (No. 53) at 10, U.N. Doc. A/41/53 (1987).

30. U.S. Dept. of State, *Country Reports on Human Rights Practices for 1979* (Washington, DC 1980), 764. See also U.S. Dept. of State, *supra* note 18 at 1379.

31. P. Johnson, ''Behind the Interpretations: Faces of the Palestinian Uprising,'' 5 *Mideast Monitor* (No. 2, 1988), 3.

32. Reicin, *supra* note 27 at 547.

33. M. Shamgar, ''The Observance of International Law in the Administered Territories,'' 1 *Israel Yearbook on Human Rights* (Tel Aviv, 1971), 262 at 276.

34. High Court of Justice Case 698/85, cited in E. Playfair, *Demolition and Sealing of Houses as a Punitive Measure in the Israeli-Occupied West Bank* (Ramallah, Palestine, 1987), 12.

35. Kawasmeh v. Minister of Defense, 36(1) *Piskei Din* (1982) 666; D. Kretzmer, *The Legal Status of the Arabs in Israel* (Boulder, CO, 1990), 145.

36. Military Order 378, Order Concerning Security Provisions (1970), arts. 84A, 87, in Playfair, *supra* note 34 at 11.

37. Military Order 815, Jan. 11, 1980, cited in E. Playfair, *Administrative Detention in the Occupied West Bank* (Ramallah, Palestine, 1986), 11.

38. Israel National Section, International Commission of Jurists, *The Rule of Law in the Areas Administered by Israel* (Tel Aviv, 1981), 73.

39. Military Order 815, Article 87, in Playfair, *supra* note 37 at 19.

40. Rabbi Kahane et al. v. Minister of Defense, 35(2) *Piskei Din* (1981), 253.

41. Ha'aretz, Mar. 20, 1988; Military Commander, Judea and Samaria, Order Concerning Administrative Arrests (Interim Instruction) (No. 1229), Mar. 17, 1988.

42. G. Frankel, ''Israeli Army Allows Press Inspection of Detention Center for Palestinians,'' *Washington Post*, June 3, 1988, A21; Al-Haq, *Ansar 3: A Case for Closure* (Ramallah, Palestine, 1988), 31.

43. Military Commander, Judea and Samaria, Amendment to Interim Order (No. 1236), June 13, 1988.

44. International Covenant on Civil and Political Rights, Article 93, entered into force Mar. 23, 1976, 999 U.N. Treaty Series 171 (hereinafter International Covenant).

45. Report of the Secretary-General under General Assembly Resolution 2252 (ES-V) and Security Council Resolution 237 (1967), 22 U.N. SCOR, Supp. (Oct.–Dec. 1967) at 80, 119, U.N. Doc. S/8158 (1967); J. Abu-Lughod, ''The Continuing Expulsions from Palestine: 1948–1985,'' in: G. E. Perry, ed., *Palestine: Continuing Dispossession* (Belmont, MS, 1986), 17 at 30, 32.

46. 23 U.N. GAOR, 622nd mtg. (Spec. Polit. Comm.) at 5, U.N. Doc. A/SPC/SR.622 (1968).

47. Report by the Secretary-General to the Security Council in pursuance of operative paragraph 3 of the Council's resolution 237 (1967), Annex I, *Note verbale* dated June 22, 1967, addressed to the Secretary-General by the Representative of Israel, 22 U.N. SCOR, Supp. (Apr.–June 1967) at 301, U.N. Doc. S/8021 (1967).

48. D. A. Schmidt, "100,000 in Jordan Said to Have Fled Across River," *New York Times*, June 12, 1967, A19.

49. P. Dodd and H. Barakat, *River without Bridges: A Study of the Exodus of the 1967 Palestinian Arab Refugees* (Beirut, 1969), 40; F. J. Khouri, *The Arab-Israeli Dilemma* (Syracuse, NY, 1976), 150; Report of the Commissioner-General of the New United Nations Relief and Works Agency for Palestine Refugees in the Near East July 1, 1966–June 30, 1967, 22 U.N. GAOR, Supp. (No. 13) 11, U.N. Doc. A/6713 (1967).

50. D. Neff, *Warriors for Jerusalem: The Six Days That Changed the Middle East* (New York, 1984), 228–229.

51. S.C. Res. 237, 22 U.N. SCOR, *Resolutions & Decisions* 5, U.N. Doc. S/INF/22/Rev.2 (1968).

52. G.A. Res. 2252, 5 U.N. GAOR (emerg. spec. sess.), *Resolutions* at 3, U.N. Doc A/6798 (1967).

53. U Thant, *View from the UN* (Garden City, NY, 1978), 282.

54. Report of the Secretary-General, *supra* note 44 at 123–124.

55. Report of the Commissioner-General, *supra* note 49 at 11, "The Middle East Activities of the International Committee of the Red Cross June 1967–June 1970," 10 *International Review of the Red Cross* (1970), 424 at 448; D. Peretz, "Israel's Administration and Arab Refugees," 46 *Foreign Affairs* (1968), 336 at 337.

56. "The Middle East Activities of the International Committee of the Red Cross June 1967–June 1970," *supra* note 55 at 450.

57. U.S. Dept. of State, *Country Reports on Human Rights Practices for 1990* (Washington, DC, 1991), 1491.

58. D. Fisher, "Arab U.S. Citizens; West Bank Has a 'Little America,' " *Los Angeles Times*, May 13, 1986, A1.

59. G. Frankel, "Israel Assailed for Family Separations; Palestinians Barred from Joining Relatives in Occupied Areas," *Washington Post*, Feb. 8, 1987, A25.

60. J. Diehl, "7,000 Palestinians with U.S. Passports Caught in Uprising; Many Americans Complain of Treatment by Israelis," *Washington Post*, Sept. 16, 1989, A15; C. Whittome, *The Right to Unite: The Family Reunification Question in the Palestinian Occupied Territories: Law and Practice* (Ramallah, Palestine, 1990), 11–12.

61. U.S. Dept. of State, *supra* note 57 at 1491.

62. Fisher, *supra* note 58.

63. Mustafa v. Military Commander of the Judea and Samaria Region, Case No. 629/82, 37(1) *Piskei Din* 158, excerpted in 14 *Israel Yearbook on Human Rights* (Tel Aviv, 1984), 313.

64. Abu El-Tin v. Minister of Defense, 27(1) *Piskei Din* (1973) 481, summarized in 5 *Israel Yearbook on Human Rights* (Tel Aviv, 1975), 376.

65. Samara and Ne'imat v. Commander of the Judea and Samaria Region, Case No. 802/79, 34(4) *Piskei Din* 1, excerpted in 11 *Israel Yearbook on Human Rights* (Tel Aviv, 1981), 362.

66. G.A. Res. 217A, Art. 13, para. 2, Dec. 10, 1948, 3 U.N. GAOR, *Resolutions* at 71, U.N. Doc. A/810 (1948).

67. International Covenant, *supra* note 44 at Art. 12(4).

68. M. Greenspan, *The Modern Law of Land Warfare* (Berkeley, CA, 1959), 217.

69. 75 U.N. Treaty Series 287 (hereinafter Geneva Civilians Convention).

70. Morgan, *supra* note 20 at 485.

71. Amb. N. Lorch, Ministry for Foreign Affairs, Statement at Symposium on Human

Rights, Faculty of Law, Tel Aviv University, July 1–4, 1971, in 1 *Israel Yearbook on Human Rights* (1971), 366; Y. Z. Blum, "The Missing Reversioner: Reflections on the Status of Judea and Samaria," 3 *Israel Law Review* (1968), 279; Reicin, *supra* note 27 at 518–519.

72. Reicin, *supra* note 27 at 520.

73. Military Prosecutor v. Halil Muhamad Mahmud Halil Bakhis et al., Israel, Military Court Sitting in Ramallah, Palestine, June 10, 1968, 47 *International Law Reports* (1974), 484.

74. 61 *Department of State Bulletin* (1969), 76; S.C. Res. 237, June 14, 1967, 22 U.N. SCOR *Resolutions & Decisions* at 5, U.N. Doc. S/INF/Rev.2 (1968); G.A. Res. 2443, preambular para. 2, 23 U.N. GAOR Supp. (No. 18) 50, U.N. Doc. A/7218 (1969); W. Olson, "UN Security Council Resolutions Regarding Deportations from Israeli Administered Territories: The Applicability of the Fourth Geneva Convention Relative to the Protection of Civilian Persons in Time of War," 24 *Stanford Journal of International Law* (1988), 611 at 620.

75. M. Qupty, "The Application of International Law in the Occupied Territories as Reflected in the Judgments of the High Court of Justice in Occupied Israel," in: E. Playfair, ed., *International Law and the Administration of Occupied Territories* (Oxford 1992), 87 at 105.

76. Hague Regulations, *supra* note 3, Art. 43; Cohen, *supra* note 4 at 43.

77. Bahij Tamimi et al. v. Minister of Defense et al. (Case of Arab Lawyers Union), High Court of Justice of Israel, No. 507/85, Ruling of Sept. 16, 1987 (Goldberg, J, with Alon and Halima, JJ, concurring), 41(4) *Piskei Din* (1987) 57, summarized in 18 *Israel Yearbook on Human Rights* (Tel Aviv, 1988), 248.

78. Convention against Torture and Other Cruel, Inhuman, or Degrading Treatment or Punishment, entered into force June 26, 1987, G.A. Res. 39/46, 39 U.N. GAOR Supp. (No. 51) 197, U.N. Doc. A/RES/39/46 (1984).

79. "Israeli Interrogation Methods under Fire after Death of Detained Palestinian," 4 *Middle East Watch Reports* (issue 6, Mar. 19, 1992), 3 (quoting letter from Legal Adviser to Foreign Ministry).

80. Legal Consequences for States of the Continued Presence of South Africa in Namibia (South West Africa) Notwithstanding Security Council Resolution 276 (1970), International Court of Justice, *Reports* (1971), 15 at 54.

81. U.S. Dept. of State, *supra* note 30 at 760–768.

82. "Question of the Violation of Human Rights in the Occupied Arab Territories, Including Palestine," U.N. Commission on Human Rights, Feb. 9, 1987, preambular para. 2, U.N. Doc. E/CN.4/1987/L.4.

Part III

Latin America

Chapter 5

Judicial Protection of Human Rights in Latin America: Heroism and Pragmatism

BRIAN TURNER

INTRODUCTION

The primary responsibility for violations of human rights in Latin America in the last 30 years falls squarely on the military and the police forces. On this question there is no doubt. However, Latin American judiciaries have also been widely blamed for the failure to act with creativity, courage or principles to even call to account, let alone stop, state-sponsored extra-legal violence against citizens. Since positive judicial behavior in defense of civil liberties and human rights is exceptional in the recent history of the region, defenders of rights may properly be considered "shining lights" in an otherwise bleak landscape.

However, positive action from the bench in defense of rights is not always a simple matter. Judges are representatives of the law, and law sometimes conflicts with a straightforward defense of individual rights. Such conflicts must be balanced according to prevailing doctrines of judicial behavior. Judges also are representatives of an institution of the state and must consider the impact of their decisions on such corporate interests as judicial independence and the maintenance of legitimacy. They must defend the prerogatives of their branch of government.

In resolving these conflicting demands, judges do not have the luxury of moral puritanism. They hold positions of authority, but their power to influence events is rather weak. To maintain power may require compromises with moral principles. Shining lights in this sense are brighter when they shine from the authoritative position of the judiciary. Moralistic criticism of state-sponsored violence from outside the institutions of the state is admirable but not especially effective in the defense of rights in specific cases. In other words, a judge may resign in protest of abuses, and in some cases resigning may be the only acceptable choice, but in doing so that judge cedes his or her position to someone less likely to act in defense of rights. Or, as Robert Cover puts it, "If a man makes a good priest, we may be quite sure he will not be a great prophet."[1] My focus here is on the "priests."

Thus judges who act to defend human rights must be viewed in the context of their institutional position and their perception of the proper role they are to play in that position. The political context of judicial behavior must also be considered, as some situations are more conducive to a defense of rights than others, regardless of how judges think and act.

This chapter reviews the behavior of Latin American judiciaries since 1964, the year of the Brazilian military coup d'état that signaled a new and distinctly brutal era of authoritarian politics in the region. I focus on the Southern Cone (Argentina, Brazil, Chile, Paraguay and Uruguay), as the situation of judges elsewhere is often so dangerous as to make heroism nearly suicidal. It makes little sense to discuss defense of human rights from the bench when judges cannot themselves expect basic personal security.[2] This chapter searches for judicial "heroes" and analyzes the contextual features of heroic defense of human rights. The primary variables influencing "context" are judicial role perceptions and legal traditions, and the country's political situation.

Role perceptions depend on such factors as the value placed on judicial independence from other branches of government, especially regarding the power of judicial review; the defense of corporate interests, such as the ability of higher-court judges to appoint lower-court judges, assign cases, determine jurisdictions and control the general administrative matters; the impact of civil law traditions on judicial training and behavior; and the likelihood of having decisions overturned by a higher court.

The period since 1964 is marked by two very distinct political periods. The first period begins with the military takeover and continues throughout a military government's time in office. During such a time the judiciary must be very conscious of the real limits to its power and the potential threats to the judiciary and to the political rights and personal security of the judges themselves. The second period comes during the transition to democracy, when new and relatively fragile governments must resolve the thorny questions resulting from past human rights abuses. Here, judges must consider the importance of the defense of rule of law and procedural justice to a democratic system, the very real and emotional claims of those seeking retributive justice for past violations and the threat posed to the new regime by an unrepentant military. In either situation, judges who hope to defend human rights must assess the political circumstances and identify allies both within and outside the judiciary to support their efforts. Heroes, it turns out, need allies.

THE CONCEPT OF JUDICIAL HEROISM

To develop the concept of judicial heroism, a brief discussion of U.S. judges' behavior will be helpful. North American history provides several dramatic examples of judges forced to choose between defending human rights and their perception of the judicial branch's role vis-à-vis the rule of law. Not surprisingly, the most poignant examples come from the struggles to end slavery in the nineteenth century and segregation in the twentieth.

Robert Cover's careful study of anti-slavery judges in the pre–Civil War North provides a very useful framework for analyzing judicial heroism.[3] Slavery placed North American judges in a position not so very different from that of their Latin American counterparts a century later. Arguments against slavery were based on natural law concepts, which provided a powerful argument against the straightforward application of statutory law. However, application of natural law was not clearly a part of the judicial tradition, in spite of its moral appeal to the anti-slavery judges. This has also been the case in Latin America, where modern international conventions regarding human rights find little reflection in antiquated penal codes. To heroically defend human rights in either context, a judge would first have to accept the idea of natural law or international human rights law, then apply these concepts to counter statutes. To a judge trained and promoted in a system based on the supremacy of statutes, the leap to a radical doctrine of judicial interpretation outside of the traditional sources will be a difficult one. Cover refers to this as the moral-formal dilemma, likely to lead to dissonance for those who accepted the basic justice of natural law claims but yet achieved high positions on the bench through judicious interpretation of statute.[4]

To reduce dissonance, Cover's judges resorted to three strategies: "(1) elevation of the formal stakes, (2) retreat to a mechanical formalism, and (3) ascription of responsibility elsewhere."[5] In the first strategy, the judge exaggerates the importance of role fidelity, becoming the dispassionate upholder of law and the social contract. Here judges believe themselves to be making a choice between individual harm (slavery) and higher reasons of state (maintenance of the federal system). Excessive formalism is also useful for reduction of dissonance because it removes from the judge the perception of having real powers to decide specific cases. While formalism seems a more likely escape for judges in civil law systems,[6] it is interesting that Cover's anti-slavery judges made extensive use of formalistic doctrines to defend their pro-slavery decisions. Finally, ascribing responsibility elsewhere further distances the judge from unpleasant decisions. Cover's judges relied on the concept of separation of powers, ascribing their decisions to bad law and its majoritarian origins in "the sovereign people."

A similar approach can be applied to Latin American judiciaries in general. Elevation of the value of formal stakes has been very widespread in the region, as judges have accepted the premise of the National Security doctrine that civilized society is under attack from subversive forces beyond the protection of civil rights. While traditions of judicial review have taken hold in parts of Latin America, and constitutions in the region often provide for some powers more typical of common-law systems,[7] judiciaries have often resorted to excessive formalism presumed to be characteristic of civil law jurisprudence. And finally, concepts of judicial independence have been used surprisingly by judges who refused to enter into "political thickets" at the risk to the autonomy of their own institution. Such an approach allowed the Argentine PJ (Poder Judicial—judicial branch) to elaborate its "*de facto* doctrine," asserting the legitimacy of the acts of *de facto* governments.

Cover focuses on presumably good men who at great personal cost to themselves and to their reputations failed to be "heroes." Jack Bass looks at a distinct type of judge, the "unlikely" Southern heroes of the U.S. Fifth Circuit Court during the civil rights movement.[8] While Bass does not develop an explicit framework for understanding judicial behavior, he clearly sees heroism as an activist extension of constitutional theory to provide greater defense of human rights. Resolving dissonance here required finding justification for creative action that, like Cover's judges, alienated the desegregation judges from many of their friends and colleagues. A key element in the political context here, of course, was the firm support the Fifth Circuit enjoyed from the Supreme Court and later from the executive branch. This was certainly not the case in the period immediately after *Dred Scott*. The judges of the Fifth Circuit were able to rely on institutional allies, while the anti-slavery judges had none.

LATIN AMERICAN JUDICIAL BEHAVIOR—RESPONSE TO MILITARY COUPS[9]

Judicial response to coup makers in the Southern Cone varied from admirable defenses of legality and human rights to near-complete submission. As Norman Nadorff notes, judges have four choices after a military coup: They can resign, capitulate to military power, resist that power or chart a pragmatic course.[10] "The last option," he observes, "best serves the judiciary's natural desire to maintain the status quo ante of the legal system to the maximum extent possible . . . [and] afford[s] the greatest possibility of survival as an effective branch of government and as individual magistrates."[11]

Nadorff finds the Brazilian Supreme Federal Tribunal's (SFT) behavior in the first years of the military regime, from 1964 to 1969, to have been a reasonably effective effort at pragmatism, with real results for individual rights. A series of decisions defended political rights and rejected military jurisdiction over civilians,[12] rejected the military's interpretations of law,[13] rejected the military's arguments about the existence of a state of war[14] and defended free speech,[15] often with reference to U.S. Supreme Court opinions. After Institutional Act No. 2 (IA-2) was decreed by the military government in 1965, the SFT was packed with five new justices and had its powers curtailed. Recognizing the new limits on its power, the high court backed down from challenging the constitutionality of the regime.[16]

When IA-2 was lifted in 1967, the SFT reasserted itself, granting *habeas corpus* petitions[17] and reversing some decisions made under the restrictive IA-2.[18] However, IA-5, decreed in 1968, declared military actions free of judicial review and largely militarized the court process. The SFT continued to exist, but defense of individual rights through *habeas corpus* and other devices virtually disappeared. The military government forced three Court Ministers, Evandro Lins e Silva, Victor Nunes and Hermes Lima, into retirement, while two other defenders of human rights, Ministers Gonçalves de Oliveira and Lafayette de Andrade, resigned in protest.[19]

The main lesson that Nadorff draws is that the "judiciary should use the Executive's need for political 'legitimization' as political leverage."[20] By judiciously recognizing the military's power, and thus its "right" to govern, a well-written decision can raise the costs to the government when it violates individual rights. Nadorff criticizes some of the intemperate and excoriating language in some of the decisions that may have provoked the military into restricting the power of the SFT.[21]

The line between pragmatism and capitulation can be rather thin. Frederick Snyder, writing on Argentina, argues that when judges treat the military as a legal government, they provide it with legitimacy but do not gain enough leverage to defend human rights. Snyder blames the legal process, and the judges that participate in it, as having been

singularly important in the mobilization of state terror in that it has enabled the junta to address society not only through the amplifier at the rally, the proclamation in the newspaper, the rifle butt on the street, and the electrode in the torture chamber, but through a vocabulary of reason and right as well.[22]

Snyder thus dismisses the importance of the few grants of *habeas corpus* petitions during the *Proceso* (1976–1983) as beneficial to the military government. Such grants indicated that the government made a few procedural mistakes but was nevertheless legal. Clearly, the PJ in Argentina did nothing to restrain the massive human rights abuses of the military, becoming "a sham jurisdictional structure, a cover to protect its image."[23]

In fairness to the civilian judiciary in Argentina, the judicial branch was purged and militarized on the first day of the coup against Isabelita Perón (March 24, 1976). All new appointees swore to uphold the objectives of the *Proceso*,[24] denying opportunity for any judicial heroes to defend rights. Tellingly, in 1981 an Appellate Court judge declared the state of siege itself unconstitutional and fled the country a few days later.[25] Under the junta led by General Juan Carlos Onganía (1966–1970), an independent civilian judiciary did act to defend rights in a fashion similar to that of the Brazilian SFT.[26]

The Uruguayan Supreme Court also cautiously resisted the creeping militarization of politics that began in 1967. Under the doctrine of avoidance of "political" decisions, the Court sought to isolate itself from conflict with the executive branch and the military. But when provoked to defend its institutional prerogatives of review and independence, the PJ did offer resistance, ordering in one case the release of two people detained by military operatives and sending to the General Assembly a list of constitutional infractions by the executive. In these cases, though, the executive and the military simply ignored the demands of the Court.[27]

On March 1, 1972, newly elected President Juan María Bordaberry submitted repressive state security legislation to the Senate. The bill proposed granting significant judicial powers to the executive branch, essentially putting the judiciary into the hands of the military. A body of jurists consulted by the Senate declared the proposed legislation unconstitutional by a vote of 17 to 1, so the Senate tabled the bill. However, under direct threat of military coup, the Senate succumbed to pressure and eventually approved the bill. After failing to rally the legislative branch to its defense, the Supreme Court likewise succumbed and renounced its previous reservations concerning the law's constitutionality. After that time, the military ran the Uruguayan courts.[28]

The most complete capitulation to military power by an independent civilian judiciary took place in Chile. The junta led by General Augusto Pinochet (1973–1990) never had to militarize the PJ, as the civilian Supreme Court continually defended the regime. This was ironic, given that Court's defense of judicial independence during the socialist government of Salvador Allende (1970–1973). Supreme Court President Enrique Urratia Manzano not only placed the presidential sash on Pinochet but announced, "I put the judiciary in your hands."[29] In a reversal of the political exchange described by Nadorff, the military junta granted the Supreme Court some respect for its autonomy, allowing it to continue to supervise the entire PJ in what was otherwise the most thoroughly militarized regime in the region.[30] Junta concerns about judges too sympathetic to the Allende government were expressed privately to the Supreme Court, leaving it to deal with the problem.[31]

Chilean judicial heroes were without institutional allies and thus could only expect to raise symbolic resistance. President Patricio Aylwin's "Truth and Reconciliation" Commission reported only a few instances of "vigorous behavior of some judges." The efforts of these judges, such as Carlos Cerda,[32] were met with dilatory actions by the police, and their decisions were overturned by higher courts. Further, "judges who were forthright in pursuing human rights violations were punished and given poor ratings"[33] by their superiors within the PJ. It is not surprising, then, that of approximately 8,700 writs of *habeas corpus* presented to the courts, only 10 were accepted.[34]

LATIN AMERICAN JUDICIAL BEHAVIOR—RESPONSE TO DEMOCRATIZATION

Democratization in the Southern Cone altered the institutional context for the judiciary and provided a more open environment for defense of rights. Argentina returned to democracy with the election of Raúl Alfonsín in 1983. In 1985, Uruguay likewise elected a civilian, Julio María Sanguinetti. Brazil returned to civilian government through indirect elections in 1985, which placed José Sarney in the Palácio do Planalto, a new Constitution in 1988 and direct presidential elections in 1989. Paraguay's democratization began with a coup d'état in 1989 and direct election of a civilian president, Juan Carlos Wasmosy, in 1993. Chile returned to civilian rule with the defeat of Pinochet's referendum in 1988 and the election of Patricio Aylwin in 1989.

These new democracies have faced a variety of difficult decisions regarding justice, most notably regarding the question of whether or not to prosecute those responsible for the commission of human rights violations under the military government. The Alfonsín government pursued prosecutions with some vigor but provoked numerous barrack revolts from the military. The still-powerful Chilean military and the Uruguayan military were able to raise credible threats to the democratic order so as to restrict the willingness of the government to prosecute. In the case of Uruguay, the military had an ally in President San-guinetti. In Brazil and Paraguay, entrenched elites have been able to deflect serious efforts to prosecute without openly raising a threat to democratic insti-tutions.[35]

More interesting for my purposes is the response of the judiciary itself to the debates over prosecutions and to efforts to reform the administration of justice. The Alfonsín government was the most active in attempting to reform the op-erations of the PJ. Alfonsín established a new trial system and removed the prosecutor's office from the control of the Ministry of Justice.

The President had the power to nominate and promote new judges in the Federal District (Buenos Aires) and used that opportunity to replace hard-line justices of the previous regime without engaging in a sweeping purge. Thus, Alfonsín could declare that "the Judiciary was the branch most successful in revitalizing social confidence in the state's capacity to be an effective force of transformation."[36]

To pursue the prosecution of the junta leaders, Alfonsín first gave jurisdiction to the military courts, allowing that appeals would be heard in the Courts of Appeal.[37] After the military courts acquitted all of the defendants, the civilian appeals courts began work on the cases. Almost all of the appeals court judges had been first appointed to the bench during the *Proceso* and had only been promoted during Alfonsín's government. While Alfonsín himself controlled the appointments to the Court of Appeal of Buenos Aires, other Courts of Appeal in the provinces were subject to a Peronist-dominated senatorial courtesy. The high-profile prosecutions took place in Buenos Aires, and the Court of Appeals there has been given high marks for its work. However, few prosecutions were obtained in cases heard in the interior. Eduardo Rabossi concludes that many judges in the provinces were not "prepared to make an ideological break with the past and to assume the advent of democracy as having the highest legal, political, and social value."[38] The U.S. State Department draws a similar con-clusion regarding efforts to prosecute police officers, noting that "the efficacy of legal actions . . . varies widely . . . depending on the court within whose ju-risdiction the case falls, the attitude of the local authorities, and the efficacy of police internal review mechanisms."[39]

Since the ascension of Peronist Carlos Saúl Menem to the presidency in 1989, judicial reforms have been rolled back to a certain degree. Menem packed the Supreme Court, adding four new judges to the five already on the bench.[40] This new Court returned to an interpretation of the Argentine Constitution that grants legitimacy to laws passed by *de facto* governments, after the same Court in the Alfonsín years had moved away from such an interpretation. Along with Menem's pardon of the generals, the new administration effectively restored impunity for the actions of the *Proceso* governments.[41] Menem also sought to bring the judiciary and the prosecutorial function back under the control of the executive branch.[42] The government also announced its intention to appeal Judge Garzón Funes's landmark 1994 decision in the *Tarnopolsky* case, which ordered the state and two former members of the military junta to pay damages to the surviving son of a family of "disappeared."[43] Carlos S. Nino's careful study of the history of the judiciary in independent Argentina concludes that the judicial branch,

even when reaching, from time to time, some good decisions in the exercise of judicial review, was more influenced by the ideological climate of the day and by the pressures of the dominant powers, than by the conscious assumption of its triple role as custodian of democracy, personal autonomy, and the existing legal practice.[44]

The Argentine judiciary since 1983 remains largely subordinate to the executive, adapting itself to both reform governments and to executives who seek institutional hegemony.

The PJ in Uruguay also appears to be reclaiming its traditional role perception, although in this case tradition favors a more active use of judicial review and defense of judicial independence. The 1967 Constitution was restored in 1985, with its provisions regarding judicial autonomy. In spite of an executive hostile to prosecutions of military officers,[45] the Supreme Court of Justice ruled that the civil courts could try violators of human rights. This caused Parliament, under military pressure, to approve an amnesty law. This law was later affirmed after a bitter campaign in a referendum in 1989.[46] The Supreme Court has continued to demonstrate its independence since that time.[47] In general, the courts have improved procedural efficiency, moving to resolve problems that are common throughout the region, such as reducing the percentage of prisoners in pretrial detention.[48]

Indeed, the court system in Uruguay is demonstrating that a willingness to investigate torture cases and defend due process rights can cause police and military authorities to reflect upon their actions and not act with absolute impunity. The human rights climate in Uruguay is the best in the region right now, and the PJ has taken an active role in creating that climate.[49]

Unlike Alfonsín, Chilean President Patricio Aylwin did not have the opportunity to replace the judiciary and in fact was presented with a last-minute court packing by the out-going junta. The Supreme Court resisted reforms and rejected the criticisms leveled at the PJ by the Truth and Reconciliation Commission's report. The Court continually wrapped itself in a very narrow legal formalism, extending the doctrine of *de facto* law to the point of virtually rejecting the concept of unconstitutional laws.[50] Efforts have been made to add four more justices to the seventeen-member Court, to provide inducements for early retirement and even to impeach some Supreme Court justices.[51]

By the end of Aylwin's term in office, the Supreme Court continued to be the primary obstacle to the judicial defense of human rights. Pinochet-appointed justices continued to support military jurisdiction in cases involving security forces. In 1993, a military court ruled for the first time in favor of a human rights victim, only to see the ruling overturned by a military appeals court. The civilian Supreme Court upheld the appeals court decision.[52] The high court also took a narrow view of privacy rights, ruling in a political espionage case that conversations over cellular telephone are not protected by anti-wiretapping and surveillance laws, since this technology has no wire to tap. In this climate, military courts have felt open to attempt to censor civilian news accounts of military affairs.[53]

One Supreme Court Justice, Hernan Cereceda, was impeached in 1993 for facilitating military court jurisdiction and the subsequent closure of a 1975 disappearance case, in which the accused was only recently extradited from Brazil. In contrast, Aylwin's appointee to the Supreme Court, Adolfo Banados, sentenced retired General Manuel Contreras and Colonel Pedro Espinoza for the 1976 assassination of Orlando Letelier and Ronni Moffitt in Washington.[54] In spite of high court truculence, the combination of executive, Chamber of Deputies and foreign pressures are enabling would-be judicial heroes to actively investigate both old and new cases of human rights violations.

Indeed, in 1994 two separate chambers of the Santiago Court of Appeals had moved to repeal amnesty for abuses committed by the military during the period before 1978. These judges accepted the military's argument that a state of internal war existed at the time but concluded that therefore the actions of the government were subject to the Geneva Convention, to which Chile is a party. These decisions increased tension within the military but were not upheld by the Supreme Court.[55]

The Paraguayan case is distinct. The traditions of an independent judiciary are non-existent.[56] The long regime of Alfredo Stroessner built a judicial branch highly subservient to the dictator, and these judges were still very much in place when Stroessner was sent into exile. The Paraguayan democratization project is one led by conservative elites, who hope to legitimize their positions of power through electoral competition. Judicial heroes have to invent new procedures, unlike their neighbors who can refer to deeper traditions of liberal jurisprudence.

The Paraguayan Supreme Court has been an obstacle to reform.[57] Prosecutions of human rights violators, who are not protected by any amnesty, have proceeded at a snail's pace, with several convictions resulting in the immediate release of the convict for time served, pre-trial detention having been longer than the sentence itself. Judicial reformers have found allies in the Parliament, controlled by the political opposition. The executive branch, on the other hand, has worked to delay reform and to keep the judiciary under its wing.

The new Constitution, approved in 1992, creates several new institutions designed to increase judicial independence. The Council of the Magistracy (Articles 262–264) is made up of eight members, appointed individually by the executive, the legislature, the Supreme Court, the bar association and the law faculties. The Jury for Judicial Impeachment (Article 253), with membership from the Supreme Court, the legislature and the Council of the Magistracy, has been functioning with increasing efficiency in removing incompetent judges. Indeed, some judges promoted by President Wasmosy have been, at the time of promotion, under review by the Jury for Judicial Impeachment (some of these have since been removed).

However, the Council of the Magistracy, which makes nominations to the Supreme Court with the approval of the Senate and the President and nominations to the rest of the bench with approval from the Supreme Court, only began to function in 1995. The enabling legislation for the Council was held up by a challenge to its constitutionality, based on a minor point regarding the selection process for the members named by the bar association. Three of the four conservative members of the five-person Supreme Court ruled the legislation unconstitutional, while Wasmosy continued to shuffle judicial nominations, removals and transfers under powers granted by the now-defunct Constitution of 1967. The only staunch supporter of an independent judiciary on the Supreme Court up to 1995 was Jerónimo Irala Burgos, appointed by General Andrés Rodríguez shortly after the 1989 coup in a demonstration of Rodríguez's commitment to multipartism. Irala comes from the tiny opposition Christian Democratic Party.

Meanwhile, lower court judges continue to tolerate police brutality in recent torture cases. Plaintiffs in these cases are best served by denouncing police treatment to the Parliamentary Human Rights Commission, as the ordinary courts are unlikely to take action, nor are the police likely to implicate themselves through investigations of torture cases. Furthermore, it took Congress two years to write enabling legislation that allowed the Human Rights Ombudsman Office (Defensoría del Pueblo) created by the Constitution (Articles 276–280) to function.

The Brazilian courts have not engaged in a particularly strong defense of judicial power in the area of human rights, although it might fairly be said that they have been more involved in the more traditional practice of defending private power. Violence by police or private individuals on behalf of the powerful is seldom prosecuted. The victims of this violence are, in general, the relatively weak and defenseless, such as street children, rural workers, indigenous populations, prisoners and women in cases of domestic violence. Corruption and intimidation of judges are widespread, particularly in the state-level military police courts, which oversee the military police.[58] At the advent of the

Collor de Mello administration (1990), the SFT showed little willingness to challenge the executive even when the very right of judicial review of executive actions was limited by a presidential decree. Initially, Congress stalled Collor's measures, but without support from the PJ, it finally ratified the president's decree.[59]

On the other hand, judicial review of detentions through writs of *habeas corpus* is generally respected. And in 1993, a courageous judge, Denise Frossard, ignored death threats to prosecute racketeers in the spectacular numbers-game case known as the *jogo de bichos*.[60] On balance, though, the Brazilian PJ lacks support for heroic measures strong enough to counter the climate of impunity created by intimidation and corruption.[61] In this sense Brazil suffers an unwelcome comparison with the situation of the judiciary in Colombia.

CONCLUSION

Judicial defense of human rights depends on two key factors. First, the judiciary must itself develop traditions that value political liberty more than formalism and provide creative justices the support necessary for positive defense of rights. When such efforts result in transfers, demotions or other threats to the judicial career, judicial heroism will only be symbolic and not effective.

The Uruguayan tradition seems to provide some support for judicial activism in human rights, whereas the Brazilian and Argentine cases show the possibility for traditions to develop, but not without the counterweight of a tradition of subservience to executive and private power. The Paraguayan judiciary is encumbered more by the weight of past dictatorship rather than elaborated judicial doctrines that stymie creativity. In this sense, backwardness in the PJ may prove to be an advantage if reformers can effectively articulate an activist doctrine of judicial behavior. The Chilean case is the most sobering for reformers. If the heads of the PJ are committed to a narrow formalism combined with judicial independence, then creating support for the efforts of heroes will be difficult. Such heroes will have to go outside of the judiciary in search of allies, causing a potential backlash against threats to the corporate interests of the PJ.

The second key factor is the political context and the power of human rights allies outside of the judiciary. It would seem to be a truism that, under military governments, human rights allies would be very weak, and indeed this is largely the case. However, the military itself can be leveraged as an ally, if the judiciary is capable and willing to provide legitimation.

The Argentine and Brazilian PJs in the 1960s were able to work with the military to a degree. It is perhaps noteworthy that in these two cases the military was more attuned to society and more politicized than in either Uruguay or Chile. In the latter two cases, the long traditions of non-involvement in politics isolated the militaries from such concepts as popular legitimacy and left the judiciaries with little leverage. In Uruguay, the Supreme Court was forced to concede after a struggle, whereas in Chile the Court did not even attempt to gain concessions and treated Pinochet as its champion. Finally, in Argentina after 1976, the military made no pretense of negotiating with the pre-existing judicial branch, purging it immediately and unleashing the region's worst Dirty War.

Democratic transitions create a very distinctive political environment. The decade of the 1980s was a period of pronounced concern for human rights, and in Argentina, Chile and most recently in Brazil, with the election of Fernando Henrique Cardoso in October 1994, victims of past abuses, or their advocates, have risen to the presidency. Human rights champions in the judiciary have greater opportunities to cultivate alliances outside of their own branch.

In both Uruguay and Brazil, the early transition process was marked by presidents who were willing to defend the military and were reluctant to act forcefully on judicial reform. In both cases, threats to the military were deflected, and in Brazil police impunity continues. However, in Uruguay the human rights situation has improved markedly, and the self-sustaining judiciary has also found support in the Parliament.

In Argentina, strong presidential reform efforts ran into weak support from the National Congress and from the judiciary itself and strong and dangerous opposition from the military. Once Alfonsín was replaced by Menem, reform advocates lost their most important ally, and the courts have returned to a role perception that serves to marginalize them. In Chile, presidential reformism had the support of Congress, but here the military is still in the strongest position in the region, and the courts themselves are the most antithetical to reform. Finally, in Paraguay, like Chile, the advocates for judicial action are stymied by the very institution they seek to strengthen but, unlike Chile, do not have the support of the executive.

Heroes who are not martyrs must work with the cards dealt them and commit themselves to stay in the game. The strongest hand, the one most likely to support efforts to defend human rights, is one where the judiciary itself is willing to support its traditions of independence and judicial review. In addition, the executive must see an independent judiciary as valuable and be strong enough to check the enemies of human rights. Ironically, a military junta seeking legitimacy may be nearly as useful to heroes as a weak but supportive civilian president.

NOTES

I would like to thank Stan Frankowski, Mark Gibney and Jerold Waltman for their careful reading and comments on this text.

1. R. M. Cover, *Justice Accused* (New Haven, CT, 1975), 259.

2. A long litany of sacrificed "heroes" can be compiled from a reading of events in Guatemala, Honduras, El Salvador, Colombia and Peru. Judges have been murdered, exiled, fired and transferred from their posts in all of these countries. See the following reports from Americas Watch: *El Salvador's Decade of Terror: Human Rights since the*

Assassination of Archbishop Romero (New Haven, CT, 1991); *Honduras: Without the Will* (New York, 1989); *Peru under Fire: Human Rights since the Return to Democracy* (New Haven, CT, 1992). Also see Americas Watch and Physicians for Human Rights, *Guatemala: Getting Away with Murder* (New York, 1991); and Andean Commission of Jurists, *Colombia: The Right to Justice* (New York, 1991).

3. Cover, *supra* note 1.

4. *Id.* at 197–200, 226–229.

5. *Id.* at 229.

6. J. H. Merryman, *The Civil Law Tradition: An Introduction to the Legal Systems of Western Europe and Latin America* (Stanford, CA, 1985), 34–35.

7. K. S. Rosenn, "The Success of Constitutionalism in the United States and Its Failure in Latin America: An Explanation," in: K. W. Thompson, ed., *The U.S. Constitution and the Constitutions of Latin America* (Lanham, MD, 1991), 73.

8. J. Bass, *Unlikely Heroes* (New York, 1981).

9. Paraguay is omitted from this portion of the chapter since that country was under the continuous rule of a single military dictatorship beginning in 1954, and in the period before that, it never developed the kind of liberal judicial traditions that allow for a discussion of judicial response to military coup d'état.

10. N. J. Nadorff, "Habeas Corpus and the Protection of Political and Civil Rights in Brazil: 1964–1978," 14 *Lawyer of the Americas* (1982–1983), 297.

11. *Id.*

12. M. Borges, 33 R.T.J. 590 (*en banc* 1964).

13. S. de Carvalho, 33 R.T.J. 381 (*en banc* 1965).

14. O. Gonçalves, 35 R.T.J. 227 (*en banc* 1965).

15. 5 Os Grandes Julgamentos do Suprêmo Tribunal Federal 7 (*en banc* 1964).

16. Nadorff, *supra* note 10 at 315–318.

17. S. Palmeira, 50 R.T.J. 558 (*en banc* 1968).

18. V. Netto, 44 R.T.J. 322 (*en banc* 1968).

19. Nadorff, *supra* note 10 at 327.

20. *Id.* at 333.

21. *Id.* at 309.

22. F. E. Snyder, "State of Siege and Rule of Law in Argentina: The Politics and Rhetoric of Vindication," 15 *Lawyer of the Americas* (1984), 503 at 519.

23. Argentina, Comisión Nacional sobre la Desaparición de Personas, *Nunca Más: The Report of the Argentine National Commission on the Disappeared* (New York, 1986), 387.

24. *Id.* at 386.

25. Snyder, *supra* note 22 at 517.

26. R. S. Barker, "Constitutionalism in the Americas: A Bicentennial Perspective," 49 *University of Pittsburgh Law Review* (1988), 891 at 893–894.

27. Servicio Paz y Justicia (Uruguay), *Uruguay: Nunca Más: Human Rights Violations, 1972–1985* (Philadelphia, 1992), 15–18.

28. *Id.* at 27–32.

29. O. Fiss, "The Right Degree of Independence," in: I. Stotzky, ed., *Transition to Democracy in Latin America: The Role of Judiciary* (Boulder, CO, 1993), 55 at 65.

30. G. Arriagada, *Pinochet: The Politics of Power* (London, 1988), 105–107.

31. Chile, Comisión Nacional de Verdad y Reconciliación, *Report Chilean National Commission on Truth and Reconciliation* (Notre Dame, IN, 1993), 117.

32. Fiss, *supra* note 29 at 71 n.40.

33. Chile, *supra* note 31 at 122–126.

34. *Id.* at 859.

35. See P. W. Zagorski, *Democracy vs. National Security: Civil-Military Relations in Latin America* (Boulder, CO, 1992).

36. R. R. Alfonsín, "The Function of Judicial Power during the Transition," in: Stotzky, *supra* note 29 at 46.

37. See P. K. Speck, "The Trial of the Argentine Junta: Responsibilities and Realities," 18 *Inter-American Law Review* (1987), 491.

38. E. Rabossi, "The Role of the Judiciary in the Review of Human Rights Violations in Argentina," in: Stotzky, *supra* note 29 at 343.

39. *Country Reports on Human Rights Practices for 1993: Report Submitted to the Comm. on Foreign Affairs of the U.S. House of Representatives and the Comm. on Foreign Relations of the U.S. Senate by the Department of State in accordance with Sections 116(d) and 502(b) of the Foreign Assistance Act of 1961, as amended*, 103rd Cong., 2nd sess. (1994), 348 (hereinafter State Dept.).

40. Fiss, *supra* note 29 at 62.

41. I. P. Stotzky and C. S. Nino, "The Difficulties of the Transitions Process," in: Stotzky, *supra* note 29 at 13.

42. A. J. D'Alessio, "The Function of the Prosecution in the Transition to Democracy in Latin America," in: Stotzky, *supra* note 29 at 200, n.15.

43. M. O'Reilly, "Freedom Writers Update," Amnesty International, Jan. 1995.

44. C. S. Nino, "On the Exercise of Judicial Review in Argentina," in: Stotzky, *supra* note 29 at 333.

45. A. Barahona de Brito, "Truth and Justice in the Consolidation of Democracy in Chile and Uruguay," 46 *Parliamentary Affairs* (1993), 579 at 587–588.

46. See A. Soto, "El plebiscito uruguayo: Un conflicto de valores éticos," 379 *Mensaje* (1989).

47. J. L. Pierce and T. J. O'Neill, "Uruguayan Judges in Conflicted Roles: A Preliminary Exploration," paper presented at the annual meeting of the Southwestern Political Science Association, San Antonio, 1994, at 21–22.

48. E. O. Smykla and J. O. Smykla, "Criminal Procedure in Uruguay, South America: A Test of the Universal Applicability of Ingraham's Six Stages of Criminal Procedure," 21 *Journal of Criminal Justice* (1994), 595 at 601.

49. State Dept., *supra* note 39 at 563–564.

50. J. Correa Sutil, "The Judiciary and the Political System in Chile: The Dilemmas of Judicial Independence during the Transition to Democracy," in: Stotzky, *supra* note 29 at 99.

51. *Id.* at 102–103, n.1.

52. State Dept., *supra* note 39 at 385.

53. *Id.* at 388.

54. *Id.* at 384–385.

55. P. Bonnefoy, "Court's Ruling Shocks Army," *Latinamerica Press*, Nov. 19, 1994, 2.

56. K. F. Johnson, "Scholarly Images of Latin American Political Democracy in 1975," 11 *Latin American Research Review* (1976), 129.

57. See *Analisis del Mes* (Asunción 1993–1994). See also B. Turner, "Judicial Reform in the Politics of Transition: The Case of Paraguay," paper presented at the International

Political Science Association Research Committee on Comparative Judicial Studies meetings, Sante Fe, NM, Aug. 1–4, 1993.

58. State Dept., *supra* note 39 at 374–383.

59. K. S. Rosenn, "Brazil's New Constitution: An Exercise in Transient Constitutionalism for a Transitional Society," 38 *American Journal of Comparative Law* (1990), 773 at 786.

60. State Dept., *supra* note 39 at 377.

61. Even Collor de Mello was found innocent of corruption charges by the SFT on Dec. 12, 1994. Many Brazilians saw this case as further evidence of the impunity enjoyed by the powerful. "Laughing in the Face of Justice," *Latinamerica Press*, Dec. 15, 1994, 7.

Part IV

India, the Philippines and China

Chapter 6

Freedom from Torture and Cruel, Inhuman or Degrading Treatment or Punishment: The Role of the Supreme Court of India

VIJAYASHRI SRIPATI

INTRODUCTION

"All human beings are born free and equal in dignity and rights. No one shall be subjected to torture or to cruel, inhuman or degrading treatment or punishment" proclaims the Universal Declaration of Human Rights. How noble in conception, and universal in scope, these words are. The practice of torture is prohibited in most of the major international human rights instruments.[1] In 1984, the United Nations unanimously adopted and opened for signature and ratification a Convention against Torture and Other Cruel, Inhuman or Degrading Treatment or Punishment as a means of implementing "the existing prohibition under international law . . . of the practice of torture and other cruel, inhuman or degrading treatment or punishment."[2] Torture is also prohibited in the constitutions of 55 nations.[3] Indeed, it is difficult to identify a more universally accepted norm than the prohibition against torture.[4]

Unfortunately, torture has not ceased despite domestic and international prohibitions. Enforcement by domestic courts might provide the most effective means of affording individuals meaningful protection of freedom from torture. This chapter will examine the role of the Supreme Court of India in enforcing freedom from torture and cruel, inhuman or degrading treatment or punishment. This analysis will take place against the backdrop of India's international obligations and in the absence of any explicit mention of this freedom in the array of "Fundamental Rights" guaranteed to every Indian citizen under the Constitution. The second section provides a brief overview of some of the human rights norms under Indian law, while the third section examines the restrictive interpretation first given to these rights soon after the Constitution was adopted. Starting in the late 1970s, however, the Indian Supreme Court began to give a broader reading to prisoners' rights, and this is the focus of the fourth section. Finally, the fifth section sets forth the meaning of this domestic litigation in terms of the advancement of international human rights.

HUMAN RIGHTS IN THE INDIAN CONSTITUTION

India emerged independent in 1947, following the disintegration of the British Empire in the aftermath of World War II. This was a seminal period in the development of international human rights, and this fact is reflected in the evocative preamble to the Indian Constitution[5] and in the impressive array of Fundamental Rights found therein. Chapter III of the Constitution enumerates six such rights in all: Right to Equality (Articles 14–18), Right to Freedom (Articles 19–22), Right against Exploitation (Articles 23–24), Right to Freedom of Religion (Articles 25–28), Right to Education and Culture (Articles 29–30), and the Right to Constitutional Remedies (Articles 32–35).

As Granville Austin points out, these rights were included in the Constitution in the expectation that ''one day the tree of true liberty would bloom in India.''[6] They reflect the humane tone of the Constitution, a document that was premised on principles of justice, equality and the dignity of the individual. Because of their unique constitutional status, these fundamental rights take precedence over all other rights.[7] In order to enforce these rights, the framers of the Constitution attempted to create an independent judiciary. The Supreme Court, as the highest court in the country, is vested with a wide range of both original and appellate jurisdiction. Any citizen whose fundamental right has been violated can directly invoke the Court's original jurisdiction under Article 32.

Human rights norms are not only protected by the Indian Constitution. Reinforcing its commitment to these principles, India has ratified a number of international agreements, such as the International Covenant on Civil and Political Rights and the International Covenant on Economic and Social Rights. The manner in which these and other rights will be available to Indian citizens depends upon the fashion in which international convention law is given domestic legal effect. The Constitution is ambiguous regarding the relationship between international law and municipal law in India. It provides in Article 51(c) that the ''State shall endeavor to foster respect for international law and treaty obligations.'' It is to be noted, however, that this article is in the chapter on Directive Principles of State Policy.[8] Further, there is some doubt whether the expression ''state''[9] is meant to include the courts as well.[10] Still, Indian courts are potentially open to a liberal absorption of customary international law.[11]

Under British rule, English common law doctrines were widely applicable in many fields. The Constitution of India did not alter that position. Instead, it provided for the continued operation of the ''law in force'' immediately preceding its commencement. Therefore, by the analogy to the English common law, the municipal courts of India may apply well-recognized principles of customary international law on the ground that they form the law of the land. Principles of international treaty law, on the other hand, will only be incorporated into municipal law through domestic legislation. In essence, Indian subscribes to the dualist view of international law. This was the Supreme Court's holding in *Jolly George Varghese v. Band of Cochin*.[12]

A RESTRICTIVE READING OF FUNDAMENTAL RIGHTS

Despite the Constitution's emphasis on human rights, the judiciary initially gave only a niggardly reading to such rights. The 1950 decision in the celebrated case of *A. K. Gopalan v. State of Madras*[13] underscores this conservative attitude. Gopalan, a prominent leader of the opposition in Parliament, was detained under the Preventive Detention Act. The petitioner challenged the validity of the Act on the ground that it violated his fundamental rights, in particular, his right to personal liberty. The petitioner argued that the expression "procedure established by law"[14] bears the same meaning as the "due process clause"[15] in the U.S. Constitution, except for one difference.[16] The phrase "procedure established by law" is limited to procedural safeguards and does not extend to questions of substantive law.[17] He therefore urged the Court to interpret the word *law* as not to mean mere state-enacted law but as *jus*, that is, law in the abstract sense of the principles of natural justice.[18] He argued that if the Court interprets the word *law* in the sense of any state-made law, any Act passed by Parliament that was otherwise within its legislative power could destroy this right.[19]

The Court rejected these arguments. What the Court essentially did was to treat each of the Constitution's fundamental rights as separate and distinct from one another. Proceeding on this assumption, the Court reasoned that when the requirements of an article dealing with the particular matter in question are satisfied and there is no infringement of the fundamental right guaranteed by that particular article, no recourse can be had to a fundamental right conferred by any another article. On this basis, the Court treated Article 22, that part of the Constitution dealing with the "Preventive Detention" cases, as a code unto itself. The Court observed that if the procedure in the Preventive Detention Act did not come into conflict with the relevant provisions of Article 22, the Preventive Detention Act would therefore be valid and would not have to satisfy further any of the other fundamental rights enumerated in the Constitution.

In interpreting the Constitution in this manner, the Court thereby gave a very narrow ruling to the fundamental rights of an individual held in detention. The Court stifled the cumulative impact of fundamental rights by treating them piecemeal rather than as an organic whole. The ultimate result of this interpretation was that the protection of individual liberty—a right deeply honored in the Constitution—suffered a serious setback. It would take more than two decades for a progressive interpretation to emerge.

A BROADER READING OF FUNDAMENTAL RIGHTS

For nearly 25 years, the Court offered little safeguard to individual liberties. However, starting in the late 1970s, judges with more liberal views ascended to the Court. In turn, the Court began to render more enlightened opinions.

Sunil Batra v. Delhi Administration

Two companion cases, *Sunil Batra v. Delhi Administration* (1978) and *Charles Sobraj v. Delhi Administration*,[20] set the stage for the law's transformation. The complainants were two prisoners who alleged torture by prison officials. They challenged their treatment as a violation of their fundamental rights.

Batra, a death-row convict, was put in a solitary cell by a prison official and held there indefinitely. Notably enough, the Court began a survey of the issues involved in the case with the observation that as a "[s]entinel on the qui vive" it would guard freedom behind bars, intolerant of torture by executive officials.[21] Analyzing the merits of the case, the Court pointed out that Batra was in the custody of the prison authorities until his execution. The Court construed such temporary custody of a prisoner awaiting execution to be "safekeeping" wherein his mind and body were to be kept in a sound condition. The Court held that infliction of torture (mental or physical) on such a prisoner by the prison officials did not amount to safekeeping.

The Additional Solicitor General, on behalf of the state, contended that solitary confinement had survived judicial scrutiny in a country like the United States where (unlike India) specific constitutional provisions protected against cruel and unusual punishment.[22] The Court made an elaborate survey of Anglo-American opinions on solitary confinement, and also canvassed the prison diaries of India's national leaders.[23] The Court concluded that solitary confinement was one of the most severe penalties and that it should only be imposed by judicial decree.[24] Responding directly to the Attorney General's analogy, the Court drew attention to the observance of procedural safeguards before solitary confinement is imposed on a prisoner and the brief periods to which it is limited in the United States.[25] In this context, the Court pointed to the combined effect of Article 14[26] and Article 19.[27] These articles are the epitome of human values. They prescribe fairness and reasonableness, and collectively they abhor capricious, discriminatory and arbitrary actions. The Court stated:

The Court will stand four square between a prisoner and the method of destroying completely the spirit and undermining the sanity of a prisoner in jail. This we do, not because of anything like the VIII Amendment but because unreasonable restrictions and arbitrary deprivations are obnoxious to part III, especially articles 14 and 19, even within the prison setting.[28]

The Court observed that even a death-row convict has human rights that are non-negotiable. The Court held that condemned prisoners like Batra should neither be kept in a solitary cell nor be put to work like those sentenced to rigorous imprisonment.[29] Instead, such prisoners are entitled to all the amenities that ordinary inmates are entitled to: food, clothing and a bed. In its conclusion, the Court focused on the prevalence of torture and cruelty in several countries. The Court pointed out that India was no exception in this regard and called upon all the courts in India to be aware of this.

The Court did not stop with humanizing life behind prison bars. Rather, the Court displayed remarkable craftsmanship by also including the notion of procedural "due process" as a constitutional right that prisoners enjoyed. In fact, this was perhaps the Court's greatest contribution to human rights, since it placed prison caprice and cruelty on a "constitutional leash."

In articulating the principle of procedural due process, the Court relied on its earlier landmark decision in *Maneka Gandhi v. Union of India*.[30] In that case, the Court held that the government had wrongfully impounded the petitioner's passport. In its decision, the Court held that fundamental rights weave together a pattern of human rights guarantees and that these rights are not mutually exclusive and distinct. In its analysis, the Court reasoned that each freedom has different dimensions. Therefore, merely because the law meets the limits of interference with one fundamental right, it is not freed from the necessity of meeting the challenge of another fundamental right.

Adopting a dynamic interpretation of Article 21,[31] the Court in *Maneka Gandhi* observed that the term "personal liberty" should be read in its widest ambit.[32] In the Court's view, this covers a plethora of rights, only some of which are raised to the status of distinct fundamental rights in the Constitution. Significantly, the Court did not confine its scrutiny to the scope of an individual's personal liberty. Breaking from the past, then, the Court examined the nature of a procedure that can be employed to deprive an individual of his life or personal liberty. The Court held that mere semblance of a procedure was insufficient to deprive a person of his life or liberty. Rather, the procedure must be "right, just and fair and not arbitrary, fanciful, or oppressive."[33]

Applying this rule of fair procedure to the prison setting, the Court in *Sunil Batra* directed that any form of harsh punishment such as solitary confinement must be severely limited in duration and must be imposed only within the bounds of natural justice.[34] The Court held that every prisoner is entitled to a hearing complying with the principles of natural justice before any benefit available to him is revoked.

Charles Sobraj v. Delhi Administration

In the companion case, the petitioner Sobraj was a pre-trial prisoner whose wrists, ankles and waist were fettered with iron chains around the clock daily for nearly two years despite medical advice to the contrary.[35] The Additional Solicitor General contended that since Sobraj was dangerous, he was confined in irons to inhibit violence and escape. The Court noted that the Prisons Act permitted bar fetters on two grounds: safe custody of the prisoner and a finding of absolute necessity by the prison superintendent.[36] In its analysis, the Court pointed out that safe custody is endangered only where the chance of escape existed, as evidenced by the prisoner's past behavior.[37] Episodes of violence, bad behavior or other forms of misconduct that lack reference to safe custody cannot be grounds for imposing fetters on a prisoner. Thus, the Court concluded that imposition of bar fetters was justified only in rare situations.

The Court treated the infraction of the prisoner's freedom by bar fetters as "too serious" to be viewed lightly.[38] Therefore, the Court extended the rule of fair procedure in the treatment of pre-trial prisoners. The Court laid down clear guidelines to be followed strictly before a prisoner could be fettered. The Court held that before placing preventive or punitive irons on a prisoner, natural justice (both *audi alteram partem* and *nemo judex* rules) must be followed.[39] The Court required prison officials to record the reasons for the use of fetters, both in the prison journal and on the prisoner's history ticket. Also, the reasons must be recorded in the language of the prisoner to facilitate his recourse to redress. Non-compliance with these rules will make prison officials liable in civil and criminal actions.[40] In addition, the Court transferred the discretion to impose fetters on a prisoner beyond a period of 24 hours from prison officials to judges.[41] After passing an interim order to remove the fetters on the prisoner immediately, the Court held:

[B]ar fetters are a barbarity generally and, like whipping, must vanish. Civilized consciousness is hostile to torture within the walled campus. . . . [T]his ferocious rule of law, rude and nude, cannot be sustained as anything but arbitrary, unreasonable and procedurally heartless. The peril to its life from the lethal stroke of Articles 14, 19 and 21 . . . needs no far-fetched argument.[42]

Sunil Batra v. Delhi Administration (1980)

The transformation of Indian constitutional law continued. Two years later the Court received yet another petition from a prisoner alleging torture; but this time the writ petition arose in an "epistolary fashion." An epistle written by Batra, a prisoner, addressed to a judge sparked the *habeas* proceedings.[43] In his letter, Batra drew the Court's attention to a heinous act committed against another prisoner, Premchand, for an unfulfilled demand for money.[44] Forms and formalities were not required, since torture was a credible charge and the letter was treated as a writ petition. The Court immediately appointed an *amicus curiae* to investigate the complaint, and on the basis of its report the Court concluded that a prison official had tortured Premchand.[45] The Court then issued a *habeas* writ to the Lt. Governor of New Delhi and the Superintendent of the

Central prison to ensure that further violence would not be inflicted on the prisoner and that he receive immediate medical attention.[46]

It is noteworthy that the Court did not confine its task to fashioning a relief for the individual prisoner. Faced with the traumatic abridgement of a prisoner's right, the Court seized the opportunity to develop "remedial processes" to prevent injustices in the future. In its opinion, the Court cited with approval the meaning of "life" provided by Justice Field of the U.S. Supreme Court in *Munn v. Illinois*.[47]

Life is more than mere animal existence. The inhibition against its deprivation extends to all those limbs and faculties by which life is enjoyed. The Provision equally prohibits the mutilation of the body by the amputation of an arm or the leg or putting out of an eye, or the destruction of any other organ of the body through which the soul communicates with the outer world.[48]

It appears that the Court adopted this meaning to emphasize the quality of life under Article 21.[49] The Court also used this definition to stress that no prisoner can be personally subjected to deprivations not required by incarceration and the sentence of the Court.

Noting that torture can take myriad forms, the Court correctly treated every affliction on the prisoner as an "infraction of his liberty or life in its wider sense."[50] Therefore, the Court required a fair and reasonable legal procedure to curtail a prisoner's liberty. In the absence of such a procedure, the infringement of the prisoner's liberty will be "arbitrary" under Article 14,[51] "unreasonable" under Article 19,[52] and "unfair" under Article 21.[53] The Court directed hearings at all stages of the grievance proceedings, as well as early judicial involvement in the case.[54] To make prisoners' rights viable, the Court directed the District Magistrate concerned to inspect the prisons in his jurisdiction once a week, to receive complaints from individual prisoners and to take remedial action if justified. The Court directed every prison ward to have a grievance box to which every prisoner is given free access. In reaching this result, the Court drew upon Article 8[55] and Article 9[56] of the 1975 United Nations General Assembly Declaration on the Protection of All Persons from Torture and Other Cruel, Inhuman or Degrading Treatment or Punishment as being particularly relevant.[57]

By treating a letter as a writ petition, the Court manifested its remarkable sensitivity to the harsh realities of the Indian sociolegal milieu, particularly within the prison setting. Owing to widespread poverty, illiteracy and ignorance throughout the country, many victims are unaware of their rights and have no access to justice. This is especially true of the country's prison population. By introducing what has come to be known as "epistolary jurisdiction,"[58] the Court has thrown its doors wide open to all those who have suffered injustices and who would have otherwise remained helpless.

The Court also displayed its flexibility to meet new challenges. The Court broadened the horizons of the *habeas* writ not only to include releasing a prisoner for illegal detention but to enforce humanism behind iron bars as well. The Court observed, ''The essence of the matter is that in our era of human rights consciousness the habeas writ has functional plurality and the constitutional regard for human decency and dignity is tested by this capability.''[59]

Prem Shankar v. Delhi Administration

Despite the clear directives the Court laid down to safeguard prisoners' rights, the abuse continued unabated. Within a few months after its decision in the *Sunil Batra* case,[60] the Court handed down another important decision respecting the rights of prisoners.[61] In this case a telegram sent by a prisoner to a judge of the Court triggered the *habeas* proceedings. The prisoner sought to invoke the Court's jurisdiction to end the humiliation and torture meted out by police officials. The main question before the Court was whether the routine imposition of handcuffs on a pre-trial prisoner while in transit between the prison and the court violated his fundamental rights. At the very outset, the Court observed that its decision should be guided by the core principles laid down in Article 5[62] of the Universal Declaration of Human Rights and Article 10[63] of the International Covenant on Civil and Political Rights. It is thus clear that although the Court was proceeding to decide the case on the basis of Indian constitutional law, it was equally desirous of conforming to international human rights norms as well.

The police officials contended that the Police Act permitted handcuffs. They also pointed out that since the petitioner was a crafty criminal, they had used handcuffs to ensure his safe custody and to prevent his escape. The Court, however, found the routine use of handcuffs to be capricious, arbitrary and restrictive of the minimal freedom of movement of a prisoner and therefore violative of Article 14[64] and Article 19[65] of the Constitution. The imposition of handcuffs also contravened Article 21, which forbids barbarities, both punitive and processual. The Court concluded:

Handcuffing is prima facie inhuman, and therefore, unreasonable, is over-harsh and at the first flush arbitrary. Absent fair procedure and objective monitoring, to inflict irons is to resort to zoological strategies repugnant to article 21. . . . [T]o bind a man hand and foot, fetter his limbs with hoops of steel, shuffle him along in the streets and stand him for hours in the court is to torture him, defile his dignity, vulgarize society and foul the soul of the constitutional culture.[66]

The Court then determined that the general rule regarding a prisoner in transit was that he should be free of handcuffs. The Court declared that the use of handcuffs must be only an extreme measure, when there is no other reasonable way of preventing a prisoner's escape. Thus, a clear and present danger of escape is the test for imposing irons on a prisoner.[67] Routine practice and convenience of the escorting authorities were not valid grounds for placing handcuffs on a prisoner. As in the previous cases, the Court vested the power to deprive a prisoner of his restricted liberty in the hands of judicial officers. In extreme circumstances, the escorting authority must record the reasons for the use of handcuffs, present those to the presiding judge and obtain the Court's approval. After this analysis, the Court concluded that the handcuffs on the petitioner in question should be removed immediately.[68]

Francis Coralie v. Union Territory of Delhi

While the preceding cases dealt with instances of torture and cruel, inhuman and degrading treatment, the case of *Francis Coralie v. Union Territory of Delhi*[69] presented a different kind of issue. Here the detained petitioner had been denied interviews with her family and her lawyer, due to the restrictions imposed in pursuance of the detention order.[70] The petitioner challenged the restrictions on the ground that they violated her fundamental right to life and personal liberty. The Court pointed out that the nature of the detention had a direct bearing in deciding the validity of the conditions of detention. Noting that the prisoner had been placed under preventive detention as opposed to punitive detention, the Court stated that the restrictions on such a detainee must be minimal.[71]

Analyzing the content of the right to life and personal liberty, the Court drew attention to its decision in the *Sunil Batra*[72] case in which it had accepted the meaning of "life" given by an American judge.[73] The Court emphasized that protection from every kind of deprivation—whether physical or mental—came within the sweep of this right, regardless of the duration of such deprivation. The Court went on to make a poignant declaration that Article 21 also embraced "the right to live with human dignity and all that goes along with it."[74] The Court acknowledged that the magnitude of this right depends on the extent of the country's economic development. Nevertheless, the Court observed that the right under any circumstances includes the right to basic necessities of life and activities that are the bare minimum expression of the human self. Thus, every act that impairs human dignity is deprivation *pro tanto* of this right to life. On this line of reasoning the Court observed:

[A]ny form of torture, or cruel, inhuman or degrading treatment would be offensive to human dignity and constitute an inroad into this right to life and it would, on this view, be prohibited by article 21 unless it is in accordance with procedure prescribed by law. But no law which authorizes and no procedure which leads to such torture or cruel, inhuman or degrading treatment can ever stand the test of reasonableness and nonarbitrariness: it would plainly be unconstitutional and void as being violative of articles 14 and 21. It would thus be seen that there is implicit in article 21 the right to protection against torture, or cruel, inhuman or degrading treatment which is enunciated in article 5 of the Universal Declaration of Human Rights and guaranteed by article 7 of the International Covenant on Civil and Political Rights.[75]

This led the Court to determine that as a part of her right to live with human dignity, which was a part of her right to life, the petitioner was entitled to meet her family and lawyer.[76] No prison regulation or procedure regulating the detainee's right to have interviews can be held as constitutionally valid under Articles 14, 19 and 21 unless it is reasonable, fair and just. Finding the restrictions imposed on the petitioner to be "unnecessary" and "cumbrous," the Court struck them down as unreasonable.[77] The Court concluded that the petitioner was entitled to at least two interviews in a week without the prior permission of the District Magistrate.[78]

Francis Coralie was not the last petitioner who was afforded relief by the Court. Consistent with its declared role of a "[s]entinel on the qui vive," the Court continued to come to the succor of victims of mayhem, crude and subtle. By the end of the 1980s, the Court had transformed prison jurisprudence and had led the country through an era of enormous change. The far-reaching impact of this new normative regime on the treatment of prisoners can be best summarized in the Court's own words:

> True, our constitution has no "due process" clause or the VIII Amendment. But in this breach of law, after . . . *Maneka Gandhi* the consequence is the same. For what is punitively outrageous, scandalizingly unusual or cruel and rehabilitatively counterproductive is unarguably unreasonable and arbitrary and is shot down by articles 14 and 19, and if inflicted with procedural unfairness falls foul of article 21. Part III of the constitution does not part company with the prisoner at the gates. Judicial oversight protects the prisoner's shrunken fundamental rights, if flouted, frowned upon or frozen by the prison authorities.[79]

CONCLUSION

A comparison of the Court's decision in the *Gopalan*[80] case with its later decisions demonstrates that although the Constitution guarantees human rights, judicial reasoning can either negate those rights or uphold them. Much credit, then, goes to the enlightened judges who overturned cases that initially had given a very restrictive reading to the fundamental rights in the Constitution. The landmark decision in the *Maneka Gandhi*[81] case triggered an unprecedented development of the fundamental right to life and personal liberty. The result is that freedom from torture and cruel, inhuman or degrading treatment and punishment falls within its fertile ambit. Thus, at present, human rights jurisprudence in India has a constitutional status and sweep.

It is interesting to note that the protection from physical or mental deprivations that Article 21 affords is in consonance with international standards. This is evident from the definition of "torture" laid down in Article 1 of the United Nations Convention against Torture and Other Cruel, Inhuman or Degrading Treatment.[82] Article 1 states:

For the purposes of this Convention, the term "torture" means any act by which severe pain or suffering, whether physical or mental, is intentionally inflicted on a person for such purposes as obtaining from him or a third person, information or a confession, punishing him for an act he or a third person has committed or is suspected of having committed, or intimidating or coercing him or a third person, or for any reason based on discrimination of any kind, when such pain or suffering is inflicted by or at the instigation of or with the consent or acquiescence of a public official or other person acting in an official capacity.

According to this definition, any act by a public official that causes severe physical or mental pain, and is intentionally inflicted on a person for any reason based on discrimination, falls within the purview of torture. Following the *Maneka Gandhi*[83] case, every act infringing on a person's life or liberty is required to fulfill the humane imperatives of the two articles, 14 and 19,[84] besides the test of fair procedure implicit in Article 21. This is clear from the methodology the Court followed in concluding its decisions in the above cases.

Article 14 interdicts discriminatory dealings and capricious cruelty. Thus, any personal harm, whether by way of punishment or otherwise, that is intentionally inflicted on a person will be unconstitutional and violative of the equality clause of Article 14, as long as it is based on some discriminatory motive or unguided discretion of a public official. Thus, torture tactics and inhuman acts that are discriminatory and arbitrary in nature can no longer jump the constitutional gauntlet, masked as mere security measures.

An examination of the Supreme Court's analysis in the above cases gives an insight into how the normative content of international human rights law has infused Indian constitutional standards. As noted earlier in this chapter, the courts in India give effect to rules of customary international law on the ground that they form part of the law of the land. Therefore, freedom from torture, being a norm of customary international law, must be binding on the Indian courts. However, in none of the cases did the Supreme Court focus on the binding effect of customary international law. Instead, the Court relied on the Constitution to afford the petitioners relief, thereby securing a remedy based on domestic law. A fundamental reason for this approach stems from the Court's unwillingness to accept that the values established by the Indian Constitution fall below those of international standards. As is apparent from its methodology, the Court explicitly pointed out that there was a constitutional basis for holding that torture was violative of prisoners' fundamental rights and inconsistent with the inherent spirit of the Constitution. This attitude of the Indian Supreme Court is not unusual. Domestic courts all over the world will be, more often than not, reluctant to base their decisions on customary international human rights law, or on laws developed outside domestic lawmaking processes, when their own constitutions are thought to suffice.[85] The concepts of state sovereignty[86] and a preference for the law of the forum are also barriers to the use of internationally developed principles.

The fact that the Court did not directly use international human rights norms to establish an independent rule of decision in its cases, however, does not mean that it was insulated from their impact. Indeed, the Court's frequent references to norms laid down in treaties and declarations reflects its awareness and underlying approach to take that body of law seriously. In *Prem Shankar v. Delhi Administration*,[87] before embarking on a survey of the issues involved, the Court observed, "The court must never forget the core principle found in Article 5 of the Universal Declaration of Human Rights . . . and . . . Article 10 of the International Covenant on Civil and Political Rights." Obviously, the Court was desirous of being guided by human rights norms in determining the content and reach of the fundamental rights. Thus, while the Court did not apply customary international law directly, it used it indirectly in determining the protection afforded by the Indian Constitution. This "indirect incorporation"[88] of the Declaration and other international human rights instruments is a sound approach and has contributed to the enrichment of the evolving constitutional precepts.

In sum, the judicial decisions analyzed here are important landmarks in the domestic enforcement of international human rights. They represent the Supreme Court's enlightened interpretation of the Indian Constitution in conformity with international human rights principles. One hopes this approach continues in India and inspires the judicial processes of other countries as well. Only then can there be a practical hope for the ultimate realization of the "noble and ageless ideal to free all persons from brutal violence."[89]

NOTES

1. The right to be free from torture has been incorporated into Article 7 of the International Covenant on Civil and Political Rights. G.A. Res. 2200, 21 U.N. GAOR, Supp. (No. 16), at 49, U.N. Doc. A/6316 (1966); Article 5(2) of the American Convention on Human Rights, Nov. 22, 1969, entered into force July 18, 1978, O.A.S. Treaty Series No. 36, at 1, O.A.S. OEA/Serv.L/V/11.23, doc. 21 rev. 2.; Article 3 of the European Convention for the Protection of Human Rights and Fundamental Freedoms, Nov. 4, 1950, entered into force Sept. 3, 1953, 213 U.N.T.S. 221; Article 5 of the African Charter on Human and People's Rights adopted June 27, 1981, O.A.U. Doc. CAB/LEG/67/3 Rev. 5, entered into force Oct. 21, 1986.

2. G.A. Res. 39/46, 39 U.N. GAOR, Supp. (No. 51) 197 (1984), adopted Dec. 10, 1984, entered into force June 26, 1987.

3. Filartiga v. Peña-Irala, 630 F.2d 876, 884 (2d Cir. 1980).

4. *Id.*

5. India Const., preamble:

WE, THE PEOPLE OF INDIA, having solemnly resolved to constitute India into a SOVEREIGN SOCIALIST SECULAR DEMOCRATIC REPUBLIC and to secure to all its citizens:
JUSTICE, social economic and political;
LIBERTY of thought, expression, belief, faith and worship;
EQUALITY of status and of opportunity;
and to promote among them all

FRATERNITY assuring the dignity of the individual and the unity and integrity of the Nation
IN OUR CONSTITUENT ASSEMBLY this twenty-sixth day of November, 1949, do HEREBY
ADOPT, ENACT AND GIVE TO OURSELVES THIS CONSTITUTION.

6. G. Austin, *The Indian Constitution: Cornerstone of a Nation* (Oxford, 1966), 50.
7. India Const. art. 13(1) and (2) in pt. III provides:

Art 13(1): All laws in force in the territory of India immediately before the commencement of this
constitution, in so far as they are inconsistent with the provisions of this Part, shall to the extent of
such inconsistency, be void.

Art 13(2): The State shall not make any law which takes away or abridges the rights conferred by
this part and any law made in contravention of this clause, shall, to the extent of the contravention
be void.

8. India Const. pt. IV, arts. 36–51 deals with Directive Principles of State Policy.
Derived from the Irish Constitution, these positive obligations cover a variety of areas
of economic and social policy providing a context for the application of Fundamental
Rights. They are not enforceable in a court of law. They are only directives to the various
government and government agencies to be followed as "fundamental" in the gover-
nance of the country.
9. India Const., pt. III, art. 12 states:

In this part unless the context otherwise requires, "the State" includes the Government and Parliament of India and the Government and the Legislatures of each of the States and all local or other
authorities within the territory of India or under the control of the Government of India.

10. See Ujjan Bai v. State of U.P., A.I.R. 1962 S. Ct. 1621 (V 49) (expressing some
doubt as to whether the definition of "State" under art. 12 excludes a court).
11. C. H. Alexander, "International Law in India," 289 *International & Comparative
Law Quarterly* (1952), 292 at 289.
12. A.I.R. 1980 S. Ct. 474 (V 67).
13. A.I.R. 1950 S. Ct. 27.
14. India Const. art. 21:

Protection of Life and Personal Liberty.
No person shall be deprived of his Life or personal Liberty except according to procedure established
by law. *Hereinafter*, the terms right to life, right to personal liberty and right to life and personal
liberty shall be used interchangeably.

15. U.S. Const. amend. V:

No person . . . shall be deprived of life, liberty or property, without due process of law.

Amend. XIV, § 1:

[N]or shall any state deprive any person of life, liberty, or property, without due process of law.

16. A.I.R. 1950 S. Ct. 37 (Judgment of Kania, CJ).
17. *Id.*
18. *Id.* at 38.
19. *Id.* at 37.
20. A.I.R. 1978 S. Ct. 1675 (V 65).
21. *Id.* at 1682.

22. *Id.* at 1690.

23. *Id.* at 1694–1700, 1702, 1706–1710. The American cases the Court examined included Sostre v. Rockefeller, 312 F. Supp. 863 (S.D.N.Y. 1970); Trop v. Dulles, 356 U.S. 86, 101 (1958); and Charles Wolf v. McDonnell, 41 L Ed 2d 935 (1974).

24. A.I.R. 1978 S. Ct. 1702 (V cs).

25. *Id.* at 1706.

26. Art. 14 (Right to Equality): "The State shall not deny to any person equality before the law or equal protection of the laws within the territory of India."

27. Art. 19 (1) confers six explicit freedoms: (1) freedom of speech and expression; (2) to assemble peaceably and without arms; (3) to form associations or unions; (4) to move freely throughout the territory in India; (5) to reside and settle in any part of the territory of India; and (6) to practice any profession or to carry on any occupation, trade or business. Clauses (2) through (6) permit the imposition of "reasonable restrictions" on the enjoyment of these freedoms. Any other restriction on these freedoms can be struck down as an "unreasonable" restriction.

28. A.I.R. 1978 S. Ct. 1710 (V 65).

29. *Id.* at 1706.

30. A.I.R. 1978 S. Ct. 597 (V 65).

31. *Supra* note 14.

32. A.I.R. 1978 S. Ct. at 622.

33. *Id.* at 624.

34. Sunil Batra v. Delhi Administration and Charles Sobhraj v. Delhi Administration, A.I.R. 1978 S. Ct. 1706, 1722 (V 65).

35. *Id.* at 1710–1711.

36. *Id.* at 1715.

37. *Id.*

38. *Id.* at 1717.

39. *Id.* at 1719.

40. *Id.* at 1719, 1724.

41. *Id.* at 1719.

42. *Id.* at 1720.

43. Sunil Batra v. Delhi Administration, A.I.R. 1980 S. Ct. 1579, 1583 (V 67).

44. *Id.* at 1583.

45. *Id.* at 1585.

46. A.I.R. 1980 S. Ct. 1591 (V 67).

47. 94 U.S. 113 (1877).

48. A.I.R. 1980 S. Ct. at 1593.

49. *Supra* note 14.

50. A.I.R. 1980 S. Ct. at 1594.

51. *Supra* note 26.

52. *Supra* note 27.

53. *Supra* note 14.

54. A.I.R. 1980 S. Ct. at 1594.

55. Art. 8:

Any person who alleges that he has been subjected to torture or other cruel, inhuman or degrading treatment or punishment by or at the instigation of a public official shall have the right to complain to, and to have his case impartially examined by, the competent authorities of the state concerned.

56. Art. 9:

Wherever there is reasonable ground to believe that an act of torture as defined in article 1 has been committed, the competent authorities of the state concerned shall promptly proceed to an impartial investigation even if there has been no formal complaint.

57. A.I.R. 1980 Ct. 1603 (V 67).

58. By epistolary jurisdiction, access to judicial redress may be obtained without a lawyer or even filing of formal papers. Several epistles were addressed to individual judges of the Supreme Court, and reports abound of individual judges soliciting petitions. This led to the creation of a "Public Interest Litigation" cell within the Supreme Court to process the paper work. See generally P. N. Bhagwati, "Social Action Litigation: The Indian Experience," in: N. Tiruchelvam and R. Coomaraswamy, eds., *The Role of the Judiciary in Plural Societies* (New York, 1987) (discussing how judges created new ways such as epistolary jurisdiction, broadened rules of standing [*locus standi*], sociolegal commissions of inquiry, etc. to bring issues affecting unrepresented people, which gave rise to Social Action Litigation, or SAL, in India).

59. A.I.R. 1980 S. Ct. at 1583.

60. *Supra* note 43 and accompanying text.

61. Prem Shankar v. Delhi Administration, A.I.R. 1980 S. Ct. 1535, 1536 (V 67).

62. Art. 5 states: "No one shall be subjected to torture, or to cruel, inhuman or degrading treatment or punishment."

63. Art. 10 reads:

(1) All persons deprived of their liberty shall be treated with humanity and with respect for the inherent dignity of the human person.

(2)(a) Accused persons shall, save in exceptional circumstances, be segregated from convicted persons and shall be subject to separate treatment appropriate to their status as unconvicted persons;

(b) Accused juvenile persons shall be separated from adults and brought as speedily as possible for adjudication.

(3) The penitentiary system shall comprise treatment of prisoners the essential aim of which shall be their reformation and social rehabilitation. Juvenile offenders shall be segregated from adults and be accorded treatment according to their age and legal status.

64. *Supra* note 26.

65. *Supra* note 27.

66. A.I.R. 1980 Ct. 1541–1542 (V 67).

67. *Id.* at 1544.

68. *Id.*

69. A.I.R. 1981 S. Ct. 746 (V 68).

70. *Id.* at 748.

71. *Id.* at 750–751.

72. A.I.R. 1980 S. Ct. at 1583 (V 67).

73. *Supra* note 48.

74. A.I.R. 1981 S. Ct. at 753.

75. *Id.*

76. *Id.*

77. *Id.* at 754.

78. *Id.*

79. A.I.R. 1978 S. Ct. 1690 (V 65). (Sunil Batra v. Delhi Administration).

80. *Supra* note 13.

81. *Supra* note 30.

82. Convention against Torture and Other Cruel, Inhuman or Degrading Treatment or Punishment, opened for signature Dec. 10, 1984, entered into force June 26, 1987; G.A. Res. 39/46, Doc. A/39/51.

83. *Supra* note 30.

84. *Supra* notes 26–27.

85. See, e.g., Rodriguez Fernandez v. Wilkinson, 654 F.2d 1382 (10th Cir. 1981).

86. Both the International Covenant on Civil and Political Rights and the International Covenant on Economic, Social and Cultural Rights express a high degree of deference for state sovereignty and domestic jurisdiction. The Preamble of the International Covenant on Economic, Social and Cultural Rights, adopted Dec. 19, 1966, entered into force Jan. 3, 1976, G.A. Res. 2200 (XXI), 2 U.N. GAOR, Supp. (No. 16) 49, U.N. Doc. A/6316 (1966), gives great deference to state sovereignty: "Realizing that the individual, having duties to other individuals and to the community to which he belongs, is under a responsibility to strive for the promotion and observance of the rights recognized in the present Covenant."

87. A.I.R. 1980 Ct. at 1539.

88. This manner of domestic enforcement of human rights has begun to receive scholarly support. See, e.g., R. Bilder, "Integrating International Human Rights Law into Domestic Law—U.S. Experience," 4 *Houston Journal of International Law* (1981), 1; G. Christenson, "The Use of Human Rights Norms to Inform Due Process and Equal Protection Analyses," 52 *University of Cincinnati Law Review* (1983), 3; R. Martineau, "Interpreting the Constitution: The Use of International Human Rights Norms," 5 *Human Rights Quarterly* (1983), 87; and J. Paust, "Human Rights: From Jurisprudential Inquiry to Effective Litigation" (book review), 56 *New York University Law Review* (1981), 227.

89. Filartiga v. Peña-Irala, 630 F. 2d 876 at 890.

Chapter 7

Judicial Defense of Human Rights during the Marcos Dictatorship in the Philippines: The Careers of Claudio Teehankee and Cecelia Muñoz Palma

C. NEAL TATE

On the morning of February 25, 1986 there were two simultaneous presidential inaugurations in Manila. In one, the officially "re-elected" longtime President/ dictator Ferdinand Marcos was sworn in on the balcony of the presidential palace, Malacanang, by Ramon C. Aquino, the man he had appointed Chief Justice of the Supreme Court only a few months earlier. In the other, the "newly elected" Corazon "Cory" Aquino,[1] the "simple housewife" who was the widow of martyred former Senator Benigino Aquino, was sworn in at the exclusive suburban Club Filipino by Claudio Teehankee, the longest-serving incumbent member of the Supreme Court (appointed by Marcos in 1968) and twice bypassed for appointment as Chief Justice. Watching over the inauguration of Cory Aquino was Cecelia Muñoz Palma, a retired Supreme Court Justice, the first woman to have served on that august body, appointed by Marcos in 1973.

The reason for the two inaugurations was the success of the Philippines' "People Power Revolution" and the combined military mutiny/popular uprising. Soon after his inauguration, Ferdinand Marcos was forced to flee the country with his family and "cronies."[2] Cory Aquino was established as the sole president of the Philippines. The presence of Teehankee and Palma at Aquino's inauguration was not a mistake; they did not become lost on their way to Malacanang. To the contrary, Palma had been intensively active in the Aquino bid for the presidency, and Teehankee had for many years been the only consistent source of opposition to Marcos in the official government of the Philippines. In recognition of their achievements and as a reward for their service to the new government, Aquino named Teehankee chief justice of the Supreme Court when she reconstituted it in April 1986. In turn, Palma was made presiding officer of the constitutional convention that in June of that year began the drafting of a replacement constitution for the new Philippine Republic.

Teehankee and Palma were not the only politically or economically note-worthy Filipinos to openly and consistently oppose Marcos's alternately permissive and repressive authoritarianism. But among the ranks of the men and women who served on the Philippine Supreme Court during this period, they emerged as the two most prominent players of the judiciary's role as defender of the rights of citizens against the abuses of powerful rulers. Their efforts were often nearly solitary; the Supreme Court as an institution failed to mount any significant challenge to the president's "constitutional authoritarianism" and eventually came to be perceived as just another prop holding up the "conjugal dictatorship of the Marcoses."[3] This chapter traces the careers of these two courageous defenders of the rights of the Filipinos. After laying out the facts of their careers, it analyzes their tenures on the Supreme Court with the objective of determining the extent to which their opposition to the Marcoses' rule is apparent from their actions during their tenures as justices.

CLAUDIO TEEHANKEE

Claudio Teehankee was born on April 18, 1918, in Manila.[4] His father was a Chinese immigrant to the Philippines, Tee Han Kee, a physician, who came to the Philippines in 1900 to accept a position in the new colonial government's Bureau of Health. As a result of an association with Sun Yat Sen begun in medical school in Hong Kong, Tee Han Kee became the leader in the Philippines of the overseas Chinese resistance to the Manchu and, after the success of Sun's revolution, was decorated for his service to the new Republic of China. Dr. Tee Han Kee also became prominent in Philippine medical circles. He organized the Chinese General Hospital and its school of nursing, adopted the Christian name Jose, married a Filipina, Julia Ong Sangroniz, and assimilated to his adopted country.[5]

Claudio Teehankee attended the prestigious Ateneo de Manila, the elite Jesuit institution that has long been regarded as one of the Philippines' best educational institutions. He graduated from the Ateneo College of Law in 1940.

Teehankee's paternal Chinese ancestry and his matriculation from the Ateneo College of Law were both important. The former led to his having to fight off persistent accusations that he was not a "natural-born" Filipino citizen, accusations intended to bring an end to his holding of various public offices, especially that of Supreme Court justice. The latter was initially a source of distinction—he was the first Ateneo law graduate to be appointed a justice of the Supreme Court. But it must also have been, especially during Teehankee's career-building years, a source of social and, ultimately, political separation from much of the nation's legal elite, graduates of the College of Law of the government-supported University of the Philippines (UP). In particular, it was undoubtedly a source of separation from Ferdinand Marcos and the other University of the Philippines College of Law graduates who became the President's faithful supporters during martial law.

If it later set him apart from the UP lawyers in Ferdinand Marcos's set, Teehankee's graduation from the Ateneo College of Law did not appear to hamper his private career. After taking first place in the 1940 bar exams, he entered private practice with a firm of very prominent attorneys, Araneta, Zaragoza and Bautista, one of whom (Bautista) was a founding member of the Philippine Civil Liberties Union (CLU), an organization that Teehankee later joined.

Teehankee remained in private practice during the Japanese occupation of the Philippines, apparently keeping a low profile as a hardworking young lawyer. His father was not so fortunate: He was shot by anti-Japanese guerrillas, allegedly because of his collaboration with the Japanese in his role as head of the Chinese Association.

After the war, Teehankee with two colleagues formed the firm of Tanada, Pelaez, and Teehankee. This, too, was important, for Teehankee's senior partners, Lorenzo Tanada and Emmanuel Pelaez, became two of the Philippines' most important post-war nationalist politicians. Especially Tanada was active in nationalist, anti-establishment politics in the 1950s and 1960s and became one of the most vocal opponents of Ferdinand Marcos during the early years of martial law. After the formation of the firm, both Tanada and Pelaez soon held national elective office in Congress, reportedly leaving Teehankee "to get the lawyering done."[6]

Although he remained for many years in the private sector, Teehankee's own sentiments may have been revealed in several of his public activities. He cofounded, along with Tanada and the patron saint of Filipino nationalists, the late Senator Claro M. Recto, the "Citizens' Party," which served briefly as an alternative to the established Liberal and Nacionalista Parties. From the 1940s Teehankee was also an active member and frequent chair of the CLU of the Philippines, an organization that combined activism in support of civil liberties with nationalist and progressive politics.[7]

Through the 1950s Teehankee represented a number of detainees held by the military for their alleged participation in rebellion against the state. His pro bono work for the CLU became well known. However, it was his involvement in defending a movie glorifying the life and career of Ferdinand Marcos against attempted government censorship that turned Teehankee from private practice to government service. The movie, *Iginuhit ng Tadhana* (Touched by Fate), was clearly intended as a tool in Marcos's 1965 Nacionalista Party campaign for the presidency, not as an example of cinemagraphic art. When incumbent President Diosdado Macapagal's campaigners sought to have the government Board of Censors ban the movie, they were ultimately overturned in a case that Teehankee took to the Supreme Court for decision. Soon Teehankee had been persuaded to be counsel to the Nacionalista Party. When the party's nominee won, Teehankee was in line for an important government appointment.

By all accounts, Teehankee left a "lucrative" law practice in January 1966 to be appointed Undersecretary of Justice in the administration of the newly elected Ferdinand Marcos. He was Undersecretary for a year and a half before being confirmed as the government's chief legal officer, the Secretary of Justice, in August 1967. His service in that position was even briefer: Marcos named him to the Supreme Court, and he was sworn in in December 1968.

The rapidity of Teehankee's rise from his first government appointment to the Supreme Court was a bit unusual; all but one[8] of Marcos's previous five appointees to the Court had come from the Presiding Justiceship of the next highest court, the Court of Appeals. Perhaps with the benefit of hindsight, some observers of Philippine politics have suggested that the rapidity of Teehankee's rise may have reflected Marcos's desire to "kick upstairs" a troublesome cabinet member who was not among his then-developing inner circle of advisers composed of Ilocano coethnics and UP College of Law classmates, fraternity brothers and alumni.

On the other hand, Teehankee did have a record of substantial accomplishments during his brief service in the Department of Justice, and it was not unprecedented to appoint to the Supreme Court a Secretary of Justice or other important executive official who lacked substantial judicial experience.[9] Furthermore, simultaneously with Teehankee, Marcos appointed to the Court another lawyer with no judicial experience, his Solicitor General Antonio Barredo. After Marcos's declaration of martial law, there could not have been two more different records of support for the President than those of Teehankee and Barredo. From the first martial law case until the end of the Marcos regime, Teehankee consistently opposed, and Barredo consistently supported, the President's one-man rule.

Teehankee's opposition to Marcos apparently never brought him into any physical danger—he was not threatened with harm or imprisonment by the President or his cronies. However, it nearly cost him position on the Court and did twice cost him the coveted position of Chief Justice to which Supreme Court tradition entitled him.

As already noted, Teehankee's Chinese ancestry was cited by his political opponents in efforts to deny him government positions. Frictions between "overseas" Chinese immigrant populations and "native" populations are common in Southeast Asian countries. In the Philippines these frictions have led to restrictive definitions of citizenship and rigidly administered naturalization procedures. Since he was not the son of two indigenous Filipinos, Teehankee's qualifications for public office came into question especially after the adoption of the 1973 Constitution, which required that officeholders be "native-born" citizens, that is, children of parents who were both Filipino citizens at the time of the children's births. Teehankee's nomination to the Supreme Court was ratified under the 1935 Constitution, which had somewhat less rigorous citizenship requirements for officeholders. But in 1982, Teehankee, along with all the other Supreme Court Justices, resigned his position after several justices were implicated in a bar exams scandal involving apparent favoritism toward the son of a sitting justice. The mass resignation was intended to cleanse the reputation of the Court and allow the President to remake it with appointees not tainted by scandal. After the mass resignation, the President reappointed Teehankee and all the justices, except the two who were most clearly implicated in the scandal. However, Teehankee's nearly ten years of oppositionist behavior on the Supreme Court led many of Marcos's supporters and advisers to openly oppose his reappointment on grounds that he was not qualified for membership on the Supreme Court under the citizenship requirements of the then-governing 1973 Constitution. Marcos nevertheless reappointed Teehankee, perhaps because he reasoned that there would be more costs to his reputation than benefits to his power in removing the only significant source of institutional opposition to his rule.

Although he weathered the attacks on his reappointment to the Supreme Court in the wake of the 1982 bar scandal, Teehankee's opposition to Marcos's authoritarian rule subsequently did cost him an appointment to the position of Chief Justice on the retirement of Enrique Fernando from that position on July 24, 1985. In the Philippines, the position of Chief Justice has always been very important and much desired: The Philippine Chief is considerably more than first among equals. Perhaps to avoid harmful conflicts over the position, a firm tradition has existed since the 1920s[10] that the most senior associate justice is always appointed Chief Justice on the retirement of the previous Chief. However, Marcos's willingness to tolerate Teehankee as one member of the Supreme Court did not tempt the President to appoint him to the Chief Justiceship. Even though it caused a modest controversy in the legal community, he bypassed Teehankee in favor of the next most senior justice, his law school classmate Felix Makasiar. When Makasiar reached age 70 less than four months later, Marcos again bypassed Teehankee for the next most senior associate justice, Ramon C. Aquino, who was also his law school classmate. Since Aquino was a few months younger than Teehankee, his appointment meant that the President would not have to face the prospect—and the controversy—of bypassing Teehankee again. It was only when the dueling inaugurations of February 25, 1986, led to Aquino's removal from the Court that Teehankee finally received—from Corazon Aquino—his appointment as Chief Justice, a position he held for just over two years before he retired on April 17, 1988.

CECELIA MUÑOZ PALMA

Cecelia Muñoz was born on November 22, 1913, in Batangas province, a short distance south of Manila. She was the daughter of Pedro Muñoz, a former member of the Philippine Congress, and Emilia Arreglado. Like other upper-middle-class Filipino women of her generation, she attended convent schools, graduating in 1931 from the St. Scholastica High School as valedictorian. She attended the University of the Philippines and its College of Law, ultimately

receiving her Bachelor of Laws in 1937. Like Claudio Teehankee, Cecelia Muñoz topped the bar examinations when she took them that same year.

At UP she was an active student leader, involved in debate and serving as
the first woman elected president of the Law Student Council. During this period
she met and married Rodolfo Palma and became Cecelia Muñoz Palma. After
completing her law degree, she became a bill drafter and researcher for the
National Assembly but apparently devoted her time primarily to family building
and child rearing.

After World War II Palma became an assistant city attorney in the new capital,
Quezon City, and continued her education, studying for a Master of Laws degree
at the University of Manila. Later, she traveled to the United States to undertake
graduate study, completing her Master of Laws degree at Yale in 1954.

Upon her return to the Philippines she began the long judicial career that was
to take her to the Supreme Court. Her first appointment was as judge of the
Court of First Instance (CFI) in Dumagete City, Negros Oriental province, in
the Visayan region of the central Philippines, far from her Manila home. To
accept this position, she had to face the separation of her family: Her two daugh-
ters came with her to Negros, whereas her son remained with her husband, a
practicing lawyer and law dean in Manila. The separation did not last very long,
as she was soon promoted to provincial CFI courts near and in the Manila area.

After fourteen years of promotion through the informal hierarchy of the CFI
courts, Ferdinand Marcos named her in September 1968 to the Court of Appeals—the second woman to hold such an appointment.[11] She served on the
Court of Appeals until October 29, 1973, when Marcos elevated her to the
Supreme Court.

Like many other of his Supreme Court appointees, excluding Claudio Teehankee, Cecelia Muñoz Palma was a contemporary of Ferdinand Marcos in the
UP College of Law in the late 1930s. She was not his classmate or co-ethnic,
however, and obviously was not his fraternity brother. As with Teehankee, these
sources of isolation from Marcos and his friends may have made Palma skeptical
of the motives and policies of the martial law–ruling President and strengthened
her determination to stand her ground against the President's developing authoritarianism and serve as a spokesperson for the human rights of Filipinos
during and after her service on the Supreme Court.

Palma came to the Philippine Supreme Court through what has been historically the most common route, a long career of service in the ranks of the
judiciary. Her appointment to the Supreme Court was hardly "automatic," however. Traditionally, the Presiding Justice of the Court of Appeals was very likely
to be appointed to the Supreme Court, albeit sometimes only for a few months,
given the usual role of hierarchical seniority in determining who held that position.[12] However, Palma was not the Presiding Justice or the most senior member of the Court of Appeals when she was elevated to the Supreme Court. Since
she was also not a classmate, co-ethnic, or fraternity brother of Marcos's, it

seems likely that her appointment represented the President's conclusion that it was high time a woman was appointed to that body.

Regardless of the President's motivation for appointing Palma to the Supreme Court, he almost immediately must have regretted having done so, as Palma became a vocal critic of the deprivations of rights that were occurring under martial law. She remained one until her retirement at the then-mandatory age of 65 in 1978.[13] Palma's retirement did not stop her persistent opposition to the Marcos dictatorship, but it did remove her ability to express that opposition through the principal institutional channel for the legal protection of citizen rights, the Supreme Court.

OPPOSITION TO DICTATORSHIP IN THE SUPREME COURT: THE RECORDS OF TEEHANKEE AND PALMA

How did these persistent critics of the Marcos dictatorship express their opposition during their service on the Philippine Supreme Court? In an institutional environment of the Supreme Court, in which they represented a minority of only one or two, their options would have been limited. The President's repressive control of society, and especially the mass media, would have meant that even had they (1) wanted to, (2) felt that their judicial role allowed them to and (3) assumed that they would be permitted to speak out publicly, they would have had few opportunities to have their words heard by any audience of a significant size. Understandably, though it need not have been so, their principal opportunities for expression of their commitment to human rights and opposition to the dictatorship thus arose out of their performance of their official duties as Supreme Court justices.

Ferdinand Marcos, despite his thoroughgoing imposition of one-man rule on Philippine society and government, did not openly attack the Supreme Court and its authority. The reasons for this have been explored elsewhere[14] and need not detain us here. But one of its consequences was that throughout Marcos's tenure the Supreme Court continued to hear and to decide important cases with substantial political content and significant implications for the state of human rights in the Philippines. Therefore, as justices, Teehankee and Palma could, when they wished, write opinions and cast votes expressing their opposition to the regime's repression. Given that the Court's majority never opposed the President's wishes on any important issue, these opinions and votes would have had to be expressed as concurrences or dissents, having no formal legal authority in the strict sense. Nevertheless, they would still have represented opportunities for supporting human rights and opposing the regime. The President's control of the mass media would have meant that they would have had little impact on the public at large. However, since the Supreme Court's decisions were continuously available to the Philippine and, indeed, the international legal community, the opinions and votes could, for this important set of elite communities, have been important indicators of opposition to Marcos.

No one appears to have conducted an analysis of the opinion writing of Tee-hankee and Palma during the Marcos period. There is little doubt that such an analysis would be interesting to students of Philippine law and history and per-haps revealing as an example of how judges produce the rhetoric of opposition in difficult circumstances. But it is not the purpose of this chapter to study the opinion rhetoric of Teehankee and Palma. Instead, the remainder of the chapter describes how they expressed (or failed to express) their opposition to Marcos and support for human rights and limited government through their voting be-havior in several Supreme Court cases.[15]

Some might argue that the votes of Supreme Court justices, separated from the arguments of their opinions, are unlikely to serve well as indicators of op-position to a dictator or support for citizen rights. Yet one can hardly deny that it is the votes of the justices that determine the outcomes of specific cases and that it is in specific cases that the claims of citizens for relief from regime oppression are decided. A justice who wishes to express his or her opposition to a dictator can write an opinion that puts that opposition into eloquent words. However, to have that opinion published as a part of the official record, he or she will also have to cast a vote that indicates a preference for a different outcome than that preferred by the majority that supports the claims of the regime. It can certainly be imagined that when an oppositionist justice is in a distinct minority, he or she will decide not to waste time, effort and possible influence on colleagues by casting "useless" votes and writing "futile" opin-ions that cannot change case outcomes. But whether that occurs is an empirical question and one that is possible to investigate in the instances of Claudio Tee-hankee and Cecelia Muñoz Palma.

The most obvious and extreme way for a Supreme Court justice to vote his or her opposition to the decisions of a majority is to dissent. However, there are less extreme ways. For example, in an environment in which dissents have fallen into institutional disfavor, a justice may choose to vote to accept the result produced by the majority decision but disagree with some or all of the justifi-cations or reasonings offered in support of that result. In the Philippines, justices also on occasion have "reserved" their votes, not joining the majority or filing a concurrence but also not dissenting. The analysis presented here examines all these behaviors as indicators of opposition to the Marcos regime.

Table 7.1 presents the career-long voting behaviors of Claudio Teehankee and Cecelia Muñoz Palma. It shows very clearly that Teehankee was much less likely to join the majority than was Muñoz Palma. Teehankee voted with the majority and joined in its opinion in only 83.5 percent of the cases he partici-pated in; the comparable figure for Palma was 96.2 percent. Or, to shift the focus of attention, Teehankee was over four times as likely as Palma not to vote with and join the majority opinion, and he was more likely than Palma to in-dicate his disagreement with the majority in every way in which it is possible to do so, from concurring without a separate opinion to casting a dissenting vote justified by a separate opinion.

Table 7.1
Career-Long Voting Behavior of Claudio Teehankee and Cecelia Muñoz Palma

Voting Behavior	Teehankee		Muñoz Palma	
	Frequency	Percent	Frequency	Percent
Voted with Majority	4,630	83.5	1,168	96.2
Concurred with No Separate Opinion	14	0.3	1	0.1
Concurred "in Result"	317	5.7	14	1.2
Concurred with a Separate Opinion	271	4.9	12	1.0
"Reserved Vote"	49	0.9	1	0.1
Dissented with No Opinion	39	0.7	3	0.2
Dissented with Opinion	226	4.1	15	1.2
Total	5,546	100.0*	1,214	100.0
Did Not Join Majority	916	16.5	46	3.8

*Numbers do not total 100 percent due to rounding.

Of course, Teehankee served on the Court for several years both before and after the period of Palma's service. Given that, it is possible to imagine that his relative unwillingness to join the majority, compared to his oppositionist colleague, is a product of a particular mix of cases that arose with the continuation and consolidation of Marcos's dictatorship in the 1980s and that his behavior during the five years of Palma's tenure would not have been different from hers. It is also possible that Teehankee's behavior is a by-product of a propensity to dissent that is, for whatever reason, simply greater than Palma's and does not represent an expression of his opposition to one-man rule.

The first of these possibilities can be investigated by examining Teehankee's voting behavior during the period of Palma's tenure. If one restricts the analysis to the subset of cases in which Palma and Teehankee both participated (N = 1,062), there is only a tiny difference in Teehankee's voting behavior: He joins with the majority and its opinion in 84.6 percent of the cases (1.1 percent more than for his whole career) and is still as likely as, or more likely than, Palma to engage in each of the possible voting behaviors that indicate disagreement with the majority opinion. Thus, one can reject the hypothesis that the difference in the oppositionist voting of the two justices is due to the composition of the congregations of cases in which they participated.

The possibility that Teehankee's greater level of oppositionist voting behavior is due to an overall propensity to dissent that is simply greater than Palma's can be examined by examining the pattern of Teehankee's voting across his career.

Table 7.2
Voting Behavior of Claudio Teehankee by Year, 1968–1987

Year	Number of Votes	Percent Majority	Year	Number of Votes	Percent Majority
1968*	5	100.0	1978	250	84.7
1969	492	97.2	1979	276	89.9
1970	386	91.4	1980	195	72.0
1971	396	88.6	1981	234	69.4
1972	182	88.7	1982	282	77.3
1973	182	80.2	1983	269	76.9
1974	195	83.0	1984	238	84.4
1975	142	77.6	1985	214	69.0
1976	173	86.9	1986	164	85.4
1977	198	88.0	1987**	67	82.7

*Teehankee appointed at end of year.
**Data cover only half of year.

A finding that he was more supportive of the majority before the imposition of martial law and also after its demise would be consistent with the hypothesis that he used his voting behavior to express his opposition to the regime.[16] The evidence needed to document such a finding is presented in Table 7.2.

Table 7.2 shows that Teehankee's tendency to join with the majority (and, conversely, his tendency to vote in oppositionist ways) did change across his career and that the change began with the first full year of martial law authoritarianism, 1973. In the five years before 1973,[17] Teehankee always joined the majority opinion in at least seven out of eight cases (87.5 percent); from 1973 on (fifteen years), he attained that level of compatibility with the majority on only two occasions, 1977 (88 percent) and 1979 (89.9 percent).

The data cover only up through June 1987, a little more than one year after the overthrow of Marcos and the reconstitution of the Supreme Court with Teehankee as its Chief Justice. In this limited period of time, they do not suggest that Teehankee found the majority as compatible as he did at the beginning of his career. However, they do suggest that his need to express opposition to the majority did decline from its level in the waning years of the dictatorship, as a comparison of the figures for 1986–1987 with those for the period 1980–1985 documents.

In the period covered by the data, 1961 through mid-1987, only one other Philippine Supreme Court justice joined the majority as infrequently and dissented as frequently as Claudio Teehankee. This justice joined the majority opinion with his vote in 83.0 percent (as compared to Teehankee's 83.5 percent) and dissented with a separate opinion in 4.0 percent (as compared to Teehankee's 4.1 percent) of the cases. Ironically, that person was Ramon C. Aquino, the man whom Marcos named Chief Justice in 1985, superseding the more senior Teehankee for the second time, and who inaugurated Ferdinand Marcos while Teehankee was inaugurating Corazon Aquino on February 25, 1986.

CONCLUSION

The analysis of the voting behaviors of Claudio Teehankee and Cecelia Muñoz Palma has shown very different patterns for the two justices who are best known for standing up for the rights of citizens and opposing Ferdinand Marcos's dictatorship during their Supreme Court tenures. There is very little trace of Palma's sentiments in her voting behavior. She only rarely exhibited any sign that she was in any way disturbed by the decision making of the Supreme Court majority during her 1973–1978 tenure. To find evidence of her opposition to the regime and its compliant Court, one would have to turn to the words of her opinions. But even there, such evidence is likely to be sparse: In only 46 of 1,168 cases in which she participated did Palma take any action that indicated anything other than agreement with the majority opinion and outcome, and only a third of these actions were dissents accompanied by opinions in which she could have explained her disagreement with the Court. The fact is that Palma's reputation as a supporter of human rights and opponent of Marcos must rest essentially on her actions after her retirement from the Court and not on what she did while a Supreme Court justice.

In contrast, Teehankee became, after the imposition of martial law, the Court's most prominent supporter of human rights and opponent of Marcos, both in words and in deeds. Since he continued on the Supreme Court throughout the entire period of Marcos's authoritarian rule and beyond, Teehankee had no other institutional setting in which to express his opposition. For most of the period of his service, he also had no allies—not even Palma—who were willing to offer him consistent support in his efforts.

NOTES

1. No relation to Ramon C. Aquino.

2. *Cronies* is the term used by Marcos's critics to refer to a small group of close associates of the president who helped him maintain his one-man rule for over thirteen years and who benefited greatly from the "plunder" of the Philippines they helped Marcos conduct. For the story of this plunder and the role of the cronies in it, see B. Aquino, *The Politics of Plunder* (Quezon City, 1987).

3. See P. Mijares, *The Conjugal Dictatorship of Ferdinand and Imelda Marcos* (San Francisco, 1976).

4. This biographical sketch of Claudio Teehankee is based on a wide variety of accounts, many cited in C. N. Tate, *The Social Background, Political Recruitment and Decision Making of the Philippine Supreme Court Justices, 1901–1968* (New Orleans, 1971); also included are V. J. Sevilla, *Justices of the Supreme Court of the Philippines*, vol. 3 (Quezon City, 1985); P. P. Sicam, "We Have to Educate Judges: Paulynn P.

Sicam Interviews Chief Justice Claudio Teehankee,'' *The Chronicle on Sunday* (Manila), Apr. 17, 1988, 18; and J. M. Flores, ''In the Hearts of Men,'' *Philippine Panorama*, Apr. 17, 1988, 6ff.

5. Flores, *supra* note 4 at 8.

6. *Id.* at 9.

7. See H. J. Abaya, *The CLU Story: Fifty Years of Struggle for Civil Liberties* (Quezon City, 1987) for an account.

8. Enrique M. Fernando, a prominent law professor from the University of the Philippines.

9. Marcos's predecessor, Diosdado Macapagal, had appointed to the Supreme Court his executive secretary, Calixto Zaldivar, a man who had neither judicial nor justice department experience.

10. With some disruption during the confused days of the Japanese Occupation.

11. The first woman appointed to the Philippine appellate courts was Natividad Almeda-Lopes, who was appointed to the Court of Appeals in 1961 and served briefly until her mandatory retirement at age 70 in 1962.

12. See Tate, *supra* note 4, ch. 3, for an extended discussion of recruitment to the Philippine Supreme Court that documents this hierarchical of recruitment pattern.

13. Under the 1935 Constitution (art. 8, sec. 9), Philippine judges had enjoyed secure tenures during good behavior until a mandatory retirement age of 70. By the time of Palma's retirement, the retirement age had been reduced to 65. Some observers of the Philippine political system have speculated that it may have been reduced to 65 to allow Marcos to get rid of Palma. In fact, the mandatory (but not retroactive) retirement age of 65 was included in the 1973 Constitution (art. 10, sec. 7), which was declared ''ratified'' as of Jan. 17 by the President and ''in force and effect'' by the Supreme Court on Mar. 31, 1973 (Javellana v. Executive Secretary, 50 Supreme Court Reports Annotated [hereafter SCRA] 30). The retirement age was returned to 70 by an amendment ratified in a plebiscite of Jan. 30, 1980, and proclaimed in President Marcos's Proclamation No. 1959 (see E. Q. Fernando, *Philippine Constitutional Law* [Quezon City, 1984], 10).

14. See C. N. Tate and S. L. Haynie, ''The Philippine Supreme Court under Authoritarian and Democratic Rule: The Perceptions of the Justices,'' 22 under *Asian Profile* (1994), 209; C. N. Tate and S. L. Haynie, ''Authoritarianism and the Functions of Courts: A Time Series Analysis of the Philippine Supreme Court,'' 27 *Law and Society Review* (1993), 707; C. N. Tate, ''The Judicialization of Politics in the Philippines and Southeast Asia,'' 15 *International Political Science Review* (1993), 183; C. N. Tate, ''Courts and Crisis Regimes: A Theory Sketch with Asian Case Studies,'' 46 *Political Research Quarterly* (1993), 311; C. N. Tate, ''Temerity and Timidity in the Exercise of Judicial Review in the Philippine Supreme Court,'' in: D. W. Jackson and C. N. Tate, eds., *Judicial Review and Public Policy in Comparative Perspective* (New York, 1992), 107.

15. The research that produced the data used in this chapter was funded by Fulbright-Hays Senior Research Fellowships to the Philippines under the auspices of the Philippine-American Educational Foundation (PAEF) and by a grant from the Law and Social Science and Political Science programs, National Science Foundation (NSF grant No. SES-8710051). The analyses presented here are those of the author and do not necessarily represent the views of PAEF or NSF.

16. In principle, one could conduct a similar test for Palma, despite the very high level of her support for the majority across her career. The problem, of course, is that her tenure (1973–1978) occurred entirely during the period of martial law dictatorship.

17. Including 1968, although Teehankee participated in only five cases that first year of his service.

Chapter 8

Legal Culture, Legal Professionals and the Future of Human Rights in China

ALBERT MELONE AND XIAOLIN WANG

INTRODUCTION

Human rights violations in China have attracted considerable attention and concern. The international community has placed demands upon the Chinese government to provide adequate protection in accordance with universally prescribed human rights standards.[1] Although a worthy subject of study, scholarly preoccupation with the litany of human rights violations may result in a failure to consider the underlying tensions inherent in contemporary Chinese legal culture. We maintain that assessing the future of human rights in China can be better understood by focusing instead upon the latent and, in some cases, the manifest conflict between the functionaries of the Chinese Communist Party and the fledgling new professional class of legal professionals. This focus requires an understanding of the relationship between Chinese political and legal history, the political and legal socialization of legal professionals and the problems and prospects associated with the creation of an independent judiciary.

   We postulate that human rights violations in China are associated with the lack of an independent judiciary. Understandably, to the extent that the judicial system is exclusively an instrument of the Communist Party, it is ill-suited to afford human rights protection. Yet there are signs that this hegemony is about to be challenged by a new and growing class of legal professionals. This tension within the present-day legal culture has come about because in the mid-1980s the government's ruling elite came to understand the political importance of creating the perception that China respects rule of law principles. Concurrently, Chinese leaders have promoted the development of the legal profession as a functional requirement for the achievement of both their domestic and interna-

tional goals. These objectives entail the creation of domestic enclaves of capi-
talist-style markets and the development of new international trading
opportunities. At the same time, political authorities seek to maintain their authoritarian and totalitarian control. Within this framework for change, Chinese
leaders hope to attain the status as a respectable member of the international
community. This significant development portends a changing role for the Chinese judiciary, and while not sufficient by itself, it is a necessary condition for
a switch in human rights policy.

China's human rights practices and judicial system bear common character-
istics with the former Leninist-oriented states of the East European bloc.[2] However, due to the country's unique culture and tradition, there are significant
differences worth noting. Consequently, it is appropriate to briefly review
China's legal history. A historical understanding is best achieved by employing
the conceptual framework offered by contemporary political scientist John R.
Schmidhauser.[3] He effectively employs the theoretical constructs of Max Weber
to describe and explain the historical movement away from traditional and charismatic legal cultures to objective/bureaucratic legal ideal types. It is the latter
ideal type that promotes and celebrates the creation and maintenance of an independent judicial system. In turn, an independent judiciary is associated with
both the development of a predictable capitalist economic order and the protection of human rights.

The Weberian perspective views law as a conflict resolution device and not
as an instrument in the hands of the powerful for their own use. According to
this paradigm, law grows from the recognition that subjective choices yield
unstable political orders. It is thought that law provides more or less objective
standards to settle disputes among competing parties.[4] Pre-Communist China
was not substantially different from Weber's traditional society. One owed obedience to individuals, whether to the emperor or warlords, and appeals to custom
and tradition made the law legitimate. Rulers in traditional societies enjoy a high
degree of discretion. Moreover, in such societies the predictability of rules governing economic relations is low. There is often little respect for precedent, and
each dispute receives particularistic and non-systemic treatment. Communist
China, particularly under Mao Zedong, resembled Weber's charismatic authority
system and differed from the traditional type in that law was made legitimate
by the particular charismatic leader. Further, outcomes in charismatic-ideal type
systems are often idiosyncratic and justified by some form of revelation. In
China's case, the word flowed from Mao, from his little *Red Book* and from the
authoritative interpretations of Mao's thoughts by members of his inner leadership circle. Finally, the administration of law under charismatic regimes is
often ad hoc and undifferentiated. The capricious practices employed by Mao
and his followers during the Cultural Revolution illustrate the point.

Weber's legal/bureaucratic authority system is significantly different from the
other ideal types. This type exhibits the characteristic of obedience to government sanctions according to enacted rules and regulations. Decision-making

standards are reportedly objective and universal. The law is made legitimate by appeals to *a priori* legal or constitutional standards, and the judicial process is ostensibly independent of outside influence. In apposition to the traditional and charismatic ideal types, in the ideal legal authority type system, judicial administration is highly bureaucratic or routinized. It employs well-trained legal professionals with limited jurisdiction, and their discretion is relatively low. Legal/bureaucratic systems, unlike the two other ideal types, afford considerable predictability of the rules governing economic life. Because law in such a system focuses on individual legal claims, the cause of human rights assumes greater importance than in either traditional or charismatic legal systems.

By officially depoliticizing dispute resolutions with the view of resolving them, to use Tocqueville's characterization of nineteenth-century America, "into judicial questions,"[5] legal professionals are in an ideal strategic position to give meaning to the law's content. This point is especially important because in contemporary China leaders hope to regularize property relations with international trading partners, while also introducing capitalist practices in a rapidly expanding economy that features both public and private sectors. Members of the new class of Chinese legal professionals are playing an important role in facilitating economic growth by applying business law rules that meet those expectations necessary to conduct commercial intercourse. But existing Party cadres represent a powerful counterforce that is in the position to maintain the old economic and political order. It is, nonetheless, axiomatic that for China a closed socialist economic system is no longer feasible. The future of China's economy is tied to its integration into the world's capitalist markets. Thus, because it is potentially the world's largest economy, as a practical matter China must operate within the rules of the global economy.

Schmidhauser points out that while it is crucial to understand how economic penetration affects the changing world order, the work of lawyers is central to the world capitalist economy. A major purpose of each national judicial system is the creation of conditions helpful to the operation of a capitalist world economy. In the new order, there is an expectation that legal professionals will be responsive to the needs of the capitalist world economy and that they are oriented toward providing legitimacy to the system. In an evolving capitalist order, therefore, legal professionals tend to place heavy emphasis upon the development of private property relations and the security of commercial intercourse. Importantly, the capitalist worldview supposes that the structure and purposes of the judicial system are to serve the requirements of the world capitalist order including, for example, an independent judiciary free from anti-capitalist influences. This requires that judges and lawyers have a cosmopolitan outlook that conditions their attitudes about law more in keeping with the needs of the world economy than with parochial national sentiments.[6]

Given Schmidhauser's conceptualization, legal protection for contractual and property relations is important. But so are human rights. After all, liberty values are consistent with the underlying assumptions of capitalist ideology. There are latent and sometimes manifest conflicts between the old Party cadres presently in control of the upper echelons of the Chinese judiciary and the new class of legal professionals now consigned to the lower reaches of the judicial hierarchy. The way these conflicts are finally resolved is crucial to the future disposition of both private property and human rights in China.

TRADITIONAL AND CHARISMATIC ELEMENTS

While historians fix the period of Imperial China with the Qin dynasty (221–207 B.C.), civilization in China can be traced as far back as 5,000 years ago. Indeed, pre-Qin political thought and practices have had a profound influence on the 2,000 years of Imperial China, and its impact continues to this day. Two major parallel thoughts of the pre-Qin era have had a continuing influence on the Chinese legal system and attitudes toward human rights that render the desire for an independent judiciary unnecessary and, indeed, dysfunctional. On one hand, the Chinese developed a political system emphasizing "Li Yi," or courtesy and righteousness among citizens. Courtesy and righteousness were largely derived from customs and moral standards collectively observed by Chinese ancestors. Those moral standards were viewed as necessary to maintain social harmony. Confucius summarized this view with the observation: "[C]ourtesy and righteousness come from the community, and accumulate into customs; justice is originated in courtesy and punishes those who stray away from custom."[7]

On the other hand, Daoism emphasized natural justice, or the way of the universe. The source of law transcends the community; both citizens and rulers should behave in accordance with the natural justice found in the universe. Any man-made law that violates natural justice is no law at all; there is only one law—it is the way of the universe, which cannot be altered or made by mere mortals. Accordingly, "making no rule is the best rule."[8] For the Daoists, government must exercise its power in conformity with natural justice, and its chief function is to maintain harmony between the rulers and the ruled, heaven and earth. Government officials must use their best judgment to govern people in accord with the "justice of nature or heaven," courtesy and righteousness. Because humans are born with heavenly blessed righteousness and justice is largely equated with that righteousness, there is no need for an independent judicial system. Instead, social stability and harmony are achieved through the self-regulating mechanism that is natural to humankind. Consequently, there is little need for externally imposed rules, with the notable exception that a good government or ruler should help citizens to live with sufficient material goods, including food and clothing.

Because Confucianism and Daoism proved incapable of dealing with the hardships brought about by continuous wars and famine during the Zhan Guo (the Nations of Wars) Period (403–221 B.C.), the so-called Legalists became a powerful intellectual force. The Legalists viewed human beings as born evil and incapable of self-regulation. Given this view of human nature, the Legalists believed that to resolve individual conflict and to maintain social stability there is a need for a highly institutionalized judicial system with a well-defined system of positive law.[9]

The Legalists achieved dominance after Emperor Yin Zheng (circa 207 B.C.) unified the nation, and with this a new Imperial China emerged. Zheng rejected Confucianism and Daoism and enacted a series of well-defined laws, giving the Chinese their first formal judicial system. Yet, in practice, the emperor behaved in a manner more consistent with the charismatic ideal type than Weber's legal/ bureaucratic model; the judicial system and law were abused by Yin Zheng to fulfill his personal desires. As a result, the Legalist experiment ended shortly after it began, leaving in its wake massive executions and human rights violations. It is little wonder, then, that the Chinese developed an abhorrence to "legalism." They quickly reverted to principles of Confucianism and Daoism, adopting a modified view of the emperor as the son of heaven and, thus, the legitimate articulator of natural justice.

During the next 2,000 years (206 B.C.–A.D.1911), positive laws were promulgated on an intermittent basis. Yet law played the ancillary role of perfecting or implementing Confucian and Daoist principles. These laws were criminal in character, and they were designed to punish the most severely immoral behavior as well as reprehensible conduct that was directed against the emperor. The concept of separation of powers was unknown. Judicial and executive powers were usually exercised by the same government functionary. There was only a limited body of positive law. Sanctions were employed only occasionally and then as a last resort for the most severe violations committed by the common man. It is widely conceded that the Confucian social-political-ethical system dominated Chinese thought and practice until the nineteenth century A.D. It was an effective social regulator throughout the Imperial Period. But in the nineteenth century the traditional political system was undermined by the combined effects of the general deterioration and corruption of the Imperial leadership, the Japanese invasion and the diffusion of foreign ideas.[10] During the nineteenth century, however, the Western conception of human rights was not an issue.

In 1911, the last Imperial Qing Dynasty came to an end, and the nationalists formed the Republic of China. Eager to re-establish social order, the nationalists realized that the Imperial legal system was inadequate to the task. Therefore, the nationalist government established a new judicial system, and they promulgated new laws that included (1) the Constitution, (2) the Civil Code, (3) the Criminal Code, (4) the Civil Procedure Law, (5) the Criminal Procedure Law and (6) the Administration Law. This "Six Law System," as it is known, was largely copied from the Western world, especially the civil law nations of France and Germany. Yet the traditional legal system founded upon Confucian thought would not be discarded altogether. Therefore, the new Chinese legal system combined both the spirit of Confucianism and continental European legal thought. However, with the outbreak of World War II and the continuing civil war between the nationalist government and their communist adversaries, the "Six Laws" and other legal reforms failed to have a significant impact on Chinese society. It might be argued, though, that the legal reforms of the nationalist government provided a foundation for the creation of democratic institutions and the modern legal system in Taiwan after the nationalists were finally defeated by the communists in 1949.

Prior to 1949, China failed to achieve, in Weberian terms, a legal/bureaucratic model of organization. Although the Chinese had several dramatic flirtations with such a system, Confucianism served as a strong counterweight to the permanent installation of such institutions. It is also clear that the tensions between the proponents and practitioners of the traditional, charismatic and legal/bureaucratic ideal types are best understood within the larger context of politics and the conflicting views about the proper role of judges as social controllers. The successful revolution led by Mao Zedong was but another chapter in that ongoing struggle.

CHARISMATIC LEADERSHIP AND THE SOCIALIST LEGAL SYSTEM

After the communists took control of China in 1949, Marxist-Leninist thought, as articulated by Mao Zedong, became the dominant ideology. Under Communist rule, the Chinese legal system passed through four stages of evolution: (1) formation and initial development, (2) destruction, (3) reestablishment and (4) "bottom-up" change.

The first stage, formation and initial development, covers sixteen years, from 1950 to 1965. During this period, new laws were enacted along with a revised basic court and prosecutorial system. The first Constitution was adopted in 1954. It prescribed certain rights such as the right to elect government officials and representatives and private property ownership. At the same time, the government launched a program of judicial transformation. It was designed to rectify and purify the peoples' judicial organs politically, organizationally and ideologically. Since the Chinese communists view themselves as the only true representatives of people, the "judicial transformation movement," as it was called at the time, resulted in a judiciary composed of Party members only. As is typical in the continental civil law tradition, members of the judiciary view themselves as part of the government administration and not as independent guardians of the Constitution. The plain words of the basic document made clear that the Constitution is the highest law in the land. Yet that same document states that the Peoples' Congress is the supreme organ of state power. Cooperation between Party and government personnel, including judges, render legal and Communist Party policies inseparable. When new policy conflicts with existing law, Party policy supersedes the law. Thus, for example, the 1954 Constitution proclaimed the existence of certain human rights. The view taken by the Communist Party, however, was that because the communist government is "duly authorized by the people," individual human rights are not needed in the "people's nation." Instead, as the unrefutable argument went, the responsibility of government is to exercise all rights collectively for the good of the entire Chinese people.

Although Mao Zedong rejected the broad outlines of Confucianism, he nonetheless embraced the traditional notion that the emperor was the embodiment of justice. This perspective was useful when justifying the central role of the Chairman himself in the exercise of unlimited Party and personal power. However, during the late 1950s and early 1960s, this power was challenged by Mao's "comrades" after the "Great Leap Forward" proved an unreasonable burden on the population. The government's financial resources were sapped by economic misfortune and mismanagement, including famine.[11] President Liu Shaoqi and other competing government leaders challenged Mao Zedong's personal power. They criticized Mao for failing to honor the Constitution and for his failure to develop a more systematic economic, political and judicial system. Mao responded by dubbing his opponents representatives of capitalist interests. In the face of this opposition, he proclaimed that the "class struggle" still exists. According to Mao, a "Cultural Revolution" was necessary to eliminate the "capitalist alter ego" then extant within the Party. It was necessary, according to Mao, to bring the practices of the Party in conformity with the precepts of communism.

The Cultural Revolution lasted from 1966 to 1976. It destroyed Mao's opposition and in the process seriously damaged the legal system. Government departments and judicial organs were obstructed, while the Constitution and laws were abolished or otherwise disabled. During the Cultural Revolution some 10 million people were unlawfully killed, and more than 20 million were arrested and imprisoned without trial. Functionaries in the newly established judicial system were powerless in the face of Mao's attacks. Judges, lawyers and law professors were among the first victims of the Cultural Revolution.[12]

After Mao's death in 1976, and the end of the Cultural Revolution, the Chinese government under the leadership of Deng Xiaopin commenced the reconstruction of the denigrated legal and economic systems. Deng set out to re-create a legal structure that would make it possible for China to re-enter the international economic market and to render improbable the recurrence of a second cultural revolution.[13]

Socialist System in the Reconstructed Age

In 1975 and 1978, the People's Congress revised China's 1954 Constitution. The revisions reflected China's continuing commitment to Mao's idea of "class struggling." But after Mao's death, the revised Constitution was ill-suited to meet the changes taking place in China's political, economic, cultural and social environments. Deng insisted it was time to end the period of class struggle. Thus, he set out to meet the needs of socialist modernization and to effectuate change in the legal system. To that end, the People's Congress adopted the current Constitution in 1982. Article 1 embodies the idea of one center (economic construction) and two basic points: (1) upholding the four cardinal principles[14] and (2) economic reform and open policy.

From 1976 to 1988, both the central and local governments enacted more than 11,400 laws, regulations and rules.[15] The government established a comprehensive judicial system. The courts consist of the Supreme Court (the nation's highest court), the Provincial Higher Courts, Middle Level Court and the Basic Level Court. There are also courts with special subject matter jurisdiction: maritime, railroad, military, traffic and forestry. As of December 31, 1991, there were 31 Provincial Higher Courts, 1 Military Higher Court, 377 Middle Level Courts, and 3,015 Basic Level Courts.[16]

The Basic Level Courts are trial courts with general jurisdiction. They consist of city, county and district courts that are divided into civil, criminal, economic, administrative and enforcement divisions.[17] These courts of first instance possess the authority to refer serious or very complicated cases to the next higher-level court. The Middle Level Courts operate in prefectures, autonomous regions and cities under central government control or large cities typically with a population of 1 million or more. These courts function as general jurisdiction appellate courts with discretionary original jurisdictions over disputes involving political questions, or significant economic matters or foreign affairs or persons. The Provincial Higher Courts function as an appellate court for cases coming from the Middle Level Courts. The panel is usually composed of three to five judges. The Provincial Higher Courts may also serve as trial courts in special cases that are referred to them by the Middle Level Courts or cases deemed to have a significant impact upon society. The Supreme Court is the highest court. It exercises general supervision over all courts and grants appellate review over Provincial and other Higher Courts. In very rare cases, the Supreme Court may hear special prosecutions brought by the Chief Procurator. There are about 90 judges in the Supreme Court, and each serves a maximum of two five-year terms. Parties to lawsuits have the right to one appeal, usually to the next higher court. Appellate court decisions are not limited to the narrow legal issues raised by the parties to the suit. The courts normally proceed de novo: They re-try both matters of fact and law. There is no formal system of judicial review wherein judges may strike down legislative or administrative acts as inconsistent with the Constitution

Judicial selection is ostensibly a matter of election. According to the Organic Law of the People's Courts of the People's Republic of China, judges shall be elected by the People's Congress.[18] However, the usual practice is that judges are nominated and appointed by their own courts or governmental units. While on rare occasion Congress has rejected nominees, the usual practice is that it rubber stamps the nominations approved by Party officials. Because Article 34 of the Constitution indicates that judges in the Basic and Middle Level Courts may be elected or appointed, there is no pretense that the selection process requires actual election. In no case are judges elected by ordinary citizens by way of an election ballot.

As a reaction to the excesses of the Cultural Revolution, human rights provisions were written into the 1982 Constitution. At the time, the leadership felt a need to avoid wholesale violations of human rights. Although minimum standards of food and clothing remain a high priority, the new Constitution reflects an acceptance of the view that the protection of human rights is also a fundamental goal of Chinese society. This understanding is the result of historical experience. It is manifest in the following provisions of the new Constitution[19]:

Article 35

Citizens of the People's Republic of China enjoy freedom of speech, of the press, of assembly, of association, of procession and of demonstration.

Article 36

Citizens of the People's Republic of China enjoy freedom of religious belief. No state organ, public organization or individual may compel citizens to believe in, or not to believe in, any religion; nor may they discriminate against citizens who believe in, or do not believe in, any religion. The state protects normal religious activities. No one may make use of religion to engage in activities that disrupt public order, impair the health of citizens or interfere with the educational system of the state. Religious bodies and religious affairs are not subject to any foreign domination.

Article 37

The freedom of person of citizens of the People's Republic of China is inviolable. No citizen may be arrested except with the approval or by decision of a people's procuratorate or by decision of a people's court, and arrests must be made by a public security organ. Unlawful deprivation or restriction of citizens' freedom of person by detention or other means is prohibited; and unlawful search of the person of citizens is prohibited.

Article 38

The personal dignity of citizens of the People's Republic of China is inviolable. Insult, libel, false charge or frame-up directed against citizens by any means is prohibited.

Article 39

The home of citizens of the People's Republic of China is inviolable. Unlawful search of, or intrusion into, a citizen's home is prohibited.

Article 40

The freedom and privacy of correspondence of citizens of the People's Republic of China are protected by law. No organization or individual may, on any ground, infringe upon the freedom and privacy of citizens' correspondence except in cases where, to meet the needs of state security or of investigation into criminal offenses, public security or procuratorial organs are permitted to censor correspondence in accordance with procedures prescribed by law.

Article 41

Citizens of the People's Republic of China have the right to criticize and make suggestions to any state organ or functionary. Citizens have the right to make to relevant state organs complaints and charges against, or exposures of, violation of the law or dereliction of duty by any state organ or functionary; but fabrication or distortion of facts with the intention of libel or frame-up is prohibited. In case of complaints, charges or exposures made by citizens, the state organ concerned must deal with them in a responsible manner after ascertaining the facts. No one may suppress such complaints, charges and exposures, or retaliate against the citizens making them. Citizens who have suffered losses through infringement of their civil rights by any state organ or functionary have the right to compensation in accordance with the law.

Clearly, the 1982 Constitution and certain statutory enactments formally limit the authority of the Chinese Communist Party. That is, Party policy and administrative regulations are no longer viewed as superior to law. The Communist Party must now either seek legislative authority to override objectionable laws, or, alternatively, they must more skillfully draft policy to get around the law. For several reasons, however, the Party still reserves considerable discretion in the implementation and enforcement of laws that are inconsistent with protecting human rights. According to the U.S. State Department:

[F]undamental human rights provided for in the Chinese Constitution frequently are ignored in practice, and challenges to the Communist Party's political authority are often dealt with harshly and arbitrarily. China took some positive but limited steps in human rights areas, including releasing prominent political prisoners. Hundreds, perhaps thousands, of political prisoners, however, remained under detention or in prison. Reports of physical abuse persisted, including torture by police and prison officials.[20]

While the Constitution explicitly protects human rights, in practice these rights are nonetheless abused. A major cause for this state of affairs is that there is insufficient independent judicial power to effectively constrain the will of the Communist Party. This is true despite the creation of judicial bodies with the ostensible authority to protect human rights. The 1982 Constitution restores the provision in the 1954 Constitution governing procurate and people's courts. Article 126 prescribes that "the people's courts shall, in accordance with the law, exercise judicial power independently, and that the judiciary is not subject to interference by administrative organs, public organizations or individuals." The Supreme Court is the highest judicial organ (Article 127). It is responsible only to the National People's Congress (Article 128). Yet the present system fails to provide mechanisms to guarantee a genuinely independent judiciary. Even without the explicit power of judicial review, an independent judiciary, as in England, may nonetheless interpret statutes and administrative actions in ways that are consistent with constitutional principles. In China, however, there are institutional factors militating against such tangible manifestations of judicial independence.

There is no life tenure for judges, and the Communist Party closely supervises their work. The personnel records of judicial officials are carefully scrutinized by the Party's personnel office/department. This office exercises the Party's disciplinary power over those judges who are Party members, and because, until recently, most judges were members of the Party, control by Party officials was nearly complete. Party members are required to take an oath subscribing to the Party's cardinal regulations, vowing that they must place the Party's interests above all other personal or political considerations. If the Party's personnel office/department decides that a member is in violation of those regulations, officers may discipline the person and even dismiss that person from the Communist Party—a very serious disciplinary punishment that has the practical effect to render the sanctioned person "unfit" for any government or public service. In 1985, 95 percent of judges were also members of the Communist Party.[21] Clearly, then, the ability of judges to exercise judicial independence is strictly limited by the terms of Party membership. Today, however, many young judges are refusing to join the Communist Party, viewing the Party oath as conflicting with their desire to uphold the law. But for those seeking a quick ascension to the highest courts, Party membership nonetheless remains a necessary requirement.

There is a Communist Party secretary in every court who usually serves simultaneously as the court's president or vice president. If a conflict should arise between the law and the Party's interests, or even a Party leader's personal interest, Party-member judges are faced with the task of balancing the law against their personal interest. Basically, cross-pressured judges must ponder the following question: If they decide the case against the Party leader's interest, will they be assigned to another court perhaps in a different location and in less comfortable surroundings? In short, if they make the wrong decision, they could fall out of favor with the Party. They may be forced to leave the bench and become, for example, a marriage registrar or some other less-than-glamorous functionary. In brief, the ability of Communist Party officials to re-assign judges from one court to another renders the Article 126 proclamation of an "independent" judicial system an inaccurate description of life on the bench.

There is also a failure of professional socialization that contributes to the problematic nature of judicial independence in China. Until recently, present and prospective legal professionals have not been exposed to views supportive of judicial independence. There have been no socializing agents to inculcate the concept of a law-governed state as opposed to rule by the Communist Party. In the first place, judges traditionally view themselves as part of the bureaucracy and not independent from it. The communist legal system reinforces this traditional perception, and the Chinese people have in the past viewed law neither as a high-status occupation nor as an independent profession. Therefore, it is usually unnecessary for Communist Party leaders to pick up the phone to suggest to judges what might be a favorable disposition in a case before them. Judicial personnel already know how to proceed. Indeed, the overlap between membership in the Communist Party and a seat on the bench reinforces role expectations.

Second, before the Cultural Revolution there were few law schools, and these institutions trained only a small number of professional judges and lawyers. During the Cultural Revolution many formally trained judges, lawyers and law professors lost their lives. Those who survived the Cultural Revolution often spent more than ten years in collective farms where they were "re-educated." During this period, few legal professionals had an opportunity to maintain their legal skills. Yet after the Cultural Revolution those few legal professionals who had survived were assigned the task of re-establishing the law schools that were closed during the previous period. As a practical matter, between the end of the Cultural Revolution in 1976 and 1982 when the law schools were re-opened, all of the judges in the People's Courts were either Party members, retired military personnel or other government officials with little or no legal training. Further, judicial salaries were then, and remain even today, very low. This fact discourages capable persons from pursuing a legal career.

One result of the dearth of legally trained personnel is a judiciary that depends upon Party ideology for guidance when making decisions. Predicating judicial decisions upon a body of pre-existing objective principles and rules is therefore a difficult, if not impossible, task. However, in the 1980s laws were promulgated based upon legal principles independent of Party doctrine. These include the Constitution, 1982; the Criminal Law, 1980; the Criminal Procedure Law, 1980; the Civil Law, 1986; and the Civil Procedure Law, 1982. Before the enactment of these laws, there was no legal standard for judges to apply. Moreover, by the end of 1986, out of more than 30,000 Chinese judges who had no formal legal training, about 10,000 of them received from six months to one year of legal training for the first time in their careers.[22]

Even without the benefit of survey data, it is safe to conclude that the Chinese people are substantially unaware of their legally protected rights. General ignorance among the people contributes to the continuing dominance of the Communist Party over the judiciary. Further, despite a modern Constitution with legally defined citizen rights, the cultural milieu remains one that eschews conflict in favor of harmony and mediation. Social stigma still attaches to those who attempt to resolve their conflicts in courtrooms rather than in private or mediation settings. Thus, many citizens ignore the law. They are either unaware of their legally protected rights, or they are unwilling to seek judicial remedies. Then, too, there is little doubt that many Chinese see little distinction between judges and other bureaucrats: both represent the state and both, therefore, should be avoided whenever possible. This situation is made even more extreme by the fact that until recently the government did not permit the private practice of law. Consequently, citizens have a tendency to view all legal professionals as government employees. They believe, as experience teaches, that if one piece of the government apparatus is against them, then the whole system, including the judiciary, can be counted upon to defeat their individual claims.

PRESENT TENSIONS IN THE CHINESE JUDICIARY

Legal change is not necessarily dependent upon mass opinion. At times, folkways may follow stateways. When elites within a society seek change, they tend to employ tactics that best suit their own objectives. But the government sought ways to muzzle ideological heresy. Within institutions of higher education during the late 1980s, Chinese intellectuals hotly debated communist and Western ideologies. When prosecuted for their offenses, intellectuals defended themselves, albeit unsuccessfully, by citing the 1982 Constitution and particularly Article 35—the freedom of speech clause. The demonstrations that took place in Tiananmen Square in 1989 featured constitutional slogans that included: "We will die for our Constitution and law!" Thousands of students were unlawfully arrested and placed in jail without trial. These events caused the international community to take notice of human rights violations in China.

Today, the international community is still working to secure the freedom of Chinese political dissidents. The 1989 events in Tiananmen Square were a consciousness-raising experience for persons in China and abroad. Nonetheless, economic factors may be even more telling as an explanation for significant changes in the judicial system since 1992. Controversies arising from commercial transactions, foreign subsidiaries and joint ventures are placing a huge burden on the judiciary. The longtime Party-oriented judges can no longer rely on their knowledge of communist doctrine to guide their decision making. New thinking is required to meet the challenge of China's new role in the global economy. Given this imperative, professional judges with formal legal training are necessary to foster and protect economic reform and ultimately attract foreign investments. An additional consequence of international trade is the diffusion of ideas from other places. Among these ideas is an awareness of the rights and privileges enjoyed by citizens in other countries.

In November 1985, the Resolution on Disseminating Legal Knowledge among Residents was adopted at the 13th Session of the Sixth National People's Congress Standing Committee. The goal of this program was to educate Chinese citizens in legal subjects with the expectation that the traditional Chinese system of self-regulation would become more effective if citizens also had some knowledge of the positive law. Because law was not viewed as a sophisticated profession, government officials believed that a nationwide campaign to spread legal knowledge presented no insurmountable hurdles. To that end, the state provided free introductory law classes in the following subjects: the Constitution, the Criminal Law, the Criminal Procedure Law, the General Principle of Civil law, the Civil Procedure Law, the Marriage Law, the Inheritance Law, the Economic Contract Law, the Military Service Law and the Regulation of Public Security. Government officials at all levels were required to attend law classes.

The legal education campaign was remarkably successful within its first two years (1986–1987). There was a serious effort to educate cadre members (those government officials who hold important positions and have the power to make decisions in their respective spheres of authority). The number of these leading government officials at the provincial level who had participated in a course of legal study was nearly 1,200, or 94 percent of all cadre members. At the city level, over 20,000, or 95 percent of the entire cadre, attended learning sessions. At the county level, 450,000 leading cadre operatives and 6.5 million officials attended law classes.[23] In state-owned enterprises, about 73 percent of the workers and staff members participated in legal education exercises. In rural areas, 30 percent of that population were afforded the opportunity to learn the basics of the law system.[24] Moreover, various cadre schools and television correspondence programs were created to provide legal courses. About 85 percent of the nation's colleges and universities also provide basic law courses to their students. All judicial officials who had no formal legal training were required to attend "on-the-job training" in special law programs designed for judges and procurators.[25]

It is difficult to assess whether the legal training sessions actually increased the professional competence of judicial officials. Nonetheless, it is safe to conclude that the legal education campaign strengthened the awareness of citizens and government officials about law. As a by-product of this activity, participants in the learning exercises also had the opportunity to discover that the Communist Party is not the only possible source of norm creation and rule interpretation. Further, the education program had the unintended consequence of preparing citizens to challenge their government and law enforcement officials in court. Most significantly, since the mid-1980s there is a growing number of students who have chosen law as their vocation. They work in the people's court, usually at the District and Middle Level Courts, and, since 1991, in private practice law firms. Their formal legal training enables them to ascend to the bench quickly.

Table 8.1 demonstrates that between 1986 and 1993 the number of accepted applications to law school increased 605 percent. The number of law students during this same period increased by 399 percent, and the number of students actually graduating from law school increased 421 percent. The dramatic increase in law school attendance and graduates clearly meets a necessary condition for changing the personnel at the bench and bar.

Moreover, as Table 8.2 indicates, the total number of lawyers in China has risen from 14,500 in 1986 to 68,834 in 1993. This represents a 375 percent increase in the number of legal professionals in China. Most lawyers, however, practice in the public sector. But there has been a dramatic increase in the number of lawyers who practice in the private sector. The number of private practice attorneys before 1991 is unknown, but it is presumed to be negligible. Since 1991, the number of private practice law firms has increased from 73 to 505, an increase of 591 percent.

Until very recently, the private practice of law was not a professional option

Table 8.1
Law School Attendance and Graduation

Year	Students in School	Accepted Students	Graduates
1993	51,622	19,603	10,695
1990	41,634	11,675	12,094
1988	11,609	3,525	3,696
1986	10,349	2,782	2,052
Percentage Increase	399%	605%	421%

Source: Chinese Department of Education, 1995.

for Chinese lawyers. Thus, the lure of personal financial gain has not been a major motivating factor to enter the legal profession. Although our evidence is mostly anecdotal, there is reason to believe that persons who have recently entered the legal profession had a clear and, to some extent, naive idea when they entered law school: That is, they wanted to uphold the law and to do justice.

Significantly, many contemporary law students have personal histories wherein family relatives or close family friends were abused during the Cultural Revolution. The results of one survey confirm what is commonly understood in China. This study conducted during a law school orientation at Xiangtan University, Department of Law, in September 1985, found that 102 out of 110 students said they enrolled in law school because they wanted to be able to work against the injustices and abuses that occurred to their families and friends during the Cultural Revolution. During the subsequent four years of study, these students receive careful instruction in the history of the Chinese Communist Party, Marxism-Leninism and the thought of Chairman Mao. But their pre-professional socialization may be operating to orient them toward remedying injustices. Furthermore, part of the four-year curriculum includes courses in Western legal history and thought.[26] Many students are exposed to Locke, Hobbes and Montesquieu, and they take such courses as Roman Law, Napoleon's Civil Code and Comparative Constitutions as well as courses in communist legal history. In sum, the combined effects of pre–law school socialization and the exposure to Western legal thought and government systems may be producing a generation of judges and lawyers with perspectives different from their older colleagues.

Because the new generation of judges is relatively young and inexperienced, they do not hold positions at the upper reaches of the judicial hierarchy. Yet their different ideology can be manifested in a variety of case situations. Where, for example, Party members had enjoyed prestige and power in almost every matter, the new generation of judges often expresses disagreement, especially in civil cases where the government and the Party exercise less control. For

Table 8.2
Lawyers and Law Firms

Year	Total Lawyers	Total Firms	Private Firms
1993	68,834	5,129	505
1992	48,094	4,176	198
1991	41,956	3,706	73
1990	38,769	3,653	n/a
1988	23,274	3,473	n/a
1987	18,308	3,291	n/a
1986	14,500	3,198	n/a
Percentage Increase	375%	60%	591%

Source: Chinese Department of Justice, 1995.

example, in one case a Party official who held a significantly higher rank than the judge was the defendant. The Party official had taken by adverse possession the plaintiff's dwelling house before the statute of limitations had expired, and the court entered a judgment for the plaintiff, an ordinary citizen. The defendant refused to move out and challenged the judge by saying: "I fought all the way from the North to here for the Party. Who gives you the power to order me? Is there still a Communist leadership?" The young judge replied: "The Constitution gives me the power. I respect you as a Party member but the Constitution[27] does not give you any privilege over other citizens before the law."[28]

Such independent judicial conduct is not unusual. Even in criminal cases, young judges often reach different opinions from the old judges and prosecutors. In the past it was not uncommon for a prosecutor to walk into a judge's office and tell the judge how a case should be processed and decided. That is no longer true. For example, in a 1987 criminal trial in Hunan province, defense lawyers raised an objection to the prosecutor's referring to the defendant as a *criminal*, although it had been customary to do so in Chinese criminal trials. The appellate judge, a graduate from Wuhan University Law School, Class of 1984, sustained the objection. The prosecutor later complained to the higher court that the people's procurators had referred to criminal defendants as criminals for many years, and as a matter of fact, the trial process almost always convicts defendants. Therefore, there is sufficient reason to continue to call such defendants, *criminals*. In responding to the higher court's inquiry, the judge in the original case who had sustained the defendant's objection explained at length the principles of "presumption of innocence" and "due process," concepts fundamentally rooted in the Western legal tradition system. They are known to contemporary Chinese law students who have studied comparative law but are, nonetheless, foreign to judges and prosecutors trained in the discredited methods of a former era.[29]

The constitutional building block for the development of a civil society is the protection of freedom of association found in Article 35. In recent years, members of the new generation of legal professionals have been involved in such cases. The Constitution grants citizens the right to associate freely, but no statutory law exists to protect freedom of association.[30] Some jurists have sought to construct an Article 35 constitutional defense to the statutory crime of "counter-revolutionary" associations or activities. It is argued that prosecutions under such laws render the Article 35 protection meaningless, and therefore, those criminal laws limiting freedom of association and activity ought to be declared unconstitutional.[31]

In 1987, a worker, Zhang Ning, organized a group of his coworkers to complain to their employer, a state-owned manufacturer, for its unfairness in housing assignments. They threatened a street demonstration. Zhang and his fellows were soon arrested and prosecuted as "organizing a counter-revolutionary organization" under Article 98 of the Criminal Law. Defense attorney Yuanzhang Wang, who was then a law professor, successfully challenged the prosecution on the ground that it violated Article 35 of the 1982 Constitution.[32]

Similar challenges have been raised by other attorneys, but their Article 35 arguments have not prevailed. Obviously, the constitutional provision is sufficiently vague to permit decisions on both sides of the issue. Indeed, when many of these cases are appealed to the higher courts, the older Party-oriented judges tend to support the government to the detriment of the freedom of association claimants. In a similar 1988 case in Ze Jiang province, the provincial Supreme Court rejected such a defense based upon Article 51 of the Constitution.[33] This Court then concluded on the basis of a 1955 Supreme Court opinion that "in criminal cases, [the Constitution] does not prescribe what kind of conduct amounts to crime, therefore, . . . it is improper to use the Constitution in a criminal case."[34]

But in February 1997 the People's Congress enacted a significant change in the criminal law. Effectively changing the anti-libertarian rule, Congress has replaced the crime of "counter-revolution" with the crime of "harm to the nation's security." Accordingly, all provisions related to "counter-revolution" have been removed.[35]

Although not as dramatic as the change in the counter-revolution law, in 1989 the People's Congress promulgated a significant change in administrative procedures. In sharp contrast to the infamous Tiananmen Square crackdown on June 4, 1989, is the enactment of the Administrative Procedure Law of the People's Republic of China on April 4 of that same year. The statute is designed to deter government corruption and to provide further protection for Chinese citizens against government abuse. Article 3 of this act prescribes the establishment of the Administration Division in the people's court. It also restates the principle of independent judicial power that is ostensibly prescribed in Article

Table 8.3
Cases Filed in Trial Courts and Appellate Courts, 1987–1993

Year	Civil-1 Trial	Civil-2 App.	Crime 1 Trial	Crime 2 App.	Econ 1 Trial	Econ 2 App.	Adms-1 Trial	Adms-2 App.
1993	2,089,275	114,997	403,267	46,947	894,410	46,038	27,911	7,426
1991	1,880,635	125,096	427,840	55,484	563,260	42,931	25,667	6,930
1990	1,851,897	116,362	459,656	57,930	588,143	35,103	13,006	3,431
1988	1,455,130	90,430	313,306	46,432	513,615	21,442	8,573	2,356
1987	1,213,219	78,382	289,614	49,793	367,156	17,483	n/a	n/a
% Inc.	72%	47%	39%	–5.7%	144%	163%	226%	215%

Source: Chinese Department of Justice, 1995.

126 of the Constitution: ''[T]he people's court shall exercise independent judicial power over administrative cases and is not subject to interference by administrative organs, public organizations or individuals.'' Article 11 of the act defines the subject matter jurisdiction of the administrative division of the People's Court. It includes the classic human rights protection against unlawful detention of citizens (Subsection 2) and invasion of an individual's person or property (Subsection 8).

As can be seen in Table 8.3, when the Administrative Procedure Law was first enacted, there were only 8,573 cases filed. In 1993, the number of cases filed increased to 27,911, or a 226 percent increase.[36] Although current data are not presently available to assess the number of cases arising under the Administrative Procedure Law, an appellate judge in Changsha Middle Level People's Court said in an interview: ''[T]he number of complaints filed in the court is growing rapidly year after year. . . . If they [citizens] are unhappy with whatever the government has done to them, they [citizens] come to the court . . . but we are not the administration organ, we have to turn down a large portion of complaints if there are other avenues [for the plaintiffs]. Even so, cases are still piled up.''[37]

In other substantive areas of the law, the number of cases filed by litigants is increasing as well. As we might expect given the emphasis upon reforming the economy to provide for greater capitalism in China, economic rights and the related field of civil litigation are experiencing an explosion in the number of cases coming before the courts. The criminal docket is substantially less busy. Between 1987 and 1993, the rate of civil litigation has increased for trials at a rate of 72 percent, whereas filings for appellate review of those cases has increased 47 percent. Filings for economic cases at the trial level have increased 144 percent during this six-year period, and appellate filings for economic cases have increased 163 percent.

During the same period, the number of filings for criminal trials has increased modestly, whereas criminal appeals have actually decreased by 5.7 percent. The criminal dockets have fluctuated for two interrelated reasons. First, since 1987, political crimes have gone down, while economic crimes have risen. But with the growth of capitalist institutions come attendant negative consequences. In China, as is also the case for the former Soviet bloc countries of Eastern Europe, there are increases in fraud and other white-collar crimes, prostitution and drug trafficking. Further, the significant increases in both criminal trial and criminal appellate cases between 1988 and 1991 are attributable to cases arising out of the 1989 events in Tiananmen Square. There were many criminal prosecutions throughout China in an attempt by political authorities to reassert their control and to teach dissidents a lesson. But since 1991 the number of criminal cases has dropped, reflecting the attrition, but not the end, of Tiananmen-related prosecutions. Yet due to increases in economic-related offenses, the overall number of criminal trial cases was 39 percent higher in 1993 than in 1987.

There is cause for guarded optimism concerning the potential for protecting human rights in China. There is a growing professionalism within the judiciary. The Chinese government has enacted legislation supportive of human rights. And the legal profession is growing and changing rapidly, attracting many bright persons interested in human rights questions. Yet this happy conclusion should not be over-stated. Particularly in cases involving nationally or internationally notable political dissidents, the law school–trained judges are usually in a relatively weak political position to exercise their discretion in support of human rights. The case of the trial of Wei Jingshen[38] is a good example. Deng Xiaoping,[39] then a retired "ordinary Party member," made it clear in a speech to Party cadres that "we will not release him."[40] It is difficult to imagine that any trial judge could do anything but convict the defendant. Also, note that many young liberally oriented judges simply do not have an opportunity to hear important government cases. The Provincial Supreme Courts and the State Supreme Court are the courts most likely to exercise jurisdiction or control over controversial human rights cases. Judges on these courts are typically members of the Party elite and not recent law school graduates. Therefore, it is too much to expect recent law school graduates to decide cases inconsistent with the will of the Party. Moreover, recent law school graduates are usually assigned to the lower-level courts, such as District and Middle Level Courts. When law graduates seek appointments to the more important Provincial Supreme Courts, they often become clerks, where they remain for many years. Meanwhile, their law school classmates have successfully become judges on a lower court. There are several reasons for this career pattern.

First, the caseload at the District and Middle Level Courts is often heavy. The relatively heavy workload obviously presents the need for more judges at the lower levels of the judicial system. Consequently, there are greater opportunities for recent law school graduates at these lower levels. Because these lower courts are relatively low in prestige and power, the government dominated by the Communist Party does not view the younger legal professionals as a significant threat. Indeed, the Party leadership knows that the young legal professionals are needed to modernize China and to cope with pressing legal problems.

Second, Party leaders keep a careful eye on the more politically important upper reaches of the judiciary. They ensure that only those persons exhibiting ideologically correct views hold positions at the upper reaches of the bench. It is difficult, therefore, for young and less experienced law school graduates without the correct ideological credentials to be promoted up the judicial hierarchy.

An innovation in the available styles of legal practice is a third factor affecting the judicial system and the future of human rights in China. The recent privatization of business enterprises and provisions for a market economy that began in 1991 have made the private practice of law possible. One consequence is that not all Chinese lawyers are government employees.

Perhaps private practice lawyers possess a higher level of professional competency and self-confidence than many of their colleagues in government service. To become private attorneys they must give up the security of their guaranteed government salary. Significantly, because they are not employed by the state, private practice lawyers experience less interference from the government and the Communist Party. Furthermore, the reputation and financial well-being of these private practice attorneys are directly dependent upon serving the interests of their clients. For these reasons, private lawyers have a blossoming reputation for aggressive courtroom behavior.

A few judges in the People's Court of the Western District of Changsha claim that without looking at that part of the written record that indicates the name of the attorney representing the clients, they can usually discern which litigants are represented by a private attorney. In such cases, the written record is better prepared, and the arguments contained in those records exhibit high professional standards.

Moreover, because private practice is professionally attractive and financially lucrative, some judges have left the bench to become private practice attorneys. One example is Tao Da Jun, who left his job as a judge in a District Court to become a private attorney. In an interview he explained that a judge is sometimes asked to sacrifice the integrity of the law to political pressure. This is too much to ask a person who has devoted years of his life to legal education. It is also too much to suffer the indignity of a low monthly salary of about 300 yuan (equal to about U.S. $40). A judge may behave dishonorably by accepting bribes, but Tao said, ''[I]f I cannot uphold the law, then at least I did not want to violate it.'' Thus, he explained that he was happy to enter private practice and that ''I not only make a nice living now, but also, I gain respect by doing my best for my clients.''[41]

Tao's statement reflects the views of many others who have left the bench to engage in private law practice. It is also true that former judges also possess a unique advantage over other private practice lawyers. By virtue of once being a judge, they not only know the law, but they also know the complexities of court management. This advantage, combined with their legal expertise, is easily converted into monetary rewards.

Between 1991 and 1996, judicial salaries tripled. This increase reflects both inflationary pressures and an awareness on the part of the government that the private market for lawyers is great and that in order to create a bench that is professionally qualified there is a genuine need for the government to offer more competitive salaries. But what might be offered in the form of remuneration for public service cannot compete with the kind of financial gain private law firms are willing to offer. The result is that increasing numbers of judges are lured off the bench to take positions as private practice lawyers. Not surprisingly, recent law school graduates are now turning to private law practice as their initial career step.

CONCLUSION

From a human rights perspective, recent changes in the Chinese judicial system seem promising. These changes may provide better legal services and greater legal protection for the Chinese people. These developments represent a trend toward a legal system that better resembles the rational legal/bureaucratic model as understood by Max Weber. It represents significant movement away from the practices inherent in traditional and charismatic systems common to centuries of Chinese legal culture.

In democratic polities, legal professionals often act as articulate spokespersons for various causes that celebrate the "rule of law, not the rule of men." This commitment to a law-governed state may manifest itself in several ways, including the manner in which judges should be selected to the bench and support for the judiciary when it comes under attack from other government institutions, politicians and the public or when forces from whatever quarter challenge or discard constitutional and ordinary legal norms. In this respect, the recent changes in China's judicial system and legal profession are striking. Clearly, the manner in which lawyers play their strategic role in society is becoming a matter of political significance.

China's 1982 Constitution contains provisions that are protective of human rights. Moreover, statutory law, most particularly the Administrative Procedure Law, represents an important step toward limiting the discretionary authority of Party functionaries—political authorities historically accustomed to denying citizens the exercise of their human rights.

Developments in the legal profession are particularly significant because they create the conditions for at least a gradual infusion of rule of law ideas into Chinese political culture. For lawyers, it is both a matter of immediate self-interest and professional dogma that legalism as an ideology is thought central to a good polity. From this perspective, it is vitally important that political actors accept and play by the constitutional rules of the game. But, significantly, legal professionals are the interpreters of the rules, no matter which side of particular controversies may happen to win the day. Herein lies the potentially striking yet, to date, unrealized influence of the Chinese legal profession.

The belief that legal rules are superior to the twists and turns of Party ideology or the caprice of emperors and warlords is at the center of efforts to move China from its traditional and charismatic past to a legal system that is principle centered. Movement toward a law-governed state is possible because the political leadership in China has on its agenda competition in a global world economy. They seek to make the nation of 1.3 billion people a central player in the developing world drama.

The belief that the law is a set of objective rules applied to particular disputants in a more or less neutral way is preferable to the highly subjective desires of a Party elite. It matters little that legalism itself is part of a myth that seriously confuses normative prescriptions for factual descriptions. What is important is that—as an alternative to the old totalitarian ways—a new legalism for China may serve as an ideology that could move it toward greater observance of human rights and democratic values.

NOTES

1. U.S. Department of State, *1993 Human Rights Report* (Washington, DC, 1994).

2. A. P. Melone, "The Struggle for Judicial Independence and the Transition toward Democracy in Bulgaria," 29 *Communist and Post-Communist Studies* (1996), 231.

3. J. R. Schmidhauser, "Alternative Conceptual Frameworks in Comparative Cross-National Legal and Judicial Research," in: J. R. Schmidhauser, *Comparative Judicial Systems: Challenging Frontiers in Conceptual and Empirical Analysis* (London, 1987), 34.

4. *Id.* at 35.

5. A. de Tocqueville, *Democracy in America* (New York, 1945), 280.

6. Schmidhauser, *supra* note 3 at 48.

7. See Y. Wang, *History of Chinese Legal Systems and Thoughts* (Changsha, 1988).

8. *Id.*

9. *Id.* at 357.

10. M. A. Civic, "A Comparative Analysis of International and Human Rights Law—Universality versus Cultural Relativism," 2 *Buffalo Journal of International Law* (1996), 285.

11. It is estimated that some 3 million Chinese died of starvation and famine after the "Great Leap Forward"; see *The History of the Chinese Communist Party* (Beijing, 1987). In Chinese language.

12. C. Bin, *The Ten Years of Disaster* (Shi Jia Zhuan, 1987). In Chinese language.

13. J. W. Dellapenna, "The Rule of Legal Rhetoric in the Failure of Democratic Change in China," 2 *Buffalo Journal of International Law* (1996), 231.

14. The leadership of the Communist Party; the socialist system; the people's democratic dictatorship; Marxism-Leninism and Mao Zedong thought. Const. of People's Republic of China, art. 1 (1982).

15. *China: Changes in 40 Years* (Shijiazhung, 1989).

16. Personnel Department, the People's Supreme Court, 1992. The statistics of Middle

Level Courts and Basic Level Courts include Courts with special subject matter jurisdiction at their respective levels.

17. The Basic Level Courts were traditionally divided into criminal and civil divisions. The economic and administrative divisions were products of economic reform and the enactment of Administrative Procedural Law.

18. See Article 35.

19. *The Constitution of the People's Republic of China—The Official English Version* (Beijing, 1982).

20. U.S. Department of State, "Overview," *1993 Human Rights Report* (Washington, DC, 1994). On Internet.

21. *The Development of a Socialist Legal System* (Fuzhou, 1987), 103–107. In Chinese language.

22. Chinese Department of Justice, 1986 Statistics.

23. In the Chinese government hierarchy, city level is higher than a county level.

24. National Statistics Bureau, 1988.

25. Chinese procuracy has no direct analog in a common law system. It is established as the state organs of legal supervision that exercise power to supervise the socialist legality by all ministries, government agencies, enterprises, social organizations and government officials.

26. In China, law school consists of four years of education, and the graduates receive a bachelor's degree in law.

27. "All citizens of the People's Republic of China are equal before the law." Const. of the People's Republic of China, art. 33 (1982).

28. Yang Shan Yen v. Zhang Zhong Guan, W. Dist. Ct. (Changsha, 1990).

29. People v. Wang, Doc. No.: (1987) Tan Xin Zhi ———.

30. G. Luoji, "Human Rights Critique of the Chinese Legal System," 9 *Harvard Human Rights Journal* (1996), 1.

31. *Criminal Law, Collection of the Law of the People's Republic of China* (Changchun, 1990). In Chinese language.

32. People v. Zhang Ning, Tan Zhong Zhi 870014 (1987).

33. "The exercise by the citizens of the People's Republic of China of their freedoms and rights may not infringe upon the interests of the state, of society and of the collective, or upon the lawful freedom and rights of the other citizens." Const. of the People's Republic of China, art. 51 (1982).

34. In re Xiang Jiang Higher People's Court: "Constitution shall not be cited as a base for criminal conviction and sentencing." The People's Supreme Court, July 30, 1955. From Department of Justice, *Laws, Regulations, and Policy, Lawyer Edition* (Beijing, 1989).

35. *Xinhua News*, Feb. 19, 1997. In Chinese language.

36. The Research Office, People's Supreme Court, 1994.

37. Telephone interview on Dec. 20, 1996.

38. Wei Jingshen is one of the most famous leaders of Chinese political dissidents.

39. Deng Xiaoping (1904–1997) was the pragmatist of China's Economical and Social Reform. He served as the General Secretary of the Chinese Communist Party and as vice premier. In 1980, he became the paramount leader, and his last official position before retirement was chairman of the Chinese Central Military Committee.

40. Luoji, *supra* note 30.

41. Telephone interview of Tao Da Jun of Changsha, China, with Xiaolin Wang of Carbondale, IL, on or about Dec. 20–25, 1996.

Part V

The Protection of Indigenous Rights: The Australian Example

Chapter 9

"Retreat from Injustice": The High Court of Australia and Native Title

GARTH NETTHEIM

The theme for this chapter is indicated by a noteworthy passage from Sir William Deane (now Governor-General of Australia) when he was a Justice of the High Court of Australia, the nation's highest court:

It would seem that the Aboriginal people had inhabited this country for at least forty millenniums before the arrival of the first white settlers less than 200 years ago. To the extent that one can generalize, their society was not institutionalized and drew no clear distinction between the spiritual and the temporal. The core of existence was the relationship with and the responsibility for their homelands which neither individual nor clan "owned" in a European sense but which provided identity of both in a way which the European settlers did not trouble to comprehend and which the imposed law, based on an assertion of *terra nullius*, failed completely to acknowledge, let alone protect. The almost two centuries that have elapsed since white settlement have seen the extinction of some Aboriginal clans and the dispersal, with consequent loss of identity and tradition, of others. Particularly where the clan has survived as a unit living on ancestral lands, however, the relationship between the Aboriginal people and their land remains unobliterated. Yet, almost two centuries on, the generally accepted view remains that the common law is ignorant of any communal native title or other legal claim of the Aboriginal clans or peoples even to ancestral tribal lands on which they still live: see *Milirrpum v. Nabalco Pty Ltd* [(1971) 17 FLR 141]. If that view of the law be correct, and I do not suggest that it is not, the common law of this land has still not reached the stage of retreat from injustice which the law of Illinois and Virginia had reached in 1823 when Marshall CJ, in *Johnson v. McIntosh*, accepted that, subject to the assertion of ultimate dominion (including the power to convey title by grant) by the State, the "original inhabitants" should be recognized as having "a legal as well as just claim" to retain the occupancy of their traditional lands. (*Gerhardy v. Brown* [1985] 159 CLR 70, 149)

Why had the common law of Australia "still not reached the stage of retreat from injustice" that American law had reached over a century and a half earlier? How did it reach that stage seven years later in the High Court's decision in *Mabo v. Queensland (No. 2)* (1992) 175 CLR 1?

204 YEARS OF INVISIBLE TITLE[1]

There are numerous reasons for the prolonged delay in the recognition and protection by the common law of the pre-existing rights of Australia's indigenous peoples in relation to land. They include factual misinformation, cross-cultural incomprehension, the intellectual currents of the period since the late eighteenth century, greed for land and racism. These factors were supported by selective extracts from the writings of eminent jurists including Vattel and Blackstone.[2]

Surprisingly, the two centuries of denial of native title had received little consideration in the courts. There were a number of judicial statements to the effect that the several Australian colonies fell within the category of "settled" colonies, as distinct from colonies acquired by "conquest" or "cession." This was in terms of Sir William Blackstone's classic exposition of the extent to which the laws of England would flow into a newly acquired colony and of the governmental authorities empowered to alter that situation:

Plantations or colonies, in distant countries, are either such where the lands are claimed by right of occupancy only, by finding them desert and uncultivated, and peopling them from the mother country; or where, when already cultivated, they have either gained, by conquest, or ceded to us by treaties.[3]

Blackstone was not specifically addressing the issue as to whether in settled colonies that were populated the rights of the existing peoples would survive annexation, although the passage may seem to assume a legal vacuum. The proposition that such of the law of England as is applicable should automatically flow into such a colony does not necessarily require that pre-existing law, and rights under that law, are immediately extinguished. Any indigenous sovereignty in the international law sense would (subject to any treaty stipulation) almost inevitably have been extinguished. But other indigenous rights might logically survive, as "the Marshall cases" in the U.S. Supreme Court had indicated.

In the early half of the nineteenth century, U. S. jurisprudence was better known to judges in the Australian colonies than it came to be in later years. This is illustrated by judgments in two cases concerning claims by Aboriginal criminal defendants to be immune from the jurisdiction of colonial courts. One judge accepted such a claim on the basis of American doctrines of the "domestic dependent nation," but a Full Supreme Court reached a different conclusion on the basis of a perceived distinction between the social organization of Aboriginal peoples in Australia and Native Americans in the United States.[4]

In several cases, judges declared that when the Crown had acquired sovereignty, it had also acquired the beneficial ownership of all the land in the colony. Yet in all but one of these cases the litigation involved no indigenous parties asserting pre-existing title. The exception was *Milirrpum v. Nabalco Pty Ltd* (1971) 17 FLR 141, a decision of a single judge of the Supreme Court of the Northern Territory. Justice Blackburn was clearly influenced by the dicta in the earlier cases. He was also influenced by decisions of the courts of British Columbia, which were subsequently rejected on appeal by the Supreme Court of Canada (*Calder v. Attorney-General [B.C.]* [1971] 13 DLR [3d] 64). In sum, then, prior to the *Mabo* litigation, the High Court of Australia had never had an opportunity to directly address the issues of native title in a case brought by indigenous plaintiffs.

The resulting view of the common law of Australia as providing no recognition of pre-existing land rights stood in stark contrast to the position established in the United States, Canada, New Zealand and other parts of the world where the common law had followed the British flag. Reynolds characterizes this view in the following vivid summation:

This was surely the distinctive and unenviable contribution of Australian jurisprudence to the history of the relations between Europeans and the indigenous people of the non-European world. It was not to provide justification for conquest or cession of land or assumption of sovereignty—others had done that before Australia was settled—but to deny the right, even the fact, of possession to people who had lived on their land for 40,000 years. Settlers in comparable countries (New Zealand, United States, Canada, South Africa) did not deny that the indigenes were the original owners of the soil, whatever else they may have done in the course of colonization.[5]

INSTITUTIONAL CONTRASTS

The Australian colonial experience contrasts with that in some comparable countries in that there were no treaties negotiated with the Aboriginal peoples, either on first contact or on the defeat of Aboriginal resistance. Also by way of contrast, no European powers other than the British established settlements in Australia. Aboriginal peoples were, accordingly, in no position to play one European nation off against another.

A third and significant contrast arises from a comparison of federal Constitutions. The Constitutions of Canada and the United States established express legislative authority for indigenous people at the national level. In Australia, the Constitution, Section 51(xxvi), conferred on the Parliament of the Commonwealth power to make laws with respect to: "The people of any race, *other than the aboriginal race in any State* for whom it is deemed necessary to make special laws." The italicized words were removed in a constitutional amendment that won massive support in a referendum in 1967. The consequence was to confer on the national Parliament a concurrent (but not an exclusive) power, and the politics of federalism have largely limited the exercise of that power.

Lastly, the Constitution of the Commonwealth of Australia, and the several state Constitutions, contain very little by way of guarantees of individual rights. The founders of the Commonwealth Constitution deliberately decided not to follow the U.S. precedent of incorporating a Bill of Rights, and there are very few provisions of that character in the Constitution. These contrasts in institutional arrangements probably contributed to the difficulty in achieving recognition of Aboriginal land rights at common law. However, the relationship of indigenous peoples to land did receive some legislative recognition.

STATUTORY LAND RIGHTS

Until well into the second half of the twentieth century, lands still occupied by Aboriginal people (and the Torres Strait Islanders whose islands had been annexed to Queensland in 1879) were regarded as Crown land, reserved for their use. The reserves in the long-settled parts of the country were usually small; although in the less hospitable lands, they could be quite large. All were managed by governments or by church missions.

From the mid-1960s, a strong re-assertion by indigenous Australians of their claims to land led to the enactment of legislation in some, but not all, Australian jurisdictions conferring on particular peoples rights to lands that had not been alienated to others. The model was set by the Aboriginal Land Rights (Northern Territory) Act (1976) (Cth). It was followed with variations by two South Australian Acts for arid lands in the north and west of the state—the Pitjantjatjara Land Rights Act (1981) (SA) and the Maralinga Tjarutja Land Rights Act (1984) (SA). The *Aboriginal Land Rights Act* (1983) (NSW) also made provision for land grants and established a fund to support purchases. In the early 1980s, the Queensland government began to modify its Land Act to permit the grant of a form of title over reserves to the Aboriginal or Islander Councils for those reserves.[6]

In order to resist the imposition of any such title over Murray Island in the Torres Strait, the *Mabo* litigation was initiated in May 1982 in the original jurisdiction of the High Court of Australia. The late Eddie Mabo and other Murray Islanders sought declarations against the State of Queensland and the Commonwealth of Australia. In effect, they were asserting the survival of their rights to the islands (and surrounding reefs, waters, etc.) based on their own Meriam law.

MABO (NO. 1)

In an early Directions Hearing, the High Court asked the parties to attempt to settle an agreed statement of facts. This proved difficult. The determination of facts was remitted for trial by a Queensland Supreme Court judge. However, in 1985 the Queensland government enacted legislation designed to kill off the litigation. The Queensland Coast Islands Declaratory Act (1985) (Qld) declared, retroactively, that the intention of the Queensland legislature in 1879 was not only to assert sovereignty over the Islands but also to extinguish any land rights without entitlement to compensation.

The High Court was required to determine whether the 1985 state act was valid and effective. No constitutional human rights guarantees were available. But the case turned ultimately on a Commonwealth human rights statute, the Racial Discrimination Act (1975) (Cth). This act was enacted to implement Australia's obligations under the International Convention on the Elimination of All Forms of Racial Discrimination. The critical provision was Section 10.

(1) If, by reason of, or of a provision of, a law of the Commonwealth or of a State or Territory, persons of a particular race, colour or national or ethnic origin do not enjoy a right that is enjoyed by persons of another race, colour or national or ethnic origin, or enjoy a right to a more limited extent than persons of another race, colour or national or ethnic origin, then, notwithstanding anything in that law, persons of the first-named race, colour or national or ethnic origin shall, by force of this section, enjoy that right to the same extent as persons of that other race, colour or national or ethnic origin.

(2) A reference in sub-section (1) to a right includes a reference to a right of a kind referred to in Article 5 of the Convention.

The particular rights in question, under Article 5(d) of the Convention, were: (v) The right to own property alone as well as in association with others; (vi) The right to inherit.

The High Court divided on the question whether the 1985 Queensland Act was inconsistent with Section 10. A minority treated the rights claimed under Meriam law as unique, so that an act extinguishing those rights for Murray Islanders did not leave the same rights in force for others. But the majority judgments treated the claimed rights as property rights in the same sense as the property rights of others, even though one set of rights derived from Meriam law and the other from Queensland law (*Mabo v. Queensland* [1988] 166 CLR 186). This decision permitted the principal action to proceed with its attempt to establish the existence and survival of such rights under Meriam law as rights to be recognized and protected under Australian common law.

THE AUSTRALIAN USE OF INTERNATIONAL HUMAN RIGHTS NORMS

The tradition of Australian law has been similar to that of English law, in the absence (in either jurisdiction) of any constitutional Bill of Rights. Human rights may derive some protection from common law traditions and presumptions such as the need for *mens rea* in criminal offenses and entitlement to compensation for compulsory acquisition of property. Judicial processes long accepted in the

Common Law would also reflect (and probably inspired) procedural standards in such instruments as the International Covenant on Civil and Political Rights.

But the approach has been the Dualist tradition of perceiving international law as a totally distinct domain from national law. Accordingly, international human rights instruments would influence Australian law only to the extent that it had been domesticated by Australian legislation. An example already noted is the Racial Discrimination Act (1975) (Cth) implementing Australia's obligations under the International Convention on the Elimination of All Forms of Racial Discrimination. Australia has ratified most of the "core" human rights treaties. Since 1991 it has taken the further step of accepting provisions for individual communications to international treaty committees, notably the Human Rights Committee, the Committee on the Elimination of Racial Discrimination and the Committee against Torture.

These developments have led to increasing reference by Australian appellate courts to international human rights law in resolving ambiguities in legislation and in developing common law principles. In tracing these relatively recent developments, Justice Michael Kirby (now a Justice of the High Court) perceives the High Court's decision in *Mabo v. Queensland (No. 2)* (1992) 175 CLR 1 as a breakthrough.[7] He draws attention, in particular, to the following passage from the judgment of Justice Brennan, writing with the concurrence of Chief Justice Mason and Justice McHugh:

Whatever the justification advanced in earlier days for refusing to recognize the rights and interests in land of the indigenous inhabitants of settled colonies, an unjust and discriminatory doctrine of that kind can no longer be accepted. The expectations of the international community accord in this respect with the contemporary values of the Australian people. The opening up of international remedies to individuals pursuant to Australia's accession to the Optional Protocol to the International Covenant on Civil and Political Rights brings to bear on the common law the powerful influence of the Covenant and the international standards it imparts. The common law does not necessarily conform with international law, but international law is a legitimate and important influence on the development of the common law, especially when international law declares the existence of universal human rights. A common law doctrine founded on unjust discrimination in the enjoyment of civil and political rights demands reconsideration. It is contrary both to international standards and to the fundamental values of our common law to entrench a discriminatory rule which, because of the supposed position on the scale of social organization of the indigenous inhabitants of a settled colony, denies them a right to occupy their traditional lands. ([1992] 175 CLR 1, 42)

MABO (NO. 2)

There were five separate judgments. A brief judgment by Chief Justice Mason and Justice McHugh substantially concurred with the judgment of Justice Brennan. Justices Deane and Gaudron each delivered a separate judgment, as did

Justice Toohey. Judge Dawson was the sole dissentient. At the risk of over-simplifying some 200 pages of careful judicial reasoning, the following summary is offered.

The High Court decided by a 6 to 1 majority that the pre-existing rights of indigenous people in relation to land ("native title") were not extinguished when the British acquired sovereignty over the several Australian colonies. Native title may have survived if the people concerned still maintained traditional ties to the land. The Crown had acquired the radical title but not the beneficial title to the land. However, the Crown had power to extinguish the native title. It could do so by granting interests in the land to others or by setting aside the land for public purposes, to the extent that such acts were inconsistent with the native title. Extinguishment would not lightly be inferred, and legislation would need to display a "clear and plain intention" to extinguish native title. Extinguishment would not of itself give rise to any entitlement to compensation.

"Native title" was not defined, as its content was left to be determined by reference to the law of the particular indigenous peoples. It was inalienable outside the indigenous legal system other than by surrender to the Crown. The common law was available to protect native title.

The earlier judicial statements denying native title were distinguished or overruled. Judicial decisions were considered from as early as the seventeenth century concerning the extension of English sovereignty over Ireland and Wales and into Asia, Africa, the Americas and the Pacific. The classification of the Australian colonies as "settled" was not disturbed. But the majority rejected the earlier view that pre-existing rights would not be recognized in the case of "backward peoples" lacking a degree of social and political organization acceptable to European standards. International law was relevant at this point, notably the decision of the International Court of Justice in its *Advisory Opinion on Western Sahara* (1975) I CJR12, and the norms against racial discrimination. The principles concerning native title were directly referable to U.S. jurisprudence built on the "Marshall cases" and Canadian jurisprudence. Alternative arguments based on possessory title within the common law[8] were considered only by Justice Toohey.

The principles declared by the High Court need not have disturbed anyone had the decision stood alone. Governments could have continued to grant interests over land without even needing to consider whether the land was subject to native title; such grants would have simply extinguished any native title, without any liability to offer compensation. However, the decision did not stand alone. The *Racial Discrimination Act* (1975) (Cth) had been in force since October 31, 1975. The decision in *Mabo (No. 1)* had shown that the act constituted a federal "safety net" against actions by state and territory governments affecting native title.

Immediate concern was expressed about the validity of interests in land that had been granted by state and territory governments since 1975. Industry groups in particular called on the Commonwealth to validate doubtful titles by amending its Racial Discrimination Act. Industry groups and governments sought action generally to resolve the uncertainties created by the *Mabo (No. 2)* decision.

There were also vehement criticisms of the High Court itself from various people who were unsettled by the decision. The Court, it was said, had usurped the function of the legislature; it had improperly disregarded precedent; the decision undermined the foundations of property law in Australia; the Court had improperly taken judicial notice of historical facts and, indeed, had gotten that history wrong; the decision should have been confined to Murray Island, or at least to the Torres Strait Islands with their Melanesian traditions of cultivation and landownership; Aboriginal societies were different, and their communal hunter-gatherer relationships to land did not merit recognition; contemporary Australians bear no responsibility for the wrongs of previous generations; the Court improperly invoked references to contemporary standards of the Australian people and of international law; and so on. Such criticisms fed into an extremely volatile debate as the Commonwealth government developed proposals for legislation.

NATIVE TITLE LEGISLATION

The Australian Labor Party (ALP) national government was led by Prime Minister Paul Keating. The more conservative Coalition parties (Liberal Party, National Party) were in opposition in the Commonwealth Parliament but held government in most states and territories. In the Commonwealth Parliament, neither the ALP nor the Coalition had a majority in the Senate—the balance of power was held by seven senators from the Australian Democrats, two senators from the Western Australian Greens, and one independent senator. Some conservative politicians at the federal, state and territory levels advocated for an effective reversal of the *Mabo* decision and the amendment or repeal of the Racial Discrimination Act (1975) (Cth), but most conservative leaders accepted the decision and simply sought to "tame" its more unsettling consequences.

On December 10, 1992, Human Rights Day, the Prime Minister delivered an important address to a largely Aboriginal gathering in Redfern, Sydney, to mark the commencement of the International Year of the World's Indigenous Peoples. In the course of this address, he acknowledged the responsibility of non-Aboriginal people for the dispossession of indigenous peoples and for much else that had been done over two centuries of colonial settlement. He made the following comments on the *Mabo* decision.

By doing away with the bizarre concept that this continent had no owners prior to the settlement of Europeans, Mabo establishes a fundamental truth and lays the basis for justice.

It will be much easier to work from that basis than has ever been the case in the past.

For that reason alone we should ignore the isolated outbreaks of hysteria and hostility of the past few months.

Mabo is an historic decision—we can make it an historic turning point, the basis of a new relationship between indigenous and non-indigenous Australians.

The message should be that there is nothing to fear or to lose in the recognition of historical truth, or the extension of social justice, or the deepening of Australian social democracy to include indigenous Australians.

There is everything to gain.[9]

Earlier, on October 27, 1992, the Prime Minister had announced a process to develop national legislation in response to the *Mabo (No. 2)* decision. A Cabinet Committee, chaired by him and supported by a team of public servants, in consultation with state and territory Governments, industry groups and Aboriginal and Torres Strait Islander organizations, would develop proposals to implement the Court's decision.

A discussion paper was published on June 3, 1993, the first anniversary of the High Court decision. More detailed proposals were announced in September 1993. The legislative proposals appeared to prioritize non-indigenous interests and to accommodate the interests of Aboriginal and Torres Strait Islander peoples only in a residual fashion. Indigenous negotiators worked with great skill to achieve a re-adjustment in the balance. In this effort they were assisted by the politics of the conservative parties. The government of Western Australia made it clear that it would not support any national legislation. The opposition parties in the Commonwealth Parliament decided to oppose any legislation that was not supported by all states and territories. They thus marginalized themselves into irrelevance to the debate. The government knew that it was futile to seek opposition support to get its bill enacted in the Senate, so it turned to the senators of the minor parties. They were much more supportive of Aboriginal and Torres Strait Islanders. After the longest debate in the Senate's history, the Native Title Bill was passed by the Senate (with an extraordinary number of amendments) on December 21, 1993. The House of Representatives accepted those amendments the following day, and the Act received the Governor-General's assent on Christmas Eve. The Act commenced operation on January 1, 1994.

The Native Title Act (1993) (Cth) has several functions. It recognizes and protects native title. It validates "past acts" of the Commonwealth government that would have been invalid because of the existence of native title, and it authorizes state and territory legislatures to do likewise. It establishes a process for determining the existence of native title and/or for determining compensation for extinguishment or impairment of native title. It provides for the future that native title holders shall be treated no less favorably than freeholders when it comes to compulsory acquisition or mining proposals and shall have an additional "right to negotiate" (but not a veto).

Complementary state and territory legislation is contemplated and is being developed in most jurisdictions. Western Australia was the exception. It rushed through its own legislation prior to the Commonwealth Act. The Land (Titles and Traditional Usage) Act (1993) (WA) extinguishes native title throughout the state and replaces it with statutory rights of traditional usage that were, ultimately, subordinated to all other interests in land. Aboriginal organizations have challenged the validity of the WA Act as inconsistent with both the Racial Discrimination Act (1975) (Cth) and the Native Title Act (1993) (Cth). The state government itself challenged the reach and the validity of the Native Title Act (1993) (Cth). In 1995 the High Court upheld the validity of the Native Title Act and held that the state act was invalid (*Western Australia v Commonwealth* [1995] 183 CLR 373).

In the meantime, the Commonwealth government is proceeding to Stages 2 and 3 of its response to the *Mabo (No. 2)* decision. Stage 2, enacted in 1995, was legislation to establish an Indigenous Land Corporation and a Land Fund to support the purchase of land on the open market to benefit the large majority of indigenous Australians who have no prospect of asserting native title. Stage 3 was to be the development of a series of ''social justice'' measures in a range of areas such as health, education, employment, economic development and so on. National indigenous bodies consulted widely and produced three major reports setting out a variety of proposals for changes at constitutional legislative and administrative levels.[10] But with the election of a coalition government on March 2, 1996, there is no longer any interest at the level of the national government in proceeding with the social justice proposals.

The coalition government, led by Prime Minister John Howard, also advanced proposals to amend the Native Title Act (1993) (Cth) to improve its ''workability.'' Although some of the proposed amendments were reasonable enough, others have given indigenous Australians considerable cause for concern. In particular, the ability of Aborigines and Torres Strait Islanders to have some control over mining activity on their lands (''the right to negotiate'') would be substantially reduced or eliminated.[11]

In the meantime, two further cases about native title have been decided by the High Court. In one, the High Court ordered the National Native Title Tribunal to accept an application for a determination of native title; the application had been rejected on the basis of administrative assessments that native title could not be established because pastoral leases had been granted over the land in question.[12] In the second case, the High Court directly addressed this issue and decided, by a 4-to-3 majority, that pastoral leases under Queensland state legislation do not necessarily extinguish native title, although the latter has to yield to any conflicting rights of the pastoralist.[13]

The response of most state politicians, some federal politicians and some industry groups to this latter decision has been extraordinary. Although the decision does create certain problems, they are not of a scale to justify the hysterical demands for legislative extinguishment of native title on pastoral lands or immoderate attacks on the High Court itself for excessive ''judicial activism.''

During the first months of 1997, the Howard government engaged in discussions with state leaders, industry groups and indigenous peoples' organizations. Some of these "stakeholders" also met with each other to explore the possibility of agreed outcomes. A Native Title Amendment Bill was introduced in the House of Representatives in 1997, incorporating the amendments proposed in 1996 together with other amendments responding specifically to the *Wik* decision. The bill was passsed in the House, where the government has a clear majority, but it does not have a clear majority in the Senate. When the bill reached the Senate, the government itself introduced some softening amendments; other amendments, moved by non-government senators, were accepted, but amendments in four key areas were held by the government and the House to be unacceptable.

Constitution s. 57 offers a special process for the resolution of deadlocks between the two houses of parliament. The House of Representatives can, after three months, pass the bill again; if the Senate rejects it, or passes it with amendments which the House deems to be unacceptable, the government may then seek a double dissolution of both houses. After the consequent election the new Parliament may vote on the bill in a special joint sitting of both houses.

At the time of writing, the bill has been twice passed by the House and twice passed by the Senate with amendments which the government and the House hold to be unacceptable. Any double dissolution election needs to be held by October 1998 (six months before a regular election is due for the House and for half the Senate). Any double dissolution election will not be confined to the issue of native title, but will turn on the general range of federal government policies and programs. It will be a matter for the political discretion of the Prime Minister when to go to the voters and whether or not to do so in the form of a double dissolution.

CONCLUSION

None of these dramatic developments would have occurred without the decision of the High Court of Australia in *Mabo (No. 2)*. Earlier proposals for national land rights legislation had foundered, in the 1980s, on the politics of federalism and the interests of the mining industry. The High Court managed to signal the beginning of the "retreat from injustice" to which Justice Deane had referred and to provide the critical basis for political and legislative follow-up. In doing so, the majority justices placed a significant degree of reliance on contemporary standards of human rights.

The nature of the political and legislative follow-up was totally dependent on the political will of governments. It was fortuitous for indigenous Australians that in 1993 the then–prime minister committed himself and the national government wholeheartedly to seeing through legislation designed to accord substantial justice to Aborigines and Torres Strait Islanders while providing substantial accommodation to other interests. It remains to be seen whether the Howard government will commence a retreat from the "retreat from injustice."

NOTES

1. The phrase is the title of an article on the *Mabo* decision by Aboriginal lawyer Noel Pearson. The sub-title for the article is even more indicative: "From the Most Vehement Denial of a People's Rights to a Most Cautious and Belated Recognition"; in: M. A. Stephenson and S. Ratnapala, eds., *Mabo: A Judicial Revolution* (Brisbane, 1993), 75.

2. The story is lucidly told by historian Henry Reynolds, *The Law of the Land*, 2nd ed. (Melbourne, 1992).

3. Blackstone, *Commentaries on the Laws of England*, Book 1 (1765), 106–108.

4. The cases of Bonjon (1841) and Murrell (1836) are discussed in J. Hookey, "Settlement and Sovereignty," in: P. Hanks and B. Keon-Cohen, eds., *Aborigines and the Law* (Melbourne, 1984), 1.

5. Reynolds, *supra* note 2 at 3.

6. For an overview of such Land Rights Acts, see H. McRae, G. Nettheim and L. Beacroft, *Indigenous Legal Issues: Commentary and Materials* (Sydney, 1997), Ch. 4; *The Laws of Australia* 1, Aborigines and Torres Straits Islanders, 1.3 Land Law.

7. M. Kirby, "The Australian Use of International Human Rights Norms: From Bangalore to Balliol—A View from The Antipodes," 16 *University New South Wales Law Journal* (1993), 363 at 384–386.

8. K. McNeil, *Common Law Aboriginal Title* (Oxford, 1989).

9. Citations for Prime Minister Keating's Redfern Address are: "Redfern Address, in 'Prime Minister speaks at Redfern' " (1992) (Dec.) Land Rights New 2. A fuller version appears in (1993) 3 (61) Aboriginal Law Bulletin 4–5 and in Aboriginal and Torres Strait Islander Social Justice Commissioner (1993) First Report, 1993 (AGPS, Canberra), 135–140.

10. P. Jull, "An Aboriginal Policy for the Millennium: the Three Social Justice Reports," 1 *Australian Indigenous Law Reporter* (1996), 1.

11. Proposed Amendments to the Native Title Act 1993. Issues for Indigenous People, Aboriginal and Torres Strait Islander Commission, Nov. 1996.

12. North Ganalanja Aboriginal Corporation v. Queensland, 135 ALR 225 (1996).

13. The Wik Peoples v. Queensland, 141 ALR 129 (1996).

Part VI

The United States

Chapter 10

U.S. Courts and the Selective Protection of Human Rights

MARK GIBNEY

On one level at least, there is reason to celebrate the protection of human rights by U.S. courts. Since the landmark decision in *Filartiga v. Peña-Irala*,[1] a number of federal courts have provided a forum for foreign plaintiffs who have successfully sued for human rights abuses occurring in other countries. This litigation has been based on the simple language of the Alien Tort Statute (ATS),[2] passed by the first Congress in 1789. The act reads in its entirety: "The district courts shall have original jurisdiction of any civil action by an alien for a tort only, committed in violation of the law of nations or a treaty of the United States." From merely this, human rights abusers from all corners of the globe have been held legally responsible under U.S. law.

Yet one should not become sanguine about the American judiciary. While U.S. courts have proven receptive to cases alleging human rights abuses committed by foreign state actors, these same courts have been unwilling to challenge, or in most instances to even examine, the human rights practices in other countries of the U.S. government or American multinational corporations. This is the focus of this chapter. The first section provides a brief overview of *Filartiga* and its progeny, much of which has been written already.[3] The second section focuses on suits brought by foreign plaintiffs alleging human rights violations committed by the U.S. government; and the third section examines the great reluctance of American courts to rein in the egregious practices of U.S.-based multinational corporations.

THE ALIEN TORT STATUTE AND THE PROTECTION OF HUMAN RIGHTS

Filartiga was a stunning decision, the repercussions of which are still being felt. The events upon which the case was based are, unfortunately, not particularly unusual. Joelito Filartiga, the son of a prominent opponent of the ruling government, was tortured and killed in Paraguay by Americo Norberto Peña-Irala, the chief of police of Asunción, Paraguay. Attempts to institute criminal action against Peña-Irala in Paraguay proved futile, resulting in the arrest and eventual disbarment of the family's attorney. At that juncture, justice did not seem possible.

Subsequent to this, in 1979 the deceased's sister, Dolly Filartiga, was living permanently in New York when she learned that Peña-Irala was visiting the United States. Filartiga filed a civil suit in federal district court against Peña-Irala on behalf of herself and her father, alleging subject matter jurisdiction under the previously moribund ATS. The district court dismissed the complaint, but the Court of Appeals for the Second Circuit reversed. In his opinion for the court, Judge Irving Kaufman held that under the "law of nations" there was a "clear and unambiguous" prohibition against official torture. On the basis of this finding, the court held that the ATS provided federal jurisdiction when "an alleged torturer is found and served with process by an alien within our borders."[4] On remand, the district court implemented the court of appeals holding, awarding the Filartigas a default judgment against Peña-Irala (who by then had returned to Paraguay) of more than $10 million.

Almost without exception,[5] courts in the United States have been receptive to "Filartiga" cases. Thus, several Argentine citizens successfully sued former Argentine General Carlos Guillermo Suarez-Mason for human rights violations committed during the "dirty war."[6] A group of Guatemalan plaintiffs were awarded a $47.5 million judgment against Guatemalan General Hector Gramajo for his responsibility for massive human rights violations.[7] In *Abebe-Jiri v. Negewo*,[8] three women who were tortured in Ethiopia in the late 1970s sued the man responsible for the abuse, now living in Atlanta. The judge awarded the plaintiffs a total of $1.5 million for torture, cruel, inhuman or degrading treatment and arbitrary detention. Six Haitians who had been detained and tortured because of their opposition to the military regime won a default judgment against a former dictator;[9] while a Haitian plaintiff who was mutilated by members of FRAPH, a paramilitary group, has a default judgment pending.[10] In *Todd v. Panjaitan*[11] the mother of a man killed in a massacre in East Timor successfully sued an Indonesian general living in Boston. Relatives of victims of the Rwandan genocide won a default judgment against the leader of a paramilitary group.[12] And in *Doe v. Karadzic* and *Kadic v. Karadzic*,[13] consolidated suits were brought against the leader of the Bosnian-Serb forces. In *Doe*, two individuals representing a class have sued for genocide, war crimes, crimes against humanity, rape and other torture, summary executions and other abuses. In *Kadic*, a Bosnian woman and two organizations sued for genocide, rape, forced prostitution, forced pregnancy and other abuses. The district court dismissed both claims on the basis that the defendant was a private actor, not acting under color of state law. However, the Second Circuit has reversed this decision.

The *Marcos*[14] litigation merits special mention. It was the first class action suit brought under the ATS, the first jury verdict and finally, the first case to be decided on the merits. The case consolidated five separate civil suits filed in three different judicial districts, all alleging various forms of human rights abuses under Ferdinand Marcos's reign. All five cases were originally dismissed by the district courts in which they were filed on the basis of the Act of State doctrine, but the Ninth Circuit reversed in a brief and unpublished opinion and at the same time consolidated the cases for trial.

In sum, "Filartiga" cases in the United States have revolutionized human rights protection. Although plaintiffs have not been able to collect on the money damages they have been awarded (*Marcos* might well prove to be the exception), these cases have raised the voices of the oppressed, and at the same time they have reminded those responsible for carrying out human rights abuses that they no longer operate with impunity. In that sense, then, the federal judiciary in the United States has done much to advance the cause of human rights in the world.[15] What we will see in the next two sections, however, is how disappointing the performance of the American judiciary has been when there have been allegations of human rights abuse by U.S. actors.

ALLEGATIONS OF HUMAN RIGHTS VIOLATIONS BY THE U.S. GOVERNMENT

As a world superpower, the United States pursues foreign policy objectives in virtually every corner of the globe, and it does so in a variety of ways. One means of achieving its national interest is through violence—either indirectly, by supporting a foreign power or army, or more directly, through the deployment of U.S. military personnel. One of the unintended consequences of the use of military measures is that "innocent" civilians are harmed or killed. The question that this has raised for U.S. courts is whether those harmed by this violence should be compensated. The answer provided thus far is no.

This issue was first raised in *Sanchez-Espinoza v. Reagan*,[16] where a group of twelve Nicaraguan civilians[17] sued nine then-present or former officials of the executive branch, including President Ronald Reagan, three non-federal defendants, and a group of unidentified officers or agents of the United States.[18] The basis of the suit was that the U.S. government was providing military and financial support to the Contra rebel forces, who were in turn committing terrorists raids in Nicaragua.[19] These nonresident aliens sought monetary relief as well as declaratory and injunctive relief prohibiting further U.S. military intervention in Nicaragua.

The district court dismissed the plaintiffs' suit on the basis of the political question doctrine: "In order to adjudicate the tort claims of the Nicaraguan plaintiffs, we would have to determine the precise nature of the United States government's involvement in the affairs of several Central American nations, namely, Honduras, Costa Rica, El Salvador, and Nicaragua."[20] The court of appeals affirmed, but did so on the basis of the doctrine of sovereign immunity.

Responding to the civilians' claim for monetary relief, then-Judge Antonin Scalia writes:

It would make a mockery of the doctrine of sovereign immunity if federal courts were authorized to sanction or enjoin, by judgments nominally against present or former Executive officers, actions that are concededly and as a jurisdictional necessity, official actions of the United States. Such judgments would necessarily interfere with the public administration, or restrain the government from acting, or . . . compel it to act.[21]

Taking up the plaintiffs' claim for declaratory or injunctive relief, Scalia simply points out how many government officials had helped to create this policy.

The support for military operations that we are asked to terminate has, if the allegations in the complaint are accepted as true, received the attention and approval of the President, the Secretary of State, the Secretary of Defense, and the Director of the CIA, and involves the conduct of our diplomatic relations with at least four sovereign states—Nicaragua, Costa Rica, Honduras, and Argentina. Whether or not this is, as the District Court thought, a matter so entirely committed to the care of the political branches as to preclude our considering the issue at all, we think it at least requires the withholding of discretionary relief.[22]

Despite the gross levels of human rights abuses committed by the Contra rebel forces, and notwithstanding the Contras' intimate link with the U.S. government, if there was to be any relief, it was not to come from the judiciary but from the political branches—the same political branches implicated in the commission of the human rights abuses.[23] The ultimate end of all this, of course, was that neither the Congress nor the executive branch (nor the judiciary) ever offered any form of compensation to the tens of thousands of innocent civilians who were caught up in the brutal civil war. The painful fact is that the litigation ultimately had no effect on the conduct of the war itself or its human toll.

Civilians in other countries have been harmed or killed during direct U.S. military intervention. To date, none have been given any relief or compensation in American courts. *Saltany v. Reagan*[24] was a suit brought by a group of 53 Libyan plaintiffs (all civilians) suing for personal and property damage from the U.S. military air strikes in April 1986 in retaliation for the bombing of a disco in West Berlin earlier that month. The defendants were the President of the United States, various civilian and military officials of the U.S. government, Prime Minister Margaret Thatcher of the United Kingdom and the U.S. and U.K. governments.

The district court dismissed the case in a summary fashion. The claim against the United Kingdom was dismissed on the basis of the Act of State doctrine, whereas the claim relating to the U.S. defendants was dismissed on the basis of sovereign immunity. The ironic thing about the court's opinion is that it readily conceded that the alleged conduct by the defendants would have been "tortious" if it were to be judged by civil law standards. Yet the court eventually did not apply *any* set of standards. Instead, it merely pointed out the obvious: that the defendants had exercised "discretion in a myriad of contexts of utmost complexity and gravity, not to mention danger."[25] In addition, each of the defendants "acted, as duty required, in accordance with the orders of the commander-in-chief or a superior order."[26] From the mere fact that the operation involved great complexity and danger and was carried out through the government's chain of command, the court held that the defendants were immune from suit.

One of the more noteworthy features of the *Saltany* opinion is the fact that while the court seemed to recognize the full extent of the plaintiffs' injuries, it also was outraged that such a suit was ever filed in the first place.

The plaintiffs, purportedly citizens or residents of Libya, cannot be presumed to be familiar with the rules of law of the United States. It is otherwise, however, with their counsel [former U.S. Attorney General Ramsey Clark]. The case offered no hope whatsoever of success, and plaintiffs' attorneys surely knew it.[27]

The court continued:

The injuries for which suit is brought is not insubstantial. It cannot, therefore, be said that the case is frivolous so much as it is audacious. The Court surmises it was brought as a public statement of protest of Presidential action with which counsel (and, to be sure, their clients) were in profound disagreement.[28]

In its haste to dismiss this "audacious" lawsuit, the court failed to realize several things. One is that there was (and continues to be) severe dispute whether Libya was ever involved in the West Berlin bombing in the first place. That is to say, Libyan civilians were killed on evidence that most of our allies question. Second, even if Libyan agents were somehow involved, the retaliatory air raids violated the laws of war. Article 25 of the Hague Regulations of 1907 states: "The attack or bombardment, by whatever means, of towns, villages, dwellings, or buildings which are undefended, is prohibited."[29] Finally, although the court was outraged that suit was ever brought (and Rule 11 sanctions applied against the plaintiffs' attorneys),[30] the court never provided any coherent reasoning why the lawsuit was so unwarranted. Is the opinion to be read that there are no limitations on U.S. activities in other countries? Or to phrase this in the alternative, is there any number of foreign civilians who would have to be killed before the judiciary would offer some measure of restitution?

The December 1989 invasion of Panama brought about the deaths of somewhere between 200 and 8,000 civilians. Yet attempts to seek compensation have proven unsuccessful. In *McFarland v. Cheney*,[31] suit was brought on behalf of a group of Panamanian civilians who suffered personal injury, property loss and death of loved ones during the American invasion. Many of the petitioners in the case had filed administrative service claims with the U.S. Army Claim. Service seeking compensation for their losses and injuries, attempting to rely upon a precedent used to compensate civilians harmed in the 1983 invasion of Grenada.[32] The Army Claims Service rejected all of the Panamanian compensation claims on the grounds that the various injuries occurred during U.S. combat operations. The district court upheld this administrative finding, and this judgment was affirmed on appeal. While Panama has received some emergency assistance, none of these funds have been set aside for the victims of the attack.[33]

The accidental downing of Iran Air Flight 655 over the Persian Gulf by missile fire from the U.S.S. *Vincennes*, killing all of the passengers and crew abroad, has also been the subject of litigation in the United States. In *Nejad v. United States*[34] the plaintiffs were the families and economic dependents of four of the passengers. The defendants were the United States and twelve defense contractors who had supplied the ship with various military equipment. The district court dismissed the plaintiffs' case, evincing the usual deference to the political branches.

[I]t is indubitably clear that plaintiffs' claim calls into question the Navy's decisions and actions in execution of those decisions. The conduct of such affairs are [*sic*] constitutionally committed to the President as Commander in Chief and to his military and naval subordinates.[35]

Koohi v. U.S.[36] was based upon the same set of facts. One of the more noteworthy aspects of this case is how the Court of Appeals went out of its way to hold that the case was justiciable. The defendants had made the claim that the case should be dismissed on the basis of the political question doctrine. The court responded first by holding that governmental operations are traditional subjects of damage actions in federal courts. Moreover, the court held that federal courts are "capable of reviewing military decisions, particularly when those decisions cause injury to civilians."[37] Beyond this, the court also noted that the plaintiffs were seeking only monetary damages for their injuries. Unlike injunctive relief, which "may require the courts to engage in the type of operational decision-making beyond their competence"[38] and outside of the court's constitutional preserve, damage actions instead are "particularly nonintrusive."[39]

Notwithstanding the justiciability of the action, however, the court upheld dismissal on the basis of sovereign immunity. The basis of the opinion was that the waiver of sovereign immunity enacted under the Federal Tort Claims Act[40] contains an explicit exception for "[a]ny claim arising out of combatant activities of the military or naval forces, or the Coast Guard, during time of war."[41] The court concluded that although there had been no declaration of war, and although the events in question long preceded what came to be known as the Persian Gulf War, there were important policy reasons for maintaining sovereign immunity.

The court first noted that tort liability is based in large part on the theory that the prospect of liability makes an actor more careful. Yet, at least in the court's view, Congress did *not* necessarily want U.S. military personnel acting with due care. "Congress certainly did not want our military personnel to exercise great caution at a time when bold and imaginative measures might be necessary to overcome enemy forces."[42] More than this, and in rather extraordinary language, the court stated that "the result would be no different if the downing of the civilian plane had been deliberate rather than the result of error."[43]

Notwithstanding the judicial treatment of these claims, some measure of justice was achieved when the U.S. government eventually made *ex gratia* payments to the families of those killed in the *Vincennes* incident, agreeing to pay $300,000 to each of the wage-earning victims and $150,000 to each of the non-wage-earning victims.[44]

In sum, although U.S. courts have readily opened their doors to foreign plaintiffs who suffered human rights abuse at the hands of other foreigners, a completely different set of standards (and perhaps no standards at all) apply when the alleged violator is the U.S. government. When the U.S. government is pursuing foreign policy objectives in other countries, it apparently can do so without any concern for the human consequences of those activities. In fact, the court in *Koohi* went so far as to claim that the United States could *deliberately* harm or kill civilians in other countries—yet there would be no basis for compensation in American courts. Obviously, the American judiciary has not been willing to address the accusation of human rights violations by the U.S. government. As we will see in the next section, it has played a similarly supine role in the face of enormous levels of harm brought about by the activities of U.S. multinational corporations.

MULTINATIONAL CORPORATIONS AND DOUBLE STANDARDS

Whatever good they might otherwise achieve, U.S.-based multinational corporations have also brought about substantial levels of harm and suffering to various peoples throughout the world. The best-known example, of course, was the deadly gas leak at the Union Carbide plant in Bhopal, India, in which over 2,000 people died and more than 200,000 were injured.[45] In Ilo, Peru, Southern Peru Copper Corporation spews out 2,000 tons of sulfur dioxide into the air each day, or about ten to fifteen times the limit for similar plants operating in the United States.[46] As a result, the smoke from the smelter is sometimes so thick that it hovers over the city like a heavy fog, forcing motorists to turn on their headlights during the day and sending residents to hospitals and clinics, coughing, wheezing and vomiting. H. B. Fuller, a St. Paul, Minnesota–based corporation and a company that prides itself on its ethical sensitivity, has continued to sell its Resistol brand of glue in Central American countries despite the fact that tens of thousands of children in those countries have become addicted to sniffing it.[47] Ecuadoran citizens have asserted that Texaco's operations in that country caused vast levels of devastation to the air, ground and water.[48]

Does U.S. law provide any form of protection or relief for these and other harms brought about by American corporations? The answer appears to be no.

Although the U.S. Congress has readily applied American law extraterritorially to protect American corporations against foreign competition,[49] there has essentially been no attempt to protect foreign citizens of those countries who might be harmed by the operations of U.S.-based corporations. Similarly, U.S. courts have repeatedly dismissed cases brought by foreign plaintiffs against U.S. corporations on the basis of the *forum non conveniens* doctrine[50]—although there have been instances where the federal courthouse is literally across the street from the multinational's world headquarters and notwithstanding the fact that the dismissal of the case in our judicial system will mean the deathknell of the legal action.[51]

The harm and destruction brought about by the U.S. pesticide industry is a good case in point of the double standards in American law and in the American legal system.[52] Despite strict regulations and registration requirements for pesticides within the United States, federal laws permit U.S. companies to manufacture and export pesticides and other chemicals unregistered for use in the United States. Thus, pesticides made in this country—regardless of their environmental and/or health risks—can be shipped to any country and used for any purpose. Moreover, with very rare exception, developing countries do not have the resources and capacity to test and regulate the pesticides that are imported.[53] What ensues from this deadly combination of factors is that entire populations in developing countries have been widely exposed to pesticides either unregistered or banned in the United States. In Guatemala, for example, the average DDT level in cow's milk is 90 times higher than the maximum allowable level in the United States, and Guatemalans generally carry 31 times more DDT in their blood than persons living in the United States.[54] For those who work directly with pesticides the situation is even more dire. It has been estimated that 40 percent of workers who handle pesticides in developing countries display symptoms of pesticide poisoning.[55]

Despite these enormous levels of harm caused by U.S. multinational corporations (and the corporations of other industrialized countries as well, although U.S. companies dominate this market), foreign plaintiffs have received extraordinarily little relief in American courts. One suit that was successfully brought was *Dow Chemical Co. v. Castro Alfaro*, in which the Texas Supreme Court allowed a personal injury suit filed by 82 Costa Rican banana workers against Dow Chemical and Shell Oil to remain in Texas state courts.[56] For more than a decade Dow and Shell had manufactured and shipped DBCP (an agricultural pesticide) to Castle & Cooke, the parent company of Standard Fruit, a Central American banana company. Although the U.S. Environmental Protection Agency had suspended DBCP's registration on November 3, 1977, for many years thereafter Dow and Shell continued to ship the chemical to Castle & Cooke, where fieldworkers applied the dangerous pesticide manually and without any safety equipment. The workers were now claiming that the pesticide had made them sterile. The defendant corporations sought to have the case dismissed on the basis of *forum non conveniens*.

Prior to the Texas lawsuit, the plaintiffs had unsuccessfully filed similar suits in Florida and California. In the Texas litigation, the trial court granted the defendants' motion to dismiss, but the Court of Appeals reversed.[57] In a bitterly divided opinion, the state Supreme Court affirmed this decision. In his lengthy concurring opinion Justice Lloyd Doggett pointed to the hypocrisy of the defendants' actions:

The banana plantation workers allegedly injured by DBCP were employed by an American company on American-owned land and grew Dole bananas for export solely to American tables. The chemical allegedly rendering the workers sterile was researched, formulated, tested, manufactured, labeled and shipped by an American company in the United States to another American company. The decision to manufacture DBCP for distribution and use in the third world was made by these two American companies in their corporate offices in the United States. Yet now Shell and Dow argue that the one part of this equation that should not be American is the legal consequences of their actions.[58]

Alfaro is the exception and not the rule. In one case after another, U.S. courts have dismissed suits brought by foreign plaintiffs against U.S. corporations on the basis of *forum non conveniens*. As a study by David Robertson has shown, this effectively ends the litigation.[59] Of the 55 personal injury cases he examined, *none* were won in foreign courts, and 1 was lost on the merits. The problem, quite simply, is that courts in developing countries are not capable of handling mass tort litigation. Very few legal systems in the developing world allow jury trials, and virtually none allow plaintiffs to recover punitive damages and compensatory damages for the loss of future earnings, pain and suffering and so on. Furthermore, few allow any form of contingency fee arrangement, so that plaintiffs would have to finance their lawsuit against corporate giants such as Dow and Shell. Finally, most countries set a severe limit in terms of the size of the judgments that plaintiffs can be awarded ($1,800 in the case of Costa Rica).

In sum, the prospects of foreign plaintiffs successfully suing U.S. multinational corporations in their home country are virtually non-existent. Yet this has not prevented U.S. courts from systematically dismissing these cases in this country. Because of the laxity in U.S. law and because American courts are so reluctant to hear suits brought by foreigners against U.S. corporations, violations to the integrity of the person continue with impunity—whether it be from unsafe working conditions, egregious environmental practices and so on.

CONCLUSION

U.S. courts have been heralded as defenders of human rights, but this has been true only in part. While it has been the case that foreign plaintiffs who have been harmed by foreign state actors have achieved some measure of success under the "Filartiga" line of cases, foreigners harmed by American actors—public or private—essentially have been offered no protection under U.S. law. Suits alleging harm by the U.S. government have been dismissed by a variety of defenses, most notably the doctrine of sovereign immunity. The end result has been that the United States has not had to attend to the human consequences of its foreign policy pursuits in other countries. In fact, *Koohi* goes so far as to hold that foreign citizens would not have a cause of action even if the harm by agents of the U.S. government had been deliberate.

American law and the American judiciary have also protected U.S.-based multinational corporations from the claims of foreigners. With the exception of the Foreign Corrupt Practices Act,[60] American law has refused to establish any standards for U.S. corporations operating in other countries. This fact, combined with the absence of any meaningful environmental and labor standards in most developing countries, has led to a situation where multinational corporations operate with virtually no legal restraints at all. In addition, foreigners who have been severely harmed by U.S. multinationals—and a conservative estimate would place this number in the hundreds of thousands—have found very little recourse in American courts. Instead, their cases have been dismissed by our courts based on the premise that these claims can be pursued in the home country. This has not happened. Legal systems in the developing world are woefully inadequate with respect to mass tort litigation. This, however, is apparently of no interest to the American judiciary, as it has repeatedly allowed U.S.-based corporations to avoid litigation in this country.

In short, while American courts have been very good at protecting the human rights of a very small and select group of foreign plaintiffs (those alleging human rights violations by foreign state actors over whom personal jurisdiction has been obtained), U.S. courts have not been willing to consider the possibility of attempting to make whole those harmed by American actors. Until this happens, it is not possible to claim that American courts are staunch defenders of human rights.

NOTES

1. 630 F. 2d 876 (2d Cir. 1980).

2. 28 U.S.C. Sec. 1350.

3. See generally B. Stephens and M. Ratner, *International Human Rights Litigation in U.S. Courts* (Irvington-on-Hudson, NY, 1996); J. Blum and R. Steinhardt, "Federal Jurisdiction over International Human Rights Claims: The Alien Tort Claims Act after Filartiga v. Peña-Irala," 22 *Harvard International Law Journal* (1981), 53; A. D'Amato, "The Alien Tort Statute and the Founding of the Constitution," 82 *American Journal of International Law* (1988), 62.

4. 630 F.2d at 884.

5. The leading case going against the long line of Filartiga cases is Tel-Oren v.

Libyan Arab Republic, 517 F. Supp. 542 (D.D.C. 1981), *aff'd*, 726 F.2d 774 (DC Cir. 1984). Tel-Oren involved a 1978 terrorist incident on the coast of Israel. Thirteen members of the Palestinian Liberation Organization (PLO) landed a boat in Israel and hijacked a bus. In a confrontation with Israeli police, the members of the PLO shot at their hostages and blew up the bus, killing 34 adults and children and wounding 75 others. Survivors of the attack brought suit in federal district court for the District of Columbia, basing jurisdiction on the Alien Tort Statute. The plaintiffs included Israeli, Dutch and American citizens.

Affirming the district court's dismissal of the case, the panel for the D.C. Circuit deciding the case on the merits issued a one-page *per curiam* opinion, accompanied by lengthy concurring opinions from each of the three judges. Judge Edwards's opinion came the closest to the reasoning in Filartiga. Edwards was of the opinion that the ATS did provide a cause of action for aliens asserting violations of the law of nations. However, Edwards based dismissal on the fact that while the law of nations prohibits torture by state actors and persons acting under color of state law, the PLO was not subject to the same standards of international law.

Judge Bork's basis for dismissal was based on a number of factors. One was that such a suit would violate separation of powers principles. Bork also took the position that while the ATS granted jurisdiction, it did not also create a cause of action for an individual alien. Finally, Bork would restrict violations of the "law of nations" to those recognized in 1789 when the ATS was created: violation of safe-conduct, infringement on ambassadorial rights and piracy.

Judge Robb voted for dismissal on the basis that the case presented a nonjusticiable political question. Under his position, federal courts would not be able to determine the legal status of international terrorism nor trace individual responsibility for any particular acts of terrorism. In addition, given the levels of violence in the world, Robb was not certain if there was any logical stopping point to litigation that could be pursued in U.S. courts.

6. Forti v. Suarez-Mason, 672 F. Supp. 1531 (N.D. Cal. 1987), *aff'd in part*, 694 F. Supp. 707 (N.D. Cal. 1988); Martinez-Baca v. Suarez-Mason, No. 87–2057 (N.D. Cal. Apr. 22, 1988); Quiros de Rapaport v. Suarez-Mason, No. C87–2266 (N.D. Cal. Apr. 11, 1989).

7. Xuncax v. Gramajo and Ortiz v. Gramajo, 886 F. Supp. 162 (D. Mass. 1995).

8. No. 1:90-cv-2010 (N.D. Ga. Aug. 20, 1993), *aff'd*, 72 F. 3d 844 (11th Cir. 1996).

9. Paul v. Avril, 812 F. Supp. 207 (S.D. Fla. 1992); 901 F. Supp. 330 (S.D. Fla. 1994).

10. Belance v. FRAPH, No. 94–2619 (E.D.N.Y. filed June 1, 1994).

11. No. 92–122555, 1994 WL 827111 (D. Mass. Oct. 26, 1994).

12. Mushikiwabo v. Barayagwiza, No. 94 Civ. 3627, 1996 U.S. Dist. LEXIS 4409 (S.D.N.Y. Apr. 9, 1996).

13. 866 F. Supp. 734 (S.D.N.Y. 1994), *rev'd*, 70 F. 3d 232 (2d Cir. 1995).

14. No. MDL 840 (D. Haw. Feb. 3, 1995), *appeal docketed*, No. 95–15779 (9th Cir. May 5, 1995).

15. By passing the Torture Victim Protection Act (TVPA), Pub. L. No. 102–256, 106 Stat. 73 (1992) (codified at 28 U.S.C. Sec 1350 note), the political branches of the U.S. government have also advanced the protection of human rights. The act has also solidified the Filartiga line of cases. The TVPA provides, in pertinent part:

An individual who, under actual or apparent authority, or under color of law, of any foreign nation—
   (1) subjects an individual to torture shall, in a civil action, be liable for damages to that individual; or
   (2) subjects an individual to extrajudicial killing shall, in a civil action, be liable for damages to the individual's legal representative, or to any person who may be a claimant in an action for wrongful death.

   16. 568 F. Supp. (D.D.C. 1983), aff'd, 770 F. 2d 202 (D.C. Cir. 1985).

   17. There were two other groups of plaintiffs whose claims will not be explored here. One group consisted of twelve members of the House of Representatives who claimed that the executive branch violated Congress's ability to declare war, as well as provisions of the War Powers Resolution. In addition, the congressional plaintiffs claimed that the activities of the executive branch violated the so-called Boland Amendment, which prohibited further funding for the Contras. The other group of plaintiffs were residents of Florida who charged that the U.S.-sponsored paramilitary training camps violated state law.

   18. Ronald Wilson Reagan, individually and in his official capacity as President of the United States; William Casey, individually and in his official capacity as Director of Central Intelligence; Alexander M. Haig, Jr.; George P. Schultz, individually and in his official capacity as U.S. Secretary of State; Thomas O. Enders, individually; Vernon Walters, individually and in his official capacity as U.S. Ambassador-at-Large; Caspar Weinberger, individually and in his official capacity as U.S. Secretary of Defense; Nestor Sanchez, individually and in his official capacity as U.S. Assistant Secretary of Defense; John D. Negroponte, individually and in his official capacity as U.S. Ambassador to Honduras.

   19. The plaintiffs' complaint and supporting briefs described their suffering in great detail, a sample of which is provided:

Twelve of the plaintiffs or their close family members have been subjected to murder, torture, mutilation, kidnapping and rape as a result U.S.-sponsored paramilitary activities designed to ravage the civilian population in Nicaragua. . . .
   The facts of the injuries to each of the plaintiffs or their family members reflect brutal, inhumane activities violative of fundamental laws of civilized nations. For example, plaintiff Maria Bustillo de Blandon, a resident of Nicaragua, saw her husband and five sons murdered and tortured by members of the Nicaraguan Democratic Front (FDN)—the main counterrevolutionary group funded by the federal defendants. On October 28, 1982, the contras entered her home, seized her husband, a lay pastor, and removed their five children from their beds. In front of the parents, the children were tied together, castrated, their ears cut off and their throats slit. The father was then killed.
   Brief for the Appellants at 7, Sanchez-Espinoza v. Reagan, 770 F. Supp. 202 (D.C. Cir. 1985) (citations omitted) (copy with author).

   20. 568 F. Supp. at 601.
   21. 770 F.2d at 738 (citations and emphasis omitted).
   22. Id. at 208.
   23. At one point in his opinion Scalia writes:

Whether or not the present litigation is motivated by considerations of geopolitics rather than personal harm, we think that as a general matter the danger of foreign citizens' [sic] using the courts in situations such as this to obstruct the foreign policy of our government is sufficiently acute that we must leave to Congress the judgment whether a damage remedy should exist.

Id. at 209.
   24. 707 F. Supp. 319 (D.D.C. 1988).

25. *Id.* at 322.

26. *Id.*

27. *Id.*

28. *Id.*

29. Annex to the Convention, Regulations Respecting the Laws and Customs of War on Land, Art. 25, Convention (No. IV) Respecting the Laws and Customs of War on Land, Oct. 18, 1907, 36 Stat. 2277, TS No. 539, 205 Parry's TS 277.

30. 866 F.2d 438 (D.C. Cir. 1989).

31. 1991 WL 43262 (D.D.C. 1991), *aff'd*, 971 F.2d 766 (D.C. Cir. 1992), *cert. denied*, 506 U.S. 1053 (1993).

32. Jeffrey Harris, "Grenada—A Claims Perspective," *The Army Lawyer* (Jan. 1986).

33. Dire Emergency Supplemental Appropriations Act, Pub. L. No. 101–302 (1990).

34. 724 F. Supp. 753 (C.D. Cal. 1989).

35. *Id.* at 755.

36. 976 F.2d 1328 (9th Cir. 1992), *cert. denied*, 113 S. Ct. 2928 (1993).

37. *Id.* at 1331.

38. *Id.* at 1332.

39. *Id.*

40. 28 U.S.C. Sec. 1346(b).

41. 28 U.S.C. Sec. 2680(j).

42. 976 F.2d at 1334–1335.

43. *Id.* at 1335.

44. "U.S. to Pay 248 Iranians Who Lost Kin to Missile," *New York Times*, Feb. 24, 1996, A4.

45. In re Union Carbide Corp. Gas Plant Disaster, 809 F.2d 195 (2d Cir.), *cert. denied*, 484 U.S. 871, *and cert. denied*, 484 U.S. 871 (1987). The case was originally brought in the United States but dismissed, the court holding that it did not wish to engage in a form of legal imperialism by inflicting its rules, standards and values on a developing nation. Left to the Indian judicial system, the case was eventually settled for $470 million. Yet to date most of the victims have not been compensated because of legal and bureaucratic tangles.

46. C. Sims, "In Peru, a Fight for Fresh Air," *New York Times*, Dec. 12, 1995, D1.

47. D. B. Henriques, "Black Mark for a 'Good Citizen,' " *New York Times*, Nov. 26, 1995, at Sec. III, 1.

48. Sequihua v. Texaco, Inc., 847 F. Supp. 61 (S.D. Tex. 1994); Aguinda v. Texaco, Inc., 1994 WL 142006 (1994).

49. For example, while the Sherman Act, Lanham Act and Security Exchange Act have all been given an extraterritorial reading, thus protecting U.S. corporations from "unfair" competition occurring abroad, a wide range of American labor and environmental laws that would protect foreign workers and foreign consumers have been restricted to the territory of the United States. For a fuller discussion of this issue, see M. Gibney and R. Emerick, "The Extraterritorial Application of United States Law and the Protection of Human Rights: Holding Multinational Corporations to Domestic and International Standards," 10 *Temple International and Comparative Journal* (1996), 123.

50. *Forum non conveniens* gives courts the discretionary power to decline jurisdiction when the convenience of the parties and the ends of justice would be better served if the action were brought and tried in another forum. In Gulf Oil Corp. v. Gilbert, 330 U.S. 501 (1947), the Supreme Court first articulated the standards that federal courts should

use to consider whether dismissal is appropriate on the basis of the doctrine. After noting a number of factors to be considered in reaching such a decision, the Court stated that "unless the balance is strongly in favor of the defendant, the plaintiff's choice of forum should rarely be disturbed." 330 U.S. at 508. However, in Piper Aircraft Co. v. Reyno, 454 U.S. 235 (1981), the Court held that foreign plaintiffs are not to be accorded the same deference in the choice of forum as domestic plaintiffs.

51. See generally J. Duval-Major, "One Way Ticket Home: The Federal Doctrine of Forum Non Conveniens and the International Plaintiff," 77 *Cornell Law Review* (1992), 650; M. White, "Home Field Advantage: The Exploitation of Federal Forum Non Conveniens by United States Corporations and Its Effects on International Environmental Litigation," 26 *Loyola of Los Angeles Law Review* (1993), 26; D. Robertson, "Forum Non Conveniens in America and England: 'A Rather Fantastic Fiction,' " 103 *Law Quarterly Review* (1987), 398.

52. See generally J. Colopy, "Poisoning the Developing World: The Exportation of Unregistered and Severely Restricted Pesticides from the United States," 13 *Journal of Environmental Law* (1995), 167; P. Correra, "Tort and the U.S.-Mexican Circle of Poison," 12 *Arizona Journal of International and Comparative Law* (1995), 12; K. Goldberg, "Efforts to Prevent Misuse of Pesticides Exported to Developing Countries: Progressing beyond Regulation to Notification," 12 *Ecology Law Quarterly* (1985), 12; M. Kablack, "Pesticide Abuses in Third World Countries and a Model for Reform," 11 *Boston College Third World Law Journal* (1991), 277.

53. Of 115 countries surveyed in 1989, one-half did not have legislation to control pesticides, and 84 percent were unable to control potentially hazardous pesticides according to international standards. E. Sebesta, "The End of the Free Reign: In Support of a Ban on the Export of Unregistered Pesticides from the United States," 26 *Texas International Law Journal* (1991), 561 at 562.

54. D. Weir and M. Schapiro, *Circle of Poison: Pesticides and People in a Hungry World* (San Francisco, 1981), 79.

55. Colopy, *supra* note 52 at 168.

56. 786 S.W.2d 674 (Tex. 1990), *cert. denied*, 111 S. Ct. 671 (1991).

57. 751 S.W.2d 208 (Tex. Ct. App. 1988).

58. 786 S.W.2d at 681.

59. Robertson, *supra* note 51.

60. Foreign Corrupt Practices Act of 1977, Pub. L. No. 95–213, 91 stat. 1494.

Concluding Remarks

As the chapters in this book have shown, the judicial branch has, at times, played a leading role protecting human rights. To recall just a few examples, it was the judicial branch, not the political branches, that was the moving force behind the belated recognition of Aboriginal rights in Australia. It has been a very active Supreme Court in India that has offered some measure of protection against the cruelties of prison life. Finally, federal courts in the United States have been willing to provide a forum for foreign plaintiffs alleging human rights violations in their home countries.

Despite these and other noteworthy achievements, there are limitations on the judiciary's ability to act in protecting human rights. Some of these limitations are political in nature. For example, Monica Macovei's chapter on the struggle to create an independent judiciary in Romania focused on the continued dominance of the other branches of government in that country, particularly the executive. As Brian Turner has shown, there is little question that political and military considerations have severely retarded the maturation of the judiciary in countries such as Chile and Paraguay, although it is also noteworthy that some of the other countries in the Southern Cone have been successful in this regard. Finally, Albert Melone and Xiaolin Wang have demonstrated how the ideology of the Communist Party has dominated the judicial system in China. However, they suggest that this dominance might very well diminish as a cadre of young legal professionals, who are less beholden to the Party, begin to assume positions of some authority.

In addition to political limitations on the courts, there are institutional restraints as well. For instance, an Alien Tort Statute suit cannot go forward in U.S. courts without personal jurisdiction over the defendant, and judgments cannot be satisfied if the defendant does not have any assets in the United States.

Thus, the number of human rights abusers who will be brought to justice will remain relatively small (unless, of course, the judiciaries of other countries begin to hear such cases as well), and the vast majority of "successful" plaintiffs will not be compensated, financially at least. The Supreme Court of India faces a different kind of institutional restraint, namely, the fact that implementation of judicially mandated prison reform is totally dependent upon the cooperation of many of the same officials who are responsible for the commission of these human rights violations in the first place.

Notwithstanding these and other limitations facing the judiciary, there is much more that courts could accomplish in promoting and protecting human rights. Most important, judges should begin to realize that the probability that coordinate branches of government will offer such protection is not always likely. This lesson should be particularly apt in countries emerging from years or even decades of repressive rule. One obvious lesson of the ugly experiences in the Southern Cone countries that Brian Turner examines is that there was no strong and independent judiciary to halt the egregious practices of the military-political alliance. The same conclusion should be drawn from the East European example as well. And as both Macovei and Igor Petrukhin have shown in these pages, this is a battle that continues to be fought today. Nevertheless, the picture these two authors have painted looks generally promising.

With respect to the so-called mature democracies, judicial protection of human rights is also needed. Consider the United States and Israel. Both of these democracies are governed by the rule of law, or so it is often said. Yet when it comes to protecting the human rights of "others"—Palestinians in the Occupied Territories and, in the case of the United States, foreigners alleging that they have been victimized by the pursuit of American foreign policy interests—the independent (or what purports to be independent) judiciary in each of these countries gives unquestioning deference to the political branches. If foreigners are to obtain any relief for the harm done to them from the foreign policy forays of the U.S. government, then-Judge Scalia blithely held in *Sanchez-Espinoza v. Reagan*, it must come from the political branches and not from the judiciary. It is important to note, however, that this relief has never been given, nor are there any discernible prospects for it. What this means in human terms is that the United States has been able to pursue foreign policy interests anywhere in the world without having to attend to the human consequences of those policies.

There is the same kind of bifurcation in Israel. As Stephen Goldstein has shown, within the domestic sphere Israel possesses a strong independent judiciary. Yet, as John Quigley has shown, in the Occupied Territories this independence gives way to judicial deference, which in turn has given the security forces license to commit gross human rights abuses against Palestinians.

In conclusion, to protect human rights not only is it essential that there be an independent judiciary, as this term is commonly defined, but it is just as essential (perhaps more so) that the judiciary not remove itself so readily from cases that are "political" or "military" or said to be "security related." For it is in these areas in particular, commonly exempted from judicial inspection, that so many human rights violations in the world take place.

For Further Reading

Baldwin, Peter. *Reworking the Past: Hitler, The Holocaust, and the Historians' Debate.* Boston: Beacon Press, 1990.

Bickel, Alexander. *The Least Dangerous Branch.* New Haven, CT: Yale University Press, 1986.

Brown, J. F. *Hopes and Shadows: Eastern Europe after Communism.* Durham, NC: Duke University Press, 1994.

Brown, J. F. *Surge to Freedom: The End of Communist Rule in Eastern Europe.* Durham, NC: Duke University Press, 1991.

Brownlie, Ian. *Principles of Public International Law* (4th ed.). New York: Oxford University Press, 1995.

Cassese, Antonio. *Human Rights in a Changing World.* Philadelphia: Temple University Press, 1990.

Cleary, Edward. *The Struggle for Human Rights in Latin America.* Westport, CT: Praeger, 1997.

Dahrendorf, Rahl. *Reflections on Revolutions in Europe.* London: Times Books, 1990.

Echikson, William. *Lighting the Night: Revolution in Eastern Europe.* New York: Morrow, 1990.

Falk, Richard. *The Role of Domestic Courts in the International Legal Order.* Syracuse, NY: Syracuse University Press, 1964.

Franck, Thomas. *Political Questions, Judicial Answers: Does the Role of Law Apply to Foreign Affairs?* Princeton, NJ: Princeton University Press, 1992.

Garton Ash, Timothy. *The Polish Revolution: Solidarity.* New York: Scribner's, 1984.

Gibney, Mark (ed.). *World Justice? U.S. Courts and International Human Rights.* Boulder, CO: Westview Press, 1991.

Goldfarb, Jeffrey C. *After the Fall.* New York: Basic Books, 1992.

Hannum, Hurst. *Guide to International Human Rights Practice* (2d ed.). Philadelphia: University of Pennsylvania Press, 1992.

Henkin, Louis. *Foreign Affairs and the Constitution* (2d ed.). New York: Oxford University Press, 1997.

Herz, John (ed.). *From Dictatorship to Democracy: Coping with the Legacies of Authoritarianism and Totalitarianism*. Westport, CT: Greenwood Press, 1982.

Hodos, George. *Show Trials: Stalinist Purges in Eastern Europe 1948–1954*. New York: Praeger, 1987.

Hoffman, Eva. *Exit into History: A Journey through the New Eastern Europe*. New York: Viking, 1993.

Jelin, Elizabeth, and Eric Hershberg. *Constructing Democracy: Human Rights, Citizenship, and Society in Latin America*. Boulder, CO: Westview Press, 1996.

Jowitt, Ken. *New World Disorder: The Leninist Extinction*. Berkeley: University of California Press, 1992.

Koh, Harold. *The National Security Constitution: Sharing Power after the Iran-Contra Affair*. New Haven, CT: Yale University Press, 1990.

Kritz, Neil (ed.). *Transitional Justice: How Emerging Democracies Reckon with Former Regimes*. 3 vols. Washington, DC: United States Institute of Peace Press, 1995.

Lillich, Richard, and Frank B. Newman. *International Human Rights: Problems of Law and Policy*. Boston: Little, Brown, 1979.

Meier, Charles. *The Unmasterable Past: History, Holocaust, and German National Identity*. Cambridge, MA: Harvard University Press, 1988.

O'Donnell, Guillermo, Philippe Schmitter, and Lawrence Whitehead (eds.). *Transitions from Authoritarian Rule*. 4 vols. Baltimore, MD: Johns Hopkins University Press, 1986.

Ramet, Sabrina P. *Social Currents in Eastern Europe: The Sources and Meaning of the Great Transformation*. Durham, NC: Duke University Press, 1995.

Randall, Kenneth. *Federal Courts and the International Human Rights Paradigm*. Durham, NC: Duke University Press, 1990.

Rosenberg, Tina. *The Haunted Land*. New York: Random House, 1995.

Rousso, Henry. *The Vichy Syndrome: History and Memory in France since 1944*. Cambridge, MA: Harvard University Press, 1991.

Sharfman, Dapha. *Living without a Constitution: Civil Rights in Israel*. Armonk, NY: M.E. Sharpe, 1993.

Simons, Thomas W., Jr. *Eastern Europe in the Postwar World*. New York: St. Martin's Press, 1991.

Steiner, Henry, and Deltev Vagts, *Transnational Legal Problems*. Westbury, NY: Foundation Press, 1994.

Stotzky, Irwin (ed.). *Transition to Democracy in Latin America: The Role of the Judiciary*. Boulder, CO: Westview Press, 1993.

Truth and Justice, The Delicate Balance: The Documentation of Prior Regimes and Individual Rights. Budapest: Institute for Constitutional and Legislative Policy, Central European University, 1993.

Index

About the Editors and Contributors

MARK GIBNEY is the Belk Distinguished Professor in the Humanities at the University of North Carolina–Asheville. He is editor of *World Justice: U.S. Courts and International Human Rights* (1991), and *Open Borders? Closed Societies? The Ethical and Political Issues* (Greenwood, 1988). He has published extensively in the area of refugee and human rights protection.

STANISLAW FRANKOWSKI is Professor of Law at St. Louis University School of Law. Prior to this he taught for many years at Warsaw University School of Law. His coedited publications include *Abortion and Protection of the Human Fetus* (1987), *Preventive Detention* (1992), and *Legal Reform in Post-Communist Societies* (1995). Professor Frankowski is Co-Director of the Center for International and Comparative Law.

STEPHEN GOLDSTEIN holds the Edward S. Silver Chair in Procedural Law at the Hebrew University in Jerusalem. He has been a visiting professor at Trinity College, Cambridge, the University of California–Berkeley, the University of Freiberg, the University of Bologna, Tulane University, and the University of Hong Kong. This year he will serve as the Heather Grierson Visiting Professor of European and Comparative Law at Oxford University. Among his publications are *Civil Procedure: Israel International Encyclopedia of Comparative Law* (1994) and *On Comparing and Unifying Civil Procedural Systems, Butterworth Lectures 1994* (1995).

MONICA MACOVEI is a Civil Rights Attorney in Romania. She is also a Legal Expert for the Council of Europe, a Lecturer at the Romanian Journalists' Association School of Journalism and serves as an International Consultant for the

United Nations. Ms. Macovei has an LL.M. in Comparative Constitutional Law from the State University of New York–Albany and the Central European University, Budapest, Hungary (1992–1993).

ALBERT MELONE is Professor of Political Science at Southern Illinois University. He is the author or co-author of eight books and has written a number of articles and other materials involving studies of American judicial politics and cross-cultural studies. His latest book is *Creating Parliamentary Democracy: The Transition to Democracy in Bulgaria* (1998).

GARTH NETTHEIM is Emeritus Professor, Chair of the Indigenous Law Centre, and Chair of the Australian Human Rights Centre at the University of New South Wales in Sydney, Australia. He is co-author (with H. McRae and L. Beacroft) of *Indigenous Legal Issues: Commentary and Materials* (1997).

IGOR PETRUKHIN is a Professor at the Academic Law University and a Researcher at the Institute of State and Law at the Russian Academy of Sciences. He has published more than 250 papers and 25 books including *Freedom of the Individual and the Rights of the State against the Person in Criminal Procedure*, *Private Life: Limits of Intervention, Justice: Time for Reform* and *A Manual on the Law Enforcement Agencies of the Russian Federation*.

JOHN QUIGLEY is Professor of Law at Ohio State University. Professor Quigley writes on a wide variety of topics in international law. With respect to the Arab-Israeli conflict his recent publications include *Palestine and Israel: A Challenge to Justice* (1990) and *Flight into the Maelstrom: Soviet Immigration to Israel and Middle East Peace* (1997).

VIJAYASHRI SRIPATI holds an LL.B. from Osmania University, India. A recipient of the 1990 Rotary Scholarship for "International Understanding," she then attended American University (U.S.), where she received an LL.M. Later, as a British Chevening Scholar, she received an M.A. in International Law & Politics from the University of Hull, England in 1997. She was also awarded the J.C. Onoh Memorial Prize for Outstanding Research and Writing in Public International Law. Her writing is in the area of Indian constitutional law and international human rights law. She has also contributed many articles on legal education and women's rights in *The Hindu*, India's prestigious English daily.

C. NEAL TATE is Dean of the Robert B. Toulouse School of Graduate Studies and Regents Professor of Political Science at the University of North Texas. He is author or co-author of numerous research articles appearing in the *American Political Science Review*, *Law & Society Review*, and other major political science and law and society journals. He coedited and contributed to *Democracy and Law* (1997), *The Global Expansion of Judicial Power* (1995) and *Compar-*

ative Judicial Review and Public Policy (1992). His research in the Philippines has been conducted with the support of two Fulbright Senior Research Fellowships and a grant from the National Science Foundation.

BRIAN TURNER is an Assistant Professor of Political Science at Randolph-Macon College in Ashland, Virginia. He has extensive field research experience in Paraguay and is the author of *Community Politics and Peasant-State Relations in Paraguay* (1993). He has written several articles addressing judicial reform and decentralization in Latin America.

XIAOLIN WANG received his LL.B at Xiangtan University, People's Republic of China in 1989. He received his M.A. degree at Ohio University in 1994 and is presently pursuing his J.D. degree at Southern Illinois University School of Law. He has worked as an Assistant Judge and Judge in the People's Court of Changsha, Western District, China.

ISBN 0-275-96011-0

HARDCOVER BAR CODE